THE LEADERSHIP PIPELINE

THE LEADERSHIP PIPELINE

HOW TO BUILD THE LEADERSHIP POWERED COMPANY

RAM CHARAN | STEPHEN DROTTER | JAMES NOEL

SECOND EDITION

JOSSEY-BASS
A Wiley Imprint
www.josseybass.com

Times Group Books

The Leadership Pipeline: How to Build the Leadership Powered Company
Second Edition

Authorised reprint by Wiley India Pvt. Ltd., 4435-36/7, Ansari Road, Daryaganj, New Delhi-110002.

Marketed and distributed exclusively in India by

Times Group Books

Times Group Books
(A division of Bennett, Coleman and Company Limited)
Times Annexe, Express Building 9-10
Bahadur Shah Zafar Marg, New Delhi - 110002

Published by Jossey-Bass, A Wiley Imprint, 989 Market Street, San Francisco, CA 94103-1741—www.josseybass.com.

Reprint: 2012

Printed at: *Sanat Printers, Kundli*

ISBN : 978-81-265-3122-6

Contents

Foreword

"This model has changed the dialogue at my table," says the CEO *of a major fast-moving consumer goods company. "We now focus more on strategy and talent, not just revenue and volume."*

"The Leadership Pipeline idea and model has helped us push accountability down the organization in a coherent way," says the CEO *of a major mining company. "It has freed us at the top to focus more on the future while lower levels drive productivity and early operating results."*

"We are now focusing our coursework on the right skills for the right level."

"Our succession planning is now anchored in reality about what potential means and what it looks like."

"I can do better coaching of my people, given the improved clarity of expectations for them and for me."

The overwhelmingly positive response to the first edition of *The Leadership Pipeline* has been most gratifying. Our discussions with readers and our work as consultants have provided us with invaluable feedback about the Pipeline model—feedback that has helped make this model even more effective in practice than when we first wrote about it. We want to pass on the lessons we've learned so that companies can maximize the Pipeline's value.

Since the first edition of this book was published, we've worked with over one hundred companies using this framework. Many of the best and most successful corporations in the world have adopted the Leadership Pipeline model as the core framework for their efforts on the human side of their businesses. Built around the common leadership "passages" all leaders go through, it helps organizations select, develop, and assess based on specific responsibilities and work values at each leadership level.

Our approach to revising this work is a bit unorthodox: we decided not to go in and change the individual chapters with all new examples and context. The reader will notice we talk about certain players in business who are no longer in the role they are cited in. Because the examples, although no longer all current, serve the point we are trying to make, we decided to leave them and instead to add two significant sections at the end of each chapter. The first, "Observations from the Field," allows us to update our model, share some additional stories, and add some advice based on almost ten years of experiences working with companies around the world. We have also included the answers to frequently asked questions.

Our hope is that this new and "improved" version of our work continues to be effective and used easily by all.

Preface to the Revised Edition: Observations from the Field

As we've worked with a variety of organizations to put the Pipeline framework into practice, we've found a number of serious flaws with development efforts that must be corrected to enable sustained operational and financial success. At a time when organizations are enormously dependent on internal development of present and future leaders, these efforts are falling short. Here are four failings the Pipeline model is designed to correct:

Deep-Seated Development Errors

1. Line managements' dissatisfaction with human resources has not abated. We believe one critically important reason is the lack of an enduring central architecture. Imagine a company that has a chief financial officer but doesn't have a general ledger, a budget process, a cost accounting system, and a capital allocation process that are tied together. That finance officer wouldn't have much success. Finance's architecture enables the entire organization to work with and talk about financial matters in a consistent way. Companies need an enduring architecture to focus human resource processes and programs. The architecture should set common standards for both performance and potential, differentiated by layer of management. It should also establish language and processes to address issues, identify problems, and exploit opportunities effectively, as well as data for making decisions about everything from job transitions to performance improvement.

We've found that most development efforts lack this central architecture. Although most HR departments make sincere and sometimes even heroic efforts at leadership development, when these efforts don't produce the desired results, they stop spending money on development, or they replace an existing program with the next one, or they try a third program and then a fourth. Changing programs often means one leader emerges speaking one language, while another leader from a different program speaks a second language. These changes in development content and philosophy create distrust. Because there's no cumulative effect from a comprehensive but flexible architecture, there's no solid base for development purposes. This book outlines a central architecture that you can adapt to your company's specific situation.

2. Leaders don't learn to do what is needed. We've found that this is a growing problem as leadership roles and responsibilities continue to evolve rapidly. Within most developmental assignments roles are poorly defined and measured. Specific content is rarely defined. The expected value-add isn't defined, and the relationship to overall results is left to the imagination. Competency models place the emphasis on activity rather than results, and this creates misleading measurements. We've also found that under many existing development models, leaders learn to think about jobs in terms of turf—what they control. This notion has led to silos, excluding the ideas of others, and has also led to a lack of teamwork even within silos. A silo mentality precludes teamwork, and it motivates leaders to focus on details (that others should handle) and address immediate concerns rather than future goals.

Jobs should be defined by accountability for a set of results, a basic tenet of the Leadership Pipeline model. Required results must change as people move up the organization. When one set of results is achieved, a new set can be established. This allows organizations to adapt more quickly to changing business requirements and to new market conditions without having to reorganize. It also helps incumbents to focus on what is critically important, enables better decisions about who can help and who can't, contributes to making jobs more doable, and greatly reduces the activities associated with defending one's turf.

Leadership models must also be capable of redefining roles continuously in response to a changing environment. For instance, an increasing percentage of work is being done by people who are not on the company's full-time payroll, because of outsourcing and other factors. The way a leader's work is defined must encourage collaboration and inclusion, particularly when traditional control methods aren't possible.

3. *There is a lack of selection skill.* We find that the intensity in producing the numbers is several orders of magnitude greater than the intensity around choosing people. Whether it's because executives no longer have the time to devote to selection or because choosing the right candidate is more difficult, they often aren't adept at selecting the right people for the right jobs. In assessment interviews, we asked about 1,300 senior executives, "How do you go about making a selection decision?" Most people answer with a brief description of (a) the kind of person they want ("honest," "hard-working"), (b) some sort of search request, and (c) an interview process.

The Leadership Pipeline model helps people make superior selection decisions. For instance, it focuses them on the triggering event that indicates why a change must be made. Some triggering events are obvious, such as when the incumbent quits or retires or gets promoted to a new job. Some aren't so obvious, such as a change in strategy, a persistent pattern of mistakes, a bad attitude, or noticeable unhappiness with the leadership requirements. The Pipeline model also helps a senior executive judge whether an individual is working at the level to which that person is assigned, as well another individual's potential for moving up to the next level.

The worst-case scenario for poor selection was always thought to be hiring the wrong person. But today that is only the third-worst-case scenario. Two even more serious problems are (1) failing to recognize and hire the right person, instead letting this ideal candidate sail invisibly through the selection process, and (2) leaving the wrong person in the job too long.

4. HR is focused on the wrong agenda. Historically, the human resource function has focused on the supply of labor. In recent years, to win an external war for talent, HR has focused more specifically on finding and getting A players. Internally, the focus has been on identifying future "stars," the "high potentials" to be put in key jobs. This focus on "input" hasn't gotten them very far.

Instead, the focus should be on the output. Output will be inappropriate unless the incumbent values the right work, unless there is a process in place to identify what the right work is for the right leadership position, and unless measures are in place to determine whether the right work is being done. Poorly designed jobs, leaders working at the wrong level, a lack of clear direction, and bad selection decisions are ubiquitous in the current organizational environment. If HR truly understood organization and assessment and helped all leaders work at the right level, the organization could make significant leaps in productivity.

Four External Pipeline Factors

It's not just internal developmental shortcomings that are making the Pipeline model so relevant to organizations. We've witnessed the emergence of four external factors that have emerged in recent years and have a huge impact on leadership effectiveness up and down the line. The following factors also increase the value of the Pipeline approach:

Outside Talent Hasn't Met Organizational Needs

For many reasons, recruiting people to fill key positions hasn't worked out as well as expected. If we define success for external recruits as full performance and acceptance after three years, the success rate is low and gets lower for positions at or near the top. Cultural mismatches, lack of a relationship network, resentment by current employees who wanted or expected the job, and new hires focused on the next promotion rather than the job are just some of the problems. The highest-risk external hire situation involves people who are changing companies and changing layers simultaneously. Learning to work at a higher layer while learning the success formula at a new company puts these new hires under extreme pressure. The new hire commonly reacts by reverting to the skills and methods of the previous layer and the former company—and this almost guarantees failure. However, a development framework that helps outside people understand the values and skills required at a given managerial level—and that helps the company transition them to this level quickly—can increase the odds that outside people will succeed.

The Critical New Markets: China, India, and Other Emerging Markets

Dealing with China, India, and other unfamiliar markets means learning to operate effectively in a new context. Executives must master different operating styles, sophistication levels, cultural nuances, and other new areas. Developing and measuring these leaders with these differences in mind is crucial. Unfortunately, they're not kept in mind, because the HR development framework doesn't accommodate the learning and measures that change as job levels change, especially from a global perspective. What skills, attitudes, values, and knowledge should be targeted for a country manager in China? For that manager's assistant? Are there coordinated recruitment, development, and measurement programs in place to help leaders transition through the levels in these global jobs? The flexibility of the Leadership Pipeline model accommodates new and changing requirements in ways that other approaches do not.

Job Content Is Changing

Flexible models are required to cope with jobs that are evolving rapidly. Innovation and collaboration have become absolutely essential in a world where traditional market leaders no longer dominate their industries and where team structures are operating in tandem with the traditional pyramid. On top of that, the growth of electronic communication often requires leaders to work virtually or to meet face-to-face with people less frequently. The ability to lead from a distance and to communicate effectively online are skills that weren't even considered until relatively recently. We observe more people at more passages being required to work outside the company structure with partners and other elements of the ecosystem. If development and measurements at all leadership levels don't reflect this changing job content, new skills won't be adopted—or adopted in a widespread and effective manner.

The Need for Role Clarity

Last but not least, this factor is paramount in a business environment that is increasingly ambiguous, paradoxical, complex, and volatile. In this rapidly changing environment, leaders are no longer sure of their roles and responsibilities. How are they to treat employees who invest so much time and energy in communicating electronically? How transparent can and should they be when it comes to issues such as downsizing and performance? How can they build trust among employees who are increasingly distrustful of management?

No leader at any level can answer these questions effectively without a framework that clearly defines his or her role. We've found that the Pipeline model helps leaders understand what is expected of them at every leadership level. As a result, they can filter the questions just asked through a framework that identifies what behaviors and values are necessary for them to do their jobs well. They know that as the head of a function, for instance, they must learn to manage and value what is new. This imperative allows them to define all their actions against it. It helps them avoid the inconsistent behaviors that sow distrust among employees. It helps them communicate a belief in a genuine and transparent manner.

A Model for the Future as Well as the Present

In recent years, organizations have become increasingly aware of the need to build sustainable enterprises, not just ones that create short-term profits. We've heard from organizations that the Pipeline model helps them focus on the future development of leaders rather than just present performance issues. We have observed many leaders at all levels working exclusively on the problems of the moment. This has been particularly true during the recession that began in 2007–2008; each day, it seems, brings another tough decision to leaders' desks. In this environment, defining and preparing for a successful future for their company, business, function, or team has been given little or no attention. Without adequate measures and role clarity, they can't prepare for the inevitable changes required for success or survival.

For this reason, many companies are failing to develop leadership bench strength and day-to-day leadership effectiveness. Leading-edge development programs, no matter how well designed, aren't sufficient to achieve these goals.

What's lacking is a connective context. In other words, the connection between leadership development training programs, succession planning, performance management, and rewards is tenuously defined at best. In most companies, human resources orchestrates these activities, and the various groups responsible for them compete for resources, management attention, and power. Human resources efforts are rarely integrated.

Standards for making judgments about people are different for different activities. Performance ratings, promotions, bonuses, and participation in development are based on varying standards, causing confusion for those trying to make judgments as well as for the judged.

When we wrote *The Leadership Pipeline*, we knew a need existed for a central architecture, a framework shared by all leaders to ensure consistency of judgment and application on the human side of the business so that a cumulative leadership effect results. What we've learned in the interim is that this need is far more compelling and widespread than we initially assumed.

The Leadership Pipeline is about how to build that architecture.

More so now than ever before, the architecture described in *The Leadership Pipeline* must be understood and used by leaders at all levels—not only those who lead the human resources department. Understanding and using the architecture will make leaders more effective, especially if they are a leader of leaders. Human resources people have a critical role to play, but it is an "engineering" role, not an "operating" role. Leaders are the operators; they make the judgments, and they will live with the successes or failures of those judgments. HR is the engineering function accountable for design and usability, the value and quality of the architecture.

Our readers have told us that *The Leadership Pipeline* has changed the way their companies approach the human side of business at a fundamental level. Our global society can't continue to withstand the enormous failure rates of those in the highest leadership positions combined with the deepening shortage of capable men and women to lead our businesses. The challenge must be addressed in ways that are significantly more systematic, so the growth of leaders becomes organic and predictably successful. Given the growing need for a more effective leadership development model and the emerging obstacles to such development, this book is even more relevant and needed today than it was ten years ago.

The Leadership Pipeline

Introduction

This is an era in which the demand for leadership greatly exceeds the supply. Signs of this imbalance are everywhere. Almost every issue of the *Wall Street Journal* carries news about a major corporation bringing in a top executive from outside the organization. Executive search firms are flourishing because of the demand for leadership talent. Consulting firms are offering six-figure starting salaries to make sure they get their fair share of newly minted MBAs from top schools. No less a consulting firm than McKinsey has spent a great deal of time formulating a strategy to cope with the "war for talent." And just about every major organization is attempting to hire "stars," offering enormous compensation to entice the best and the brightest.

These overly aggressive, sometimes desperate attempts to recruit outsiders suggest that the leadership pipeline is inadequate. Internal training, mentoring, and other developmental programs aren't keeping the pipeline full, making it necessary to look outside. The problem, of course, is that there are only so many full-performing leaders to go around. Everyone is fighting over a relatively small group of stars who, even when successfully recruited, tend to move from company to company with alacrity.

What's needed, therefore, is an approach that will allow organizations to keep their own leadership pipelines full and flowing. This is easier said than done because the requirements of leadership have changed so dramatically, and most development models are ill-suited for these changing requirements. We've found, however, that an approach that takes into account the different requirements at distinct leadership levels is viable. Before we talk about our pipeline model and how it works, we'd like to give you a better sense of how the demand for leadership has risen while the supply of leaders has not kept pace.

The Trouble with Finding and Developing Leaders: The New Economy, Globalization, and Organizational Perspectives

While there are many factors that have increased the demand for leaders, one of the most significant ones is the information technology revolution.

The New Economy has raised organizational consciousness about the human side of the business. New Economy companies have not only preached that people have tremendous value in this economy, but they've practiced it. Dot.com companies have lured highly talented individuals with the promise of great wealth through stock options, immediate involvement in meaningful work, and other perks. MBA students have taken summer jobs with these companies and never returned to complete their degrees. Unlike traditional companies, dot.coms continue the courtship of their employees after they hire them by providing empowering work, ongoing learning, and clear, continuous communication.

While these New Economy companies have siphoned leadership talent away from mainstream organizations, they've also spawned a new set of leadership problems:

Founders and CEOs Must Change What They Work on as the Company Grows As these companies grow fast, their leaders must move to new leadership levels with amazing speed. One day they're doing first-line manager work, the next they're integrating with alliances and representing the enterprise to the world around it. Needless to say, many of these dot.com founders have difficulties with these lightning-like transitions.

There Aren't Enough Leaders and Few Are Being Grown Internally Search firms estimated that there could have been as many as a thousand dot.com CEO openings in late 1999. When Meg Whitman, president of eBay, was asked what her biggest early mistake was, she answered that it was failing to bring in enough heavyweight leaders fast enough.

New Horizontal Leadership Skills Are Necessary New Economy companies grow horizontally through alliances and partnerships. Effective integration (managing organizational interfacing) of these partners is a crucial requirement, one that managers accustomed to vertical growth may have difficulty meeting.

Old Economy Companies Are Competing for New Economy Talent A number of mainstream organizations have made great strides in Internet endeavors. Almost all the "old economy" industries—for example, autos, financial services, travel—have taken major steps to become e-commerce companies. As a result, the battle for e-commerce leadership talent has become even more intense.

What all this means is that finding the right types of leaders with the right types of skills is becoming an increasingly difficult task. The New Economy has also made development of these leaders more difficult, in that people need to acquire new skills that aren't part of the traditional leadership package.

Just as significantly, over the past twenty years organizations have become aware of the need for local leadership because of increasing globalization. Edicts and strategies from the home office require local interpretation and application. Leaders rooted in these environments (rather than those removed from them) must address issues, such as differences in culture, customer demands, and local work habits. Local leadership, then, has become a prized commodity. Equally important is the need for leaders who manage the balance between global and local issues.

What is perhaps most significant, the lack of effective talent development within organizations has contributed to the leadership deficit. It's not simply that companies have failed to train frontline people to use the power bestowed on them by the information revolution or to develop managers capable of local leadership. The issues are broader and deeper. Part of the problem is historical, going back to the late 1970s, when companies cut costs to become more competitive in response to dramatic increases in the price of oil and a flood of goods made in countries with cheaper labor. They dramatically reduced their investment in talent development. Training programs, developmental assignments, and management time for coaching were greatly reduced or even eliminated. Though some of these efforts were restarted in the 1990s, many people in key roles are the product of this "no money for development" era. In addition, there was a wave of faddish development programs that lacked much substance. As a result, many executives were never fully trained or developed for their roles.

Furthermore, organizations often don't look at development as integral to business strategy, viewing it purely as part of the human resources function. CEOs don't invest their time in it because they perceive it as outside their domain. A common organizational mindset is to view jobs as "work to be done" and not as developmental assignments. Even worse, a rather simplistic definition of leadership governs development. There is little acknowledgment that different levels of leadership exist and that people need to make skill and value transitions at each level. Relatively few organizations are thinking about the core competencies and experiences necessary to be successful at each level. Few of them are considering the leadership development needs of a first-time manager versus those of a functional manager. Instead, there is a focus on personal traits and technical competence. Organizations promote people with the expectation that they have the knowledge and skills to handle the job rather than the knowledge and skills to handle a particular level of leadership. They assume that if they've performed well at one job, they'll likely perform well at the next one.

Given all this, it should come as no surprise that the leadership pipeline is dry. What is surprising is the organizational response to this situation: adopting a "best and brightest" strategy. Company after company has decided that it can solve its leadership problem by finding and nurturing the top talent. Hiring gifted people makes sense as a tactic but not as a strategy. Certainly if there's an enormously talented individual you can recruit for your organization, you should do so. Strategically, however, this approach falls apart because of the scarcity of highly talented individuals. Not only will you have to pay through the nose for these people, but what is more important, they will probably never develop fully. The stars of the business world usually change jobs or companies so frequently that they have difficulty finishing what they started. They don't stay in one place long enough to learn from mistakes, master the right skills, or gain the experience needed for sustainable performance.

Although star performers can contribute a great deal to any company, there are not enough to go around. Today's companies need effective leaders at every level and in every location. Because of the information technology revolution, globalization, and other factors, leadership is a requirement up and down the line. To deliver on increasingly ambitious promises to customers, shareholders, employees, and other stakeholders, we need more fully performing leaders than ever before. This means finding a method that ensures that more managers than ever before will be prepared for and placed at the right leadership levels.

Untapped Leadership Potential

If we need more leaders at more levels than ever before—and if we need to build them rather than buy them—the question of potential naturally arises. Can today's average salesperson become tomorrow's "right-for-the-job" sales leader? Even though the work is different, our experience demonstrates that he can, because *potential is not fixed.* We believe in human beings' ability to grow; society cannot achieve economic as well as cultural progress without it. Too often, however, executives view potential as an abstract concept that defies definition. As such, it's difficult to see it as something that changes over time. When you define potential as the kind of work someone can do in the future, it becomes easier to see it as a dynamic concept. This future work potential is based on accumulated skills and experience as evidenced by past achievement, ability to learn new skills, and willingness to tackle bigger, more complex, or higher-quality assignments. The more people achieve, the more learning takes place; willingness to tackle new challenges increases as current challenges are met. Fueled by the rapidly changing nature of work, global opportunities, and on-line learning via the Internet, people's potential changes several times over the course of a career. They can and do reinvent themselves.

What all this means is that you need to keep an open, optimistic mind about who might become the right person for a given leadership position. People who are skilled technicians might have the potential to be managers; managers who seem entrenched in their functions might have the potential to lead cross-functional teams.

To capitalize on this potential, you need to discern the true work requirements at key leadership levels and what's needed to make the transition from one layer to the next successfully. Matching an individual's potential with a series of requirements is how pipelines are built. The Leadership Pipeline model will help you achieve these objectives.

Passages Through the Pipeline

To build your leadership base, the starting point is understanding the natural hierarchy of work that exists in most organizations (the focus here is on managerial-leadership work rather than technical or professional contributions). In a large, decentralized business organization, this hierarchy takes the form of six career passages or pipeline turns. The pipeline is not a straight cylinder but rather one that is bent in six places. Each of these passages represents a change in organizational position—a different level and complexity of leadership—where a significant turn has to be made. These turns involve a major change in job requirements, demanding new skills, time applications, and work values.

The chart in Figure I.1 illustrates the six major passages leaders face.

Though there are other, minor passages between these six major ones, we don't want to become bogged down in detail at this point. For our purposes here, it's important simply to understand what these six are all about. In the following pages, we'll explore these six leadership passages in detail, identifying the skills, use of time, and work values unique to each. Recognizing the requirements and pitfalls associated with each one is crucial, not only for the leaders themselves but also for their bosses and subordinates. With a universal understanding of the model, bosses will provide better coaching and differentiated accountability, and subordinates can be more supportive when they recognize the issues with which their bosses are struggling.

As you become familiar with each leadership passage, you'll find yourself thinking about careers and planning development from a fresh perspective. What is more significant, this new perspective will provide you with the insights necessary to keep your leadership pipeline filled and flowing. Not only will it help you structure a process to develop leaders on all levels, but it will also enable you to ensure that they're working at the right levels. As

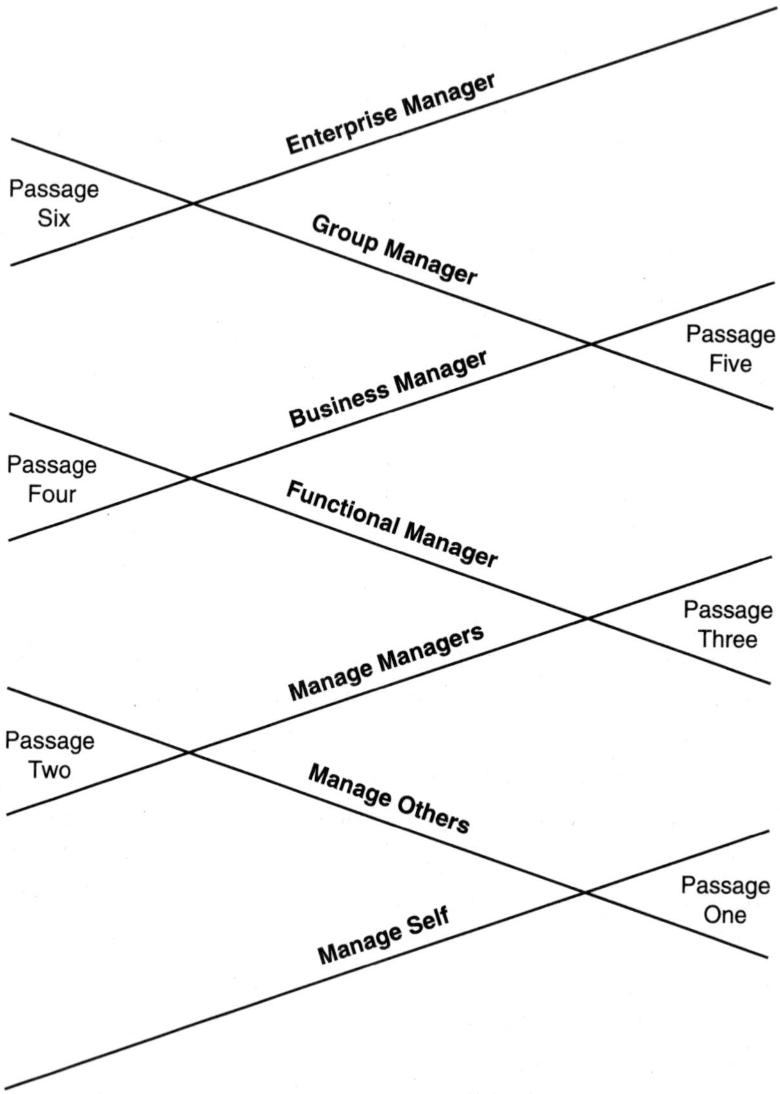

Figure 1.1. Critical Career Passages in a Large Business Organization.
Note: Each passage represents a major change in job requirements that translates to new skill requirements, new time horizons and applications, and new work values. Based on work done initially by Walter Mahler and called Critical Career Crossroads.

you'll discover, each passage requires that people acquire a new way of managing and leading and leave the old ways behind in the following three areas:

- Skill requirements—the new capabilities required to execute new responsibilities
- Time applications—new time frames that govern how one works
- Work values—what people believe is important and so becomes the focus of their effort

The challenge for organizations is to make sure that people in leadership positions are assigned to the level appropriate to their skills, time applications, and values. Unfortunately, many managers often work at the wrong level: they're clinging to values appropriate to Passage One (managing others) even though they're working at Passage Two (managing managers), or they haven't acquired the skills or time application expertise appropriate to their current level. As a result, not only are they less effective (or ineffective) leaders but the people they manage are negatively affected as well.

If you keep the metaphor of a pipeline in mind, you can see how things might become clogged at the turns. Imagine a company where more than half the managers at each turn are operating with skills, time applications, and values inappropriate to their level; either they've skipped a level and never learned what they need to know, or they're clinging to an old mode of managing that was successful for them in the past. In some companies, at least 50 percent of the people in leadership positions are operating far below their assigned layer. They have the potential to be leaders, but that potential is going unfulfilled. In short, they're stuck and clogging up the system (staying too long in one passage also can clog up the system).

Let's look at two people with leadership potential who have become stuck in this manner.

Two Leadership Turns That Give Many People Trouble

Bob is at Passage One—From Managing Self to Managing Others—having recently been promoted to the manager of his group. Previously, Bob had proven to be a crackerjack engineer, the best problem solver in the department. Technically, he was superior, and this fact earned him his promotion. As a manager, however, Bob relied on a hands-on, problem-solving approach that had worked for him as an individual contributor engineer over the past seven years. It is a work style that he enjoys and is comfortable with; his work values dictate that he figure out the engineering solution himself. But it is also what prevents him from demonstrating the leadership of which he is capable. Typically, Bob ends up competing with his own direct reports when he gives them an assignment. It smothers them psychologically, thus wasting his time and theirs. He needs to stop relying on his work skills and valuing his ability to solve problems himself and instead learn to plan the work that needs to be done, select good people to do it, set objectives, hold people accountable for results, and offer feedback. Bob needs to learn all this to be an effective leader not only now but later as well. This first turn is where he'll acquire people management and team leadership skills—skills that will be essential for him when he arrives at future passages.

Mary, a former sales manager, is now the head of a business unit; she's at Passage Four—From Functional Manager to Business Manager. Over the course of her career Mary has aggressively pursued new customers, and she relishes the supplier-customer dynamic, spending a great deal of time in one-on-one customer interactions; she's been highly innovative with her service ideas and has consistently hit or exceeded sales targets for her group because of her approach. As the head of a business unit, Mary is encountering a number of problems. She's finding it difficult to communicate with people in functions other than her own and to create a business model that her people can understand and relate to. She doesn't understand why Engineering and Manufacturing are always in disagreement and why deliveries are so late on new products. Frustrated by her inability to do what's required, Mary decides that she can "bull" her way through by relying on her strength. By focusing on deepening and securing customer relationships, she is back in her comfort zone. Unfortunately that's only one of many roles she needs to play in her current leadership position. This is the first time Mary has ever headed a multifunctional team, and she doesn't value the contributions of each function or understand their contribution to the success of the enterprise. She has to become a more strategic and less transactional manager if she's going to be an effective leader at her current level.

Making the Commitment to Fill the Leadership Pipeline

Helping people like Bob and Mary negotiate turns requires a commitment—a commitment of not only time and money but also energy and emotion. It means recognizing that poaching leaders and offering simplistic training programs isn't going to fill the pipeline. To build effective leadership at all levels, organizations need to identify leadership candidates early, provide them with growth assignments, give them useful feedback, and coach them. What is more important, they need to do these and other things within the Leadership Pipeline framework. Without a process that helps managers adopt the skills, time applications, and values appropriate to each leadership level, no type of training or coaching will have much impact.

Over the years, we've worked with many companies that have made a commitment to this pipeline concept (though they don't always use the terminology we'll use here). Let us briefly tell you about two of them.

At General Electric, there's a strong commitment to facilitating the leadership transitions we've discussed (though their leadership levels are labeled a bit differently from those in our model; they use "new manager," "functional leader," "general manager" and "officer/multiple group of businesses"). Their famed Crotonville facility plays an important role in GE's leadership development experiences. GE has a succession planning process called "Session C," part of which is designed to evaluate each individual's readiness to make a career or leadership turn, as well as training programs that help them learn business, leadership, and cultural skills at each turn. It's not a coincidence that the organization has always had several highly qualified candidates waiting in the wings to succeed the CEO when he retires and that it also has a well-deserved reputation as being a launching pad for leaders (both within GE and at other organizations). GE doesn't have a smarter or more inherently talented workforce than other companies. GE's leadership advantages stem from the investment they have made in growing their own leaders and their recognition that leadership revolves around mastering certain skills and values at each leadership level.

Citigroup is another company that had made this commitment in the 1990s. They were especially adept at helping people make the difficult transition from a transaction orientation to their first profit-and-loss positions as business managers. A year-long program for these individuals—many of whom have just been appointed chief country managers—helped them develop "hard" skills such as strategic cost management, as well as the softer values and thought processes. In the latter regard, the program provided them with a significant amount of coaching as well as interaction with senior Citigroup officers. As you might imagine, a year-long program for an entire layer of management represents a significant investment, but it's an investment with a tremendous return, especially if you measure it in leaders working at full capacity.

Understanding the Passages and How to Use Them

This book is informally divided into two sections. The first (Chapters One through Seven) focuses on defining each leadership passage and illustrating the skills, time applications, and values that are required to make the passage successfully. To keep the leadership pipeline filled and flowing, it's crucial that you are aware of the specific requirements, the common problems managers experience in making a passage, and behaviors or attitudes that identify someone as having difficulty with a passage. When organizations start to think in terms of pipeline requirements rather than job-title responsibilities, they are in a much better position to develop their leaders.

The second section concentrates on how to apply the pipeline to leadership problems and opportunities within an organization. Chapters Eight through Fourteen will help you diagnose pipeline problems, create development plans, and more effectively manage leadership performance. Within this second section, you'll also find tools and techniques for coaching leaders, dealing with succession issues, preventing leadership failures, and maintaining the flow in the functional offshoot of the pipeline.

No matter what type of organization you're in or your level of responsibility, you'll find the information in the following chapters applicable in your environment. The pipeline is a very flexible model that organizations can adapt to their own situations and concerns. It's also a model designed with changing leadership accountabilities in mind. The traditional notions of what a leader needs to be and do are no longer valid. The New Economy and other factors we've discussed are creating new requirements at all leadership levels.

To use the Leadership Pipeline approach effectively, you need to challenge traditional notions of leadership. You can't grow leaders unless you have an accurate development target, and this means acknowledging that the roles and responsibilities of leaders have shifted. The multilevel, multidimensional concept of leadership is a reality of modern business life. Once you start developing leaders with this new reality in mind, it will be that much easier to make this model work for you and your organization.

Finally, we would like to warn you away from a "mechanical" implementation of the pipeline concept. In other words, avoid three-ring binders and the paper exercise mentality that comes with them. We've seen too many companies equate succession planning with leadership development. The criteria the Pipeline establishes for leadership are different from what succession planning often dictates. We ask you to think holistically and with the complexity of people in mind.

1

Six Leadership Passages

An Overview

The six turns in the pipeline that we'll discuss here are major events in the life of a leader. They represent significant passages that can't be mastered in a day or by taking a course. Our goal here is to help you become familiar with the skills, time applications, and work values demanded by each passage, as well as this particular leadership gestalt. Once you grasp what these passages entail and the challenges involved in making each leadership transition, you'll be in a better position to use this information to unclog your organization's leadership pipeline and facilitate your own growth as a leader. Going through these passages helps leaders build emotional strength as they take on tasks of increasing complexity and scope. The following six chapters will provide you with ideas and tools to achieve full performance at all leadership levels in your organization.

As you read about each passage, you'll naturally apply it to your own organization and may question how we've defined and divided each turn in the pipeline. The odds are that you'll immediately think of at least one (and probably more) leadership transitions that apply to your own company that we have not addressed in the Leadership Pipeline model. While there certainly are other transitions, they are too small or incomplete to qualify as a major passage.

For instance, many global companies have business general managers at the country level and regional executives with responsibility for several countries. These regional executives report to a person with a title such as global consumer products head. Although this global consumer products head manages group managers (the regional executives, in this case), she isn't an enterprise manager, because she reports to a CEO or president and has little accountability for total corporate profit-and-loss matters. For our purposes here, we would categorize her as a group manager, even though she may have responsibility for other group managers.

Similarly, you may wonder why the transition from team member to team leader isn't worthy of its own passage. First, this is usually a subset of Passage One (from managing self to managing others). Second, team leaders frequently lack the decision-making authority on selection and rewards that first-line managers receive. Third, team leaders usually focus on technical or professional matters (getting a project or program completed) and aren't tested in more general management areas.

Each organization is unique, and each probably has at least one leadership passage with distinctive aspects. It's likely, however, that you can fit that distinctive passage into one of our six passages. As you become more attuned to each of them, we believe you'll see how they apply to your own situation and organization. If there is a passage in your business that doesn't fit our model, create your own definition of the transition and tell us about it.

Passage One: From Managing Self to Managing Others

New, young employees usually spend their first few years with an organization as individual contributors. Whether they're in sales, accounting, engineering, or marketing, their skill requirements are primarily technical or professional. They contribute by doing the assigned work within given time frames and in ways that meet objectives. By sharpening and broadening their individual skills, they make increased contributions and are then considered "promotable" by organizations. From a time application standpoint, the learning involves planning (so that work is completed on time), punctuality, content, quality, and reliability. The work values to be developed include acceptance of the company culture and adopting of professional standards. When people become skilled individual contributors who produce good results—especially when they demonstrate an ability to collaborate with others—they usually receive additional responsibilities. When they demonstrate an ability to handle these responsibilities and adhere to the company's values, they are often promoted to first-line manager.

When this happens, they are at Passage One. Though this might seem like an easy, natural leadership passage, it's one where people often trip. The highest-performing people, especially, are reluctant to change; they want to keep doing the activities that made them successful. As a result, people make the job transition from individual contributor to manager without making a behavioral or value-based transition. In effect, they become managers without accepting the requirements. Many consultants, for instance, have skipped this turn, moving from transitory team leadership to business leader without absorbing much of the learning in between. The result, when business leaders miss this passage, is frequently disaster.

The skills people should learn at this first leadership passage include planning work, filling jobs, assigning work, motivating, coaching, and measuring the work of others. First-time managers need to learn how to reallocate their time so that they not only complete their assigned work but also help others perform effectively. They cannot allocate all of their time to putting out fires, seizing opportunities, and handling tasks themselves. They must shift from "doing" work to getting work done through others.

Reallocating time is an especially difficult transitional requirement for first-time managers. Part of the problem is that many neophyte managers still prefer to spend time on their "old" work, even as they take charge of a group. Yet the pressure to spend less time on individual work and more time on managing will increase at each passage, and if people don't start making changes in how they allocate their time from the beginning, they're bound to become liabilities as they move up. It's a major reason why pipelines clog and leaders fail.

The most difficult change for managers to make at Passage One, however, involves values. Specifically, they need to learn to value managerial work rather than just tolerate it. They must believe that making time for others, planning, coaching, and the like are necessary tasks and are their responsibility. More than that, they must view this other-directed work as mission-critical to their success. For instance, first-line knowledge managers in the financial services industry find this transition extremely difficult. They value being producers, and they must learn to value making others productive. Given that these values had nothing to do with their success as individual contributors, it's difficult for them to make this dramatic shift in what they view as meaningful. While changes in skills and time applications can be seen and measured, changes in values are more difficult to assess. Someone may *appear* as though he's making the changes demanded by this leadership turn but in fact be adhering to individual-contributor values. Value changes will take place only if upper management reinforces the need to shift beliefs and if people find they're successful at their new jobs after a value shift.

Passage Two: From Managing Others to Managing Managers

This leadership passage is frequently ignored, especially relative to the previous passage (where the transition to new responsibilities is more obvious). Few companies address this passage directly in their training, even though this is the level where a company's management foundation is constructed; level-two managers select and develop the people who will eventually become the company's leaders.

Perhaps the biggest difference from the previous passage is that here, managers must be pure management. Before, individual contributions were still part of their job description. Now they need to divest themselves of individual tasks. The key skills that must be mastered during this transition include selecting people to turn Passage One, assigning managerial and leadership work to them, measuring their progress as managers, and coaching them. This is also the point where managers must begin to think beyond their function and concern themselves with strategic issues that support the overall business.

All this is difficult to do if a given manager at this passage still values individual contributions and functional work to the exclusion of everything else. Too often, people who have been promoted to manager-of-manager positions have skipped Passage One; they were promoted to first-line managers but didn't change skills, time applications, or work values. As a result, they clog the leadership pipeline because they hold first-line managers accountable for technical work rather than managerial work. Because they themselves skipped the first passage and still value individual contributions above managerial ones, they poison the managerial well. They help maintain and even instill the wrong values in those individuals who report to them. They choose high technical achievers for first-line managerial spots rather than true potential leaders; they are unable to differentiate between those who can do and those who can lead.

Managers at Passage Two need to be able to identify value-based resistance to managerial work, which is a common reaction among first-line managers. They need to recognize that the software designer who would rather design software than manage others cannot be allowed to move up to leadership work. No matter how brilliant he might be at software design, he will become an obstacle in the leadership pipeline if he derives no job satisfaction from managing and leading people. In fact, one of the tough responsibilities of managers of managers is to return people to individual-contributor roles if first-line managers don't shift their behaviors and values.

Coaching is also essential at this level because first-line managers frequently don't receive formal training in how to be a manager; they're dependent on their bosses to instruct them on the job. Coaching requires time—they need to go through the instruction-performance-feedback cycle with their people repeatedly before lessons sink in—and some managers aren't willing to reallocate their time in this way. In many organizations, coaching ability isn't rewarded (and the lack of it isn't penalized). It's no wonder that relatively few managers view coaching as mission-critical.

Passage Three: From Managing Managers to Functional Manager

This transition is tougher than it seems. While on the surface the difference between managing managers and functional management might appear negligible, a number of significant challenges lurk below the surface. Communication with the individual-contributor level now requires penetrating at least two layers of management, thus mandating development of new communication skills. What is just as significant, functional heads must manage some areas that are outside their own experiences. This means they must not only endeavor to understand this "foreign" work but also learn to value it.

At the same time, functional managers report to multifunctional general managers and therefore have to become skilled at taking other functional concerns and needs into consideration. Two major transitional skills are team play with other functional managers and competition for resources based on business needs. At the same time, managers at this turn should become proficient strategists, not only for their function but also for blending their functional strategy with the overall business strategy. From a time-application standpoint, this means participating in business team meetings and working with other functional managers. All this takes away from time spent on purely functional responsibilities, thus making it essential that functional managers delegate responsibility for overseeing many functional tasks to direct reports.

This leadership passage requires an increase in managerial maturity. In one sense, maturity means thinking and acting like a functional leader rather than a functional member. But it also means that managers need to adopt a broad, long-term perspective. Long-term strategy, such as state-of-the-art, futuristic thinking for their function, is usually what gives most managers trouble here. At this level, their leadership entails creating functional strategy that enables them to do something better than the competition. Whether it's coming up with a method to design more innovative products or devising a way to reach new customer groups, these managers must push the functional envelope. They must also push it into the future, looking for a sustainable competitive advantage rather than just an immediate but temporary edge.

> Tom's experiences illustrate the challenges new functional managers face. Six months ago, Tom was named the director of plant operations. In this capacity he has five direct reports: four who run large factories and one who runs purchasing of raw materials. Although Tom's experiences have made him appreciative of sales, financial, and other functional areas, Tom has trouble planning beyond immediate functional requirements and keeping in touch with line workers where the action is. Not only is it difficult for Tom to define the steps necessary for the plants to become a more integrated manufacturing facility, but he's also finding that he's lost touch with many of the workers he used to

communicate with on a regular basis. At many organizations, a guy like Tom would just muddle through, and his strengths would compensate for his weaknesses, at least on the surface. But on closer inspection, Tom would not be a full performer in his leadership position. For instance, it's important that Tom develop the skill of skip-level communication; he needs to know, without diminishing the authority of the plant managers and the first-line manager, what individual contributors are working on and how well they're being managed. If Tom doesn't develop this skill, he may alienate the plant manager and the first-line managers by usurping their authority, or he may be out of touch with how well his direct reports are supervising their people.

Luckily, Tom's organization has an assessment program in place that has identified his struggle with Passage Three and is providing him with coaching and the chance to attend a first-rate executive development program that will help him build the skills required at this leadership level.

Passage Four: From Functional Manager to Business Manager

This leadership passage is often the most satisfying as well as the most challenging of a manager's career, and it's mission-critical in organizations. Business mangers usually receive significant autonomy, which people with leadership instincts find liberating. They also are able to see a clear link between their efforts and marketplace results. At the same time, this is a sharp turn; it requires a major shift in skills, time applications, and work values. It's not simply a matter of people becoming more strategic and cross-functional in their thinking (though it's important to continue developing the abilities rooted in the previous level). Now they are in charge of integrating functions, whereas before they simply had to understand and work with other functions. But the biggest shift is from looking at plans and proposals functionally (Can we do it technically, professionally, or physically?) to a profit perspective (Will we make any money if we do this?) and to a long-term view (Is the profitability result sustainable?). New business managers must change the way they think in order to be successful.

There are probably more new and unfamiliar responsibilities here than at other levels. For people who have been in only one function for their entire career, a business manager position represents unexplored territory; they must suddenly become responsible for many unfamiliar functions and outcomes. Not only do they have to learn to manage different functions, but they also need to become skilled at working with a wider variety of people than ever before; they need to become more sensitive to functional diversity issues and communicating clearly and effectively. Even more difficult is the balancing act between future goals and present needs and making trade-offs between the two. Business managers must meet quarterly profit, market share, product, and people targets, and at the same time plan for goals three to five years into the future. The paradox of balancing short-term and long-term thinking is one that bedevils many managers at this turn—and why one of the requirements here is for thinking time. At this level, managers need to stop *doing* every second of the day and reserve time for reflection and analysis.

When business managers don't make this turn fully, the leadership pipeline quickly becomes clogged. For example, a common failure at this level is not valuing (or not effectively using) staff functions. Directing and energizing finance, human resources, legal, and other support groups are crucial business manager responsibilities. When managers don't understand or appreciate the contribution of support staff, these staff people don't deliver full performance. When the leader of the business demeans or diminishes their roles, staff people deliver halfhearted efforts; they can easily become energy-drainers. Business managers must learn to trust, accept advice, and receive feedback from all functional managers, even though they may never have experienced these functions personally.

Passage Five: From Business Manager to Group Manager

This is another leadership passage that at first glance doesn't seem overly arduous. The assumption is that if you can run one business successfully, you can do the same with two or more businesses. The flaw in this reasoning begins with what is valued at each leadership level. A business manager values the success of his own business. A group manager values the success of other people's businesses. This is a critical distinction because some people only derive satisfaction when they're the ones receiving the lion's share of the credit. As you might imagine, a group manager who doesn't value the success of others will fail to inspire and support the performance of the business managers who report to him. Or his actions might be dictated by his frustration; he's convinced he could operate the various businesses better than any of his managers and wishes he could be doing so. In either instance, the leadership pipeline becomes clogged with business managers who aren't operating at peak capacity because they're not being properly supported or their authority is being usurped.

This level also requires a critical shift in four skill sets. First, group managers must become proficient at evaluating strategy for capital allocation and deployment purposes. This is a sophisticated business skill that involves learning to ask the right questions, analyze the right data, and apply the right corporate perspective to understand which strategy has the greatest probability of success and therefore should be funded.

The second skill cluster involves development of business managers. As part of this development, group managers need to know which of the function managers are ready to become business managers. Coaching new business managers is also an important role for this level.

The third skill set has to do with portfolio strategy. This is quite different from business strategy and demands a perceptual shift. This is the first time managers have to ask these questions: Do I have the right collection of businesses? What businesses should be added, subtracted, or changed to position us properly and ensure current and future earnings?

Fourth, group managers must become astute about assessing whether they have the right core capabilities. This means avoiding wishful thinking and instead taking a hard, objective look at their range of resources and making a judgment based on analysis and experience.

Leadership becomes more holistic at this level. People may master the required skills, but they won't perform at full leadership capacity if they don't begin to see themselves as broad-gauged executives. By broad-gauged, we mean that managers need to factor in the complexities of running multiple businesses, thinking in terms of community, industry, government, and ceremonial activities. They must also prepare themselves for the bigger decisions, greater risks and uncertainties, and longer time spans that are inherent to this leadership level. They must always be cognizant of what Wall Street wants them to achieve in terms of the financial scorecard. Group managers can't take a specialist mentality into a realm that mandates holistic thinking. They need to evolve their perspective to the point that they see issues in the broadest possible terms.

We should also point out that some smaller companies don't have a group manager passage. In these companies, CEOs usually undertake a group manager's responsibilities.

Passage Six: From Group Manager to Enterprise Manager

When the leadership pipeline becomes clogged at the top, it negatively affects all leadership levels. A CEO who has skipped one or more passages can diminish the performance of not only the managers who report directly to him but also individuals all the way down the line. Such a CEO not only fails to develop other managers effectively but also doesn't fulfill the responsibilities that come with this position.

The transition during the sixth passage is much more focused on values than on skills. To an even greater extent than at the previous level, people must reinvent their self-concept as an enterprise manager. As leaders of an institution, they must be long-term, visionary thinkers. At the same time, they must develop operating mechanisms to know and drive quarter-by-quarter performance that is in tune with longer-term strategy. The trade-offs involved can be mind-bending, and enterprise leaders learn to value these trade-offs. In addition, this new leadership role often requires well-developed external sensitivity and the ability to manage external constituencies, sense significant external shifts, and do something about them proactively (rather than reactively). Again, CEOs value this outward-looking perspective.

Enterprise leaders need to come to terms with the fact that their performance as a CEO will be based on three or four high-leverage decisions annually; they must set these three or four mission-critical priorities and focus on them. There's a subtle but fundamental shift in responsibility from strategic to visionary thinking and from an operations to a global perspective. There's also a "letting go" process that should take place during this passage if it hasn't taken place previously. Enterprise leaders must let go of the pieces—that is, the individual products and customers—and focus on the whole (How well do we conceive, develop, produce, and market all products to all customers?).

Finally, at this level a CEO must assemble a team of high-achieving and ambitious direct reports, knowing that some of them want his job and picking them for the team despite this knowledge. This is also the only leadership position in the organization for which inspiring the entire employee population through a variety of communication tools is essential.

Leadership pipeline problems occur at this level for two common reasons:

- CEOs are often unaware that this is a significant passage that requires changes in values.
- It's difficult to develop a CEO for this particular leadership transition.

In terms of the latter, preparation for the chief executive position is the result of a series of diverse experiences over a long time. The best developmental approach provides carefully selected job assignments that stretch people over time and allow them to learn and practice necessary skills. Though coaching may be helpful as an adjunct to this development process, people usually need time, experience, and the right assignments to develop into effective CEOs.

The former point is a matter of will and conscious effort. We've seen too many CEOs fail because they didn't view this leadership turn as a necessary one to make—or to make fully. They sustain the same skills, time applications, and work values that served them well as group managers and never adjust their self-concept to fit their new leadership role. They behave as though they are running a portfolio of businesses, not one entity.

Adapting the Model to Small Business Requirements

This model was built primarily in large organizations, but we have used it successfully in medium-sized and small companies (some with as few as twenty employees). Essentially, this model reflects the hierarchy of work that exists in any company. Even small companies grow into this hierarchy as they become successful. We'd like to summarize how the model applies to smaller, growing organizations.

In a small company with fewer than twenty people, the only real leadership passage is a variation on our first one: from managing self to *owner* (instead of *managing others*). This owner-founder usually has to move from individual contributor to manager of other people. After designing a product or creating a service that is successful, she must hire more people, and thus begins this leadership passage. If the business is to survive, she must learn, allow time for, and value skills such as coaching, planning, and rewarding employees. If she doesn't, people will either quit or (even worse) stay and perform poorly. A significant percentage of owner-founder enterprises fail to become large organizations. In many instances, their longevity is limited to one or two generations past the founder. In the venture capital–funded companies, founders are frequently replaced by more experienced managers from larger companies sooner rather than later. Given all this, a small company's leadership passages are limited by both size and circumstance.

If the business evolves and more people and offices or stores are added, the owner must again go through a leadership passage. Because she can't be everywhere at once, she must appoint additional managers and hold them accountable for managerial work. She must ascertain that the work of the entire enterprise is integrated so that customers are properly served and resources are used efficiently. Essentially, this business owner is going through Passage Two: from managing others to managing managers. In this role, she must make sure the total effort is profitable and sustainable. Setting goals externally based on what customers want and what the competition is doing is another new responsibility.

Small businesses often fail when a new level of leadership-management must be added. We worked closely with a financial service institution that did acquisitions lending to small business, and they asked us to help them determine, before the loan was made, whether the borrowing company could manage a larger company postacquisition. We studied almost fifty loans and found that the companies that failed to handle the increased size were headed by people who were reluctant to change their own work habits; they found it difficult to give up their hands-on involvement or trust a new layer of management. In other words, they were unable or unwilling to make a crucial leadership passage.

As a business continues to grow, understanding the passages in this expanding organization is crucial. We have worked with small company owners who have successfully adopted the model shown in Figure 1.1.

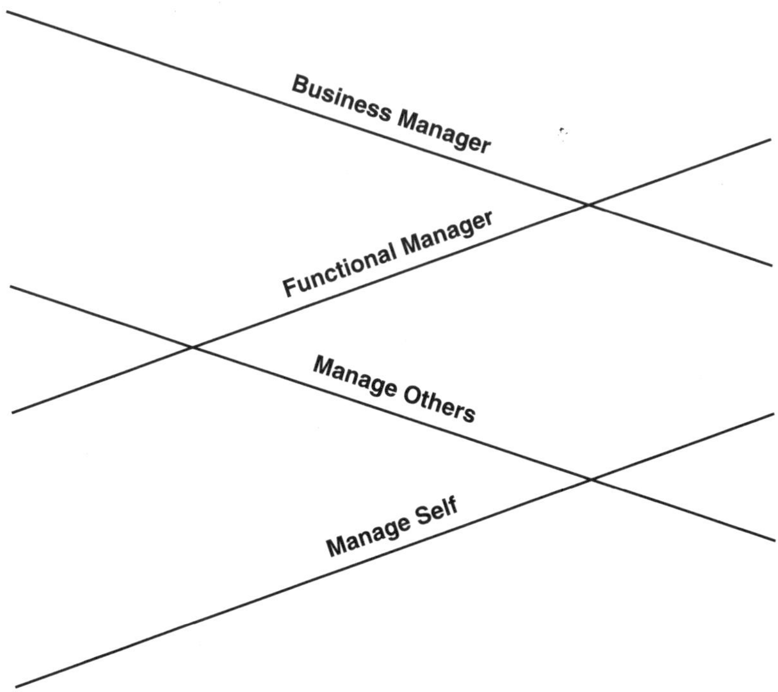

Figure 1.1. Small Business Pipeline Model.

The group level (managers of several businesses) doesn't apply to the small business model, and the work of the enterprise manager is done by the business manager (who runs the business for short-term and long-term results and deals with government agencies, key customers, and so on). Similarly, in this small business model the manager-of-managers layer is usually absorbed by the functional manager.

With these differences in mind, smaller companies can reap the same leadership development benefits as larger organizations.

Passages Through the Pipeline

Knowledge about each passage helps reveal "hidden" leadership problems at every organizational layer; this knowledge also provides a way to solve these problems. Too often, organizations don't realize that their leaders aren't performing at full capacity because they aren't holding them accountable for the right things. Companies focus only on the economic requirements of a given job rather than the skills, time applications, and values of a specific leadership level. As a result, a business manager is allowed to spend most of his time acquiring new customers rather than developing an effective business strategy. Or the business manager's boss, the group manager, never questions or explores what the business manager values about his work and whether those values are appropriate for the leadership the company requires from him. But when this manager's strategy is flawed and important goals aren't achieved, he isn't held accountable (or he isn't held accountable for the right thing).

If, however, the organization was acutely aware of these leadership passages, the problem could be quickly diagnosed and the manager developed accordingly. The organization would be aware that this business manager is still doing his job as though he's at Passage One, that he values face-to-face selling above all else, and that he has never acquired basic strategic skills crucial to his current leadership level. A development program could be created targeting these deficiencies. Concurrently, this business manager's boss, the group manager, would be held accountable for developing the business manager and coaching him about the importance of strategic planning and how he should be allocating his time.

By establishing appropriate requirements for the six leadership levels, companies could greatly facilitate the succession planning, development, and selection processes in their organizations. Individual managers could clearly see the gap between their current level of performance and the desired level; they could also see gaps in their training and experience and where they may have skipped a passage (or parts of a passage) and how that's hurting their performance. The clarity of leadership requirements would also help the human resources function, in that HR could make development decisions based on where people fall short in skills, time applications, and values rather than relying on generalized training and development programs. In addition, an individual's readiness for a move to the next leadership level could be clearly identified rather than inaccurately tied to how well they performed in their previous position. These leadership passages provide companies with a way to "objectify" selection. Rather than selecting based on past performance, personal connections, and personal preferences, managers can be held to a higher, more effective standard. Organizations can select someone to make a leadership turn when he's clearly working at the level to which he is assigned and demonstrating some of the skills required at the next level. And of course, the Pipeline model provides organizations with a diagnostic tool that helps them identify mismatches between individual capabilities and leadership level and remove the mismatched person if necessary.

You should also be aware of three other benefits to the pipeline. First, having a leadership pipeline in place can reduce emotional stress for individual employees. When someone skips leadership passages and is placed in a position for which he lacks the skills, time applications, and work values, it takes a large emotional toll. The Pipeline model makes skipping passages unlikely. Second, this model helps people move through leadership passages at the right speed. People who ticket-punch their way through jobs don't absorb the necessary values and skills; people who get stuck in a passage never "go" places where they can acquire new skills and evolve their leadership capacity. The Pipeline model provides a measurement system identifying when someone is ready to move to the next leadership level. Third, the Pipeline model reduces the typical time frame needed to prepare an individual for the top leadership position in a large corporation. Because the Pipeline model clearly defines what is needed to move from one level to the next, there's little or no wasted time on jobs that merely duplicate skills.

From a pure talent perspective, however, the most significant benefit of the Pipeline methodology is that you don't need to bring in stars to prime the leadership pump and unclog the pipeline. You can create your own stars up and down the line, beginning at the first level when people make the transition from managing themselves to managing others.

Frequently Asked Questions

Q. Does this model cover everyone in the company?

A. In the companies we have worked with, this model covers about 80 to 85 percent of the positions. Many positions in the corporate staff—typically high-level specialists such as strategy analysts, tax lawyers, benefits designers, insurance specialists, and treasury experts—may not fit within the Pipeline framework, because the Pipeline was originally created for operational people who move up to run businesses and the company. It is possible to amend the Pipeline model to indicate where key staff positions fit.

Q. If I am a corporate specialist who wants to move into operational leadership, how do I get into the flow of the pipeline to be considered for leadership positions in the future?

A. Corporate specialists usually have company-wide or close to company-wide accountability for a narrow (relative to the whole company) subject area. If they don't have a deep understanding of the workings of the business or businesses, they need to acquire it. They also must acquire experience in leading large numbers of people with diverse skills and backgrounds. Because you want to move into operational leadership, it is best to move early in your career out of a corporate specialty and into a position leading to management. You should also prepare to take a pay cut if necessary. This learning may require swallowing one's pride, but it is critical to success in moving from a corporate specialty into operational leadership.

Q. Can I use this if my company or business doesn't fit the model?

A. Few companies will fit the Leadership Pipeline model perfectly. We don't suggest that you fit your company or business or function into the model. Rather, adapt the model to your company while keeping the principles intact. For example, many marketing functions and HR functions don't have all the passages; the marketing function manager may have to deliver both function manager and manager of managers results. Don't create a new passage to fit the model. Instead, create a passage when size, scope, and good organization design requires it.

Q. What are the biggest problems in producing a pipeline of leaders that is full and flowing?

A. The following are the three biggest problems that we have observed:

1. Companies fail to recognize when inappropriate work values cause leaders to do work themselves that others should be doing. They may be able to do it faster and better than direct reports, but they aren't growing themselves or their people.

2. Senior management doesn't require that all leaders develop other leaders. Yet this is in everyone's best interest, because in the end it frees up valuable time.

3. Senior leaders spend all their time on today's rather than tomorrow's issues. As a result of this focus on the present, the company is not prepared to cope with future developments.

Q. What should I do if I missed a passage?

A. Many successful leaders working in finance or HR missed passages because their organizations are small and don't have all the passages. Examine your work habits to see whether you are working at the right level. If not, pay special attention to whichever chapter discusses your missing passage. Examine your mistakes and misses. If they are caused by lack of skill from a previous layer, ask for help from your boss or HR to fill the gap.

Q. How does this model account for our company's competency model?

A. Competency models seem to be everywhere, so we have to account for them. Unfortunately, most competency models are not differentiated by layer or are differentiated inappropriately. They suffer from a "one size fits all" construction. We suggest you align them by layer where possible by connecting them to the work of that layer. That will improve the value of your competency models. If your competencies are not or cannot be connected to specific work, call them what they are—values. We observe line managers ignoring them in most companies because they don't have a clear connection to the work.

Observations from the Field

- The size of the Leadership Pipeline depends on the size of the company. All companies have a "basket" of leadership work to do. Big companies have a big basket; small companies have a small one. As we've worked with organizations of all sizes, we've learned that there are more "break points" between old and new jobs in larger companies, so the Pipeline expands to fit the size of the organization.

- Pipeline principles translate across geographical boundaries. The Leadership Pipeline model has helped both fast-paced, highly successful companies in developed countries as well as companies in developing countries, including formerly communist countries. These passages are universal, as are the requirements for each passage.

- The number of passages varies by company. Some companies have six passages, some seven, some four. The concept doesn't change. We've found that because we listed six passages, people became fixated on six as the right number for every organization. It's not. What is required is proper differentiation, with even spacing between the layers.

- Companies often have too many leadership positions and too little leadership in all functions. We have found that one of the great benefits of the Pipeline model is spotlighting the "too many leaders" syndrome. It identifies how companies reward individual contributors with promotions to leadership roles. Strong technical people are given a title, two people to manage, and more money. They still spend most of their time doing technical work.

- Defining a technical pipeline is a great idea. Given the previous points, we discovered that strong technical people need to have their own passages, with concomitant rewards. It doesn't take much work to define the technical pipeline. It is actually an old concept that isn't used much these days. It offers an alternative for those who want more challenging work or more rewards but can't or won't lead. It really helps in unclogging the pipeline.

- A greater emphasis should be placed on the future at the functional layer and above. As we alluded to earlier, working on the future is hard but must be done to assure long-term success. Getting trapped into solving today's problems uses up leaders' time. Leaders at the functional layer and above should get their people to solve those problems and free themselves to grapple with challenges down the road.

2

From Managing Self to Managing Others

When people are appointed to their first management positions, they often think they have it made. All their hard work as an individual contributor has finally been rewarded, and they see a management assignment as a cause for celebration. They call their spouse, make reservations at a favorite restaurant, and generally believe that they're more than ready to take on a management role.

In fact, to be successful as a first-time manager requires a major transition for which many people are not adequately prepared. Perhaps the most difficult aspect of this transition is that first-time managers are responsible for getting work done through others rather than on their own. While new managers may recognize this transition intellectually, they reject it psychologically, as evidenced by their behaviors. Typically they overpower their direct reports with their expertise. For instance, a neophyte investment banking firm manager might structure a complex transaction himself rather than helping his direct report do it, relishing the thrill of showing everyone his extraordinary skill in this area. In other situations, new managers end up competing with direct reports on assignments and sometimes complete the assignments themselves when they're frustrated by how their people approach it. Giving up the tasks and responsibilities that earned them a manager title in the first place is a tremendously difficult aspect of this leadership passage.

In a world in which knowledge-worker companies are multiplying, this is an especially crucial passage. Today's twenty-two-year-old individual contributor is tomorrow's CEO. She no longer has to wait thirty years to ascend to the top spot; she may be ready in five or ten years. Plus, first-time managers in knowledge-worker companies have a tremendous impact on productivity (in terms of cost efficiency and revenue growth). If they're acting like individual contributors, their impact will be reduced. For these reasons alone, organizations must do more than just give lip service to the importance of this passage.

To help your people make this challenging passage successfully, you need to be familiar with the targeted shift in skills, time applications, and work values and how to facilitate this shift. First, however, you should understand how events at the individual contributor level have recently reshaped the skill, time, and value requirements.

The Rising Power and Expectations of Individual Contributors

Frontline employees have unprecedented access to incredible amounts of information via the Internet and other sources, and they possess great freedom to innovate, affect operating results, and serve customers. But they won't use this freedom—or use it wisely—unless first-line managers recognize that the day of the "military manager" has passed.

Managers who issue orders, jealously guard information, and make unilateral decisions won't get the best performance from their people. The old-line manager who controlled people by controlling information is an anachronism. Today, employees expect to have access to what was formerly considered privileged information and to be involved in the decision-making process. They also want a certain amount of latitude in the way they carry out assignments. In other words, they want direction but also the freedom to reach a destination in their own way.

Recognize, too, that most employees are more savvy and sophisticated about career issues than in the past. They've seen parents and friends lose jobs through downsizing, and they're aware that the only true job security is to possess in-demand skills and be knowledgeable about career paths in their profession. Because of all this, they expect career development opportunities.

First-line managers need to make the transition to these new realities and not to the old ones. This isn't always easy, in part because many of the people who are promoted to this first managerial level are technicians; they have spent their time developing great skill at carrying out a given assignment rather than being in touch with the needs and expectations of their peers. They haven't undergone the workplace socialization that would provide useful insights and experiences for a new manager.

In lieu of that socialization, they must become cognizant of the first-level leadership characteristics that will help them meet the needs and maximize the performance of their people.

Three Achievements of Terrific First-Time Managers

Table 2.1 provides an overview of the transition that must take place at this level.

As you can see, the shift here is not only qualitative but quantitative. The number of skills alone may appear daunting. A quick look at this table also demonstrates, however, that this transition can be summed up as follows: Managers must cease thinking only about themselves and start thinking about others. Of course, all this is easier said than done, especially in light of the numerous changes listed on this table.

We've found that all these changes can be boiled down to the following three areas:

Table 2.1. Passage One: First-Time Management.

Individual Contributor	vs.	First-Line Manager
Skills • Technical or professional proficiency • Team play • Relationship building for personal benefits, personal results* • Using company tools, processes, and procedures		Skills • Planning—projects, budget, workforce • Job design • Selection (of people) • Delegation • Performance monitoring • Coaching and feedback • Performance measurement • Rewards and motivation • Communication and climate setting • Relationship building up, down, sideways for the unit's benefit • Acquisition of resources
Time Application • Daily discipline—arrival, departure • Meeting personal due dates for projects—usually short-term by managing own time		Time Application • Annual planning—budgets, projects • Making time available for subordinates—both at your request and at theirs • Setting priorities for unit and team • Communication time with other units, customers, suppliers
Work Values • Getting results through personal proficiency* • High-quality technical or professional work • Accepting the company's values		Work Values • Getting results through others • Success of direct reports • Managerial work and disciplines • Success of unit • Self as manager • Visible integrity

Source: Drotter Human Resources, Inc.

*Items to be dramatically reduced or left behind when person becomes a first-line manager.

1. Defining and assigning work to be done, including communicating with the boss and others about needs or expectations, planning, organizing, choosing people, and delegating.
2. Enabling direct reports to do the work by monitoring, coaching, providing feedback, acquiring resources, problem solving, and communicating.
3. Building social contracts through establishing relationships with direct reports, bosses, and support groups that facilitate open dialogues and trust.

Let's examine each area so that you can recognize the optimum skills, time applications, and values for this level as well as where first-time managers typically fall short.

Defining and Assigning Work to Be Done

Job design and delegation are rarely the focus of training. Perhaps it's because people consider them inherent skills or ones that are easily acquired. It may be that organizations assume that there are natural dividing lines for work—geography for salespeople or process steps for manufacturing people—and that job assignments flow from these natural divisions. Though it's true that existing parameters make it easier to assign some tasks, there is also a need for judgment—especially when first-line employees feel tremendously overworked and cut off from their bosses. Downsizing, delayering, merging companies, and other factors have made employees feel as though they have too much to do and no one to ask how to do it. First-line managers who know how to design a job effectively can diminish employees' negative feelings and make them feel positive about an assignment; they can give employees a sense that they're developing highly marketable skills that will enhance their career prospects.

Unfortunately, many first-time managers stumble when it comes to defining and assigning work because they don't have the right discussions with the right people. These discussions should help them obtain a good understanding of what is required of their unit and create assignments so that people are working at tasks that are appropriate to them and that they can complete on time and with a high level of quality.

The logical person for a manager to discuss these issues with is his boss. It's more and more important, however, that he also talk with peers, customers, suppliers, partners, and other relevant parties. A sales manager, for instance, can be much more effective if she is aware of what customers do with the products or services her unit sells. She can learn more about specific customer needs and make assignments recognizing which salespeople are best able to meet those needs.

These discussions take time, of course, and first-time managers who are used to spending their time *doing* rather than *discussing* may charge ahead and create assignments without sufficient knowledge.

Delegation presents another formidable challenge to novice managers. It's one thing to figure out what needs to be done and who needs to do it; it's quite another, and much more psychologically difficult, to let go of work that you were trained to do and that has helped you become successful. This is a very difficult step for first-time managers to take, and they're usually able to take it only when they realize that delegation is not abdication. They need to be trained and coached in how to delegate and become skilled at regular review and follow-up, problem solving, measurement, rewards, and coaching their own people.

As part of these defining and assigning responsibilities, new managers must learn to hire the right people to do the assigned tasks. Though many of them quickly learn how to hire people with the talent and experience to do a given job properly, they find it more difficult to hire people who "fit" a company's work values and practices. This is an important responsibility: in most cases in which people early in their career leave or are asked to leave an organization, it's because the individual doesn't fit. Although some people depart because they lack the talent for a specific job, most simply lack the beliefs, values, and ability to conform to an established style of working. Becoming astute about hiring people who are well matched to the work style and beliefs of the organization can greatly enhance a first-time manager's effectiveness.

Enabling Direct Reports to Do the Work

A sure sign of a clogged leadership pipeline at this first level is high stress among individual contributors. When they feel overwhelmed and think their boss isn't doing much to help them deal with their work, it's likely that this manager is missing a crucial first-level skill. Here are some common signs that a manager hasn't mastered this skill:

- Views questions from his people as interruptions
- Fixes their mistakes rather than teaching them to do the work properly
- Refuses to take ownership of the success of his people, distancing himself from their problems and failures

Part of helping people do their work involves paying attention. Monitoring what is getting done and how it's getting done requires both time and effort. Managers need to engage in regular discussions with people as well as keep tabs on work flow. They have to ask questions about what's getting in the way of completing tasks effectively or what might facilitate the process. Monitoring needs to be an active rather than a passive process. It's not enough just to take notes. The information gleaned from monitoring should be translated into a pat on the back and positive feedback when results are good and into training, rescheduling, redesign of methods, and requests for more resources when results aren't so good.

Perhaps the simplest skill—and the one that many new managers never valued as individual contributors—is just being available. This doesn't just mean keeping your door open and grudgingly answering questions. It's much more of an attitude than an event. People sense when a boss is approachable. Everything from his speech to his body language communicates accessibility (or the lack of it). This is really much more of a value- and time-application issue than a skill set. When managers believe that being approachable is crucial to their leadership role, they make themselves available, both physically and emotionally.

Building Social Contracts

The changes required here are primarily rooted in values. Although there is some skill necessary to build strong relationships with bosses, direct reports, customers, suppliers, and so on, the main issue has to do with a value transformation. When you're an individual contributor, relationship-building is often of secondary importance. In recent years, the Internet and other factors have given individual contributors much more independence to apply their technical skills. Though they are sometimes asked to work as members of a team, they still receive great freedom to work on their own.

Managers, however, are highly interdependent creatures. They need to build trust and open lines of communication vertically and horizontally. This is a significant hurdle during this passage, not only because they may not have valued relationship building as individual contributors but also because their corporate culture may not value it. In some companies, relationship-building has political overtones, suggesting brown-nosing and other manipulative behaviors. In these instances, it takes a concerted effort by managers and strong coaching by their boss to overcome this hurdle.

The other big issue is that a manager must learn to value and build relationships with three types of people:

The Boss (and by Extension, the Management Structure) The big transition here is from an individual contributor's often adversarial view of management to becoming part of the establishment. It's not just connecting with a boss who is the lifeline to resources, information, and so on. It's connecting with the larger management structure and understanding how it works.

Direct Reports This isn't about liking subordinates or socializing with them but about building mutual respect and support. First-line managers need to become accountable for the success of their subordinates (and vice versa). In this way, a relationship is built that has mutual benefits. Demonstrating personal integrity is another aspect of relationship-building with direct reports. First-line managers who are perceived as devious and manipulative will never form productive relationships with their people.

Suppliers, Customers, and Other Relevant Individuals This type of relationship demands broader thinking and a wider perspective than was necessary for an individual contributor. Establishing "common purpose" relationships with these people—relationships in which both parties work toward the success of the business—is often a new experience. Supplying information and providing early warnings on problems to an "outsider" requires an adjustment in perception.

Two Examples of Transition Troubles

To help you understand the difficulties people experience at this first leadership passage—and also to give you some insight into how organizations need to respond to these difficulties—we'd like to share two stories with you. These real-world examples will give you a sense of the challenges and struggles first-line managers face and how they can often occupy positions at this level and lack the requisite skills.

> When Barry became a regional sales manager for a large pharmaceutical company, he saw it as an opportunity to earn more money and have more influence within the organization. When the position was offered, he didn't hesitate for a second, even though he had loved his previous job as a salesperson; he'd enjoyed the autonomy given him, largely working out of his home office, traveling the region, and meeting a variety of physicians and hospital administrators.
>
> As a sales manager with eight sales representatives reporting to him, Barry has had to spend much of his time in the field observing his reps, hiring and training new people, going to meetings with other sales managers, and doing a great deal of paperwork (assessments, reports, and the like). Not only was he upset that his autonomy had been taken away, but he was also frustrated by all the paperwork. The psychological narcotic of closing a sale evaporated when he became a sales manager. For two years Barry struggled with this role, and his people also struggled because he didn't provide them with the guidance they desperately needed. Even though he knew certain reps were making mistakes with customers, he found it difficult to communicate what they were doing wrong. At first he did attempt to help people correct mistakes, but he quickly grew tired of his people's defensive reactions. Eventually Barry quit to take a sales rep position with another company where he would be given a larger territory and greater compensation.

The leadership pipeline problems at Barry's managerial level were both preventable and resolvable. It's possible that Barry might have made this first managerial passage successfully if he had been given training to gain the communication and other skills he lacked; it would have also given him an understanding of what was expected of him as a manager, and he might have taken himself off of the managerial track. Though it's possible that Barry wasn't cut out to be a manager, it's also possible that he could have adjusted to that role if someone had coached him and helped him question and reconfigure his values. As Barry matures and gains experience, his values might naturally shift so that he realizes the importance of communication and building mutually beneficial relationships with direct reports. Unfortunately, Barry's company had no assessment system in place to identify what Barry's values were and how entrenched he was in his work beliefs. If they had done so, they might have either put him on a "super-salesman" career track or designed a development program that would have allowed him to assume a managerial role when he was emotionally ready to do so.

> Though Barry didn't make his passage successfully, Mary has overcome significant obstacles and has changed in a way that has helped her take this leadership turn. As a computer programmer for a telecommunications company, Mary found great satisfaction and success working on technical problems and creating solutions. Mary was a bit awkward and unsure when she was asked to deal with people issues but quite confident when confronted with technical matters. After three years, she was promoted to the manager of the group of seven that she had been part of.
>
> Unlike Barry's company, Mary's company provided her with some training that helped her develop some of the skills she needed as a first-time manager. She learned how to design and assign work, and HR worked with her on interviewing and hiring skills. Still, this training was insufficient. When Mary's boss began putting significant

pressure on her group to develop new systems, she responded by becoming overly involved in her people's work. She demanded daily reports on her group's progress and often insisted that they follow her ideas rather than coaching them on how to come up with viable ones themselves. It was almost as though Mary thought she could impose her will on the group, that if she returned to her former role as a member of the team, everything would be OK. In reality, Mary's intrusiveness alienated other team members and robbed them of the guidance they required. Not only did they miss the first deadline for developing new systems, but the systems they eventually developed were seriously flawed.

Mary's boss recognized that she was having problems with her managerial role and used coaching and 360 degree feedback to help her deal with this leadership transition. Mary was surprised to hear that her group—people she had known and worked with well in the past—found her intrusiveness and inability to delegate off-putting. More than that, their comments demonstrated that Mary's managerial style was preventing them from achieving their objective. This feedback forced Mary to confront the issues in a way she had never done before. Though she recognized intellectually that she was micromanaging her people, the emotional recognition caused her to want to change her behaviors. Through coaching, Mary began understanding how to delegate and forced herself to do so. The combination of the coaching and feedback also helped her shift her values; she came to realize that as much as she enjoyed the technical part of her job, she also found satisfaction in combining her technical knowledge with her new managerial skills to help people successfully complete an assignment. Mary didn't change overnight—it took several months before she was able to delegate effectively and keep her hands off an important assignment. Her boss recognized she was making progress and provided her with time, advice, and encouragement to make this transition.

Pipeline-Unclogging Tactics

Measures need to be put in place so that first-time managers make a smooth transition from their individual contributor roles. These measures need to prepare people for this transition, monitor whether they're making it successfully, and intervene when there are problems. Although there is some overlap between all three of these measures, let's look at them separately so you can understand how to implement them effectively.

> Preparation: Clearly communicate the skills, time applications, and work values required at this passage and provide training that helps people make necessary changes.

This is an easy first step and one that's frequently overlooked. Individual contributors need to understand what's required of them as they move through this first leadership level, and they need to understand it in specific rather than general terms. You can use Table 2.1 or the list in the earlier section, Three Achievements of Terrific First-Time Managers, as a tool to delineate the requirements for a first-line manager in your organization. It's also useful to communicate the behaviors that need to be left behind (as indicated in Table 2.1). Some people find that modeling—live demonstrations of a required skill that the manager can observe—helps bring the paper list to life. A boss should discuss these issues with a first-time manager and answer any relevant questions.

In articulating these leadership goals and expectations, it's important to go beyond a listing of skills. As we've emphasized, individual contributors are focused on technical competence. Getting the job done quickly and effectively is what they value. If first-time managers focus only on skills, they may not see a need for a shift in what they value; they'll simply find a way to become competent in a given area without learning to value the new skill. This can cause all sorts of problems, as skills applied without concomitant values are not applied with enthusiasm, energy, and innovation.

General Electric used a model that you may find useful when it comes to the skills-versus-values question (see Figure 2.1).

Obviously, the best place to be in this matrix is the high-values, high-results quadrant. At GE, the tough issue was what do you do with someone who has high results but low values? The answer was that you let him go if he can't shift his values because ultimately his contribution will be undermined by his incompatible belief system. You can adapt this matrix to impress upon first-time managers that it's not enough to acquire the skills needed at this level, but they must also refocus their values; that if they don't

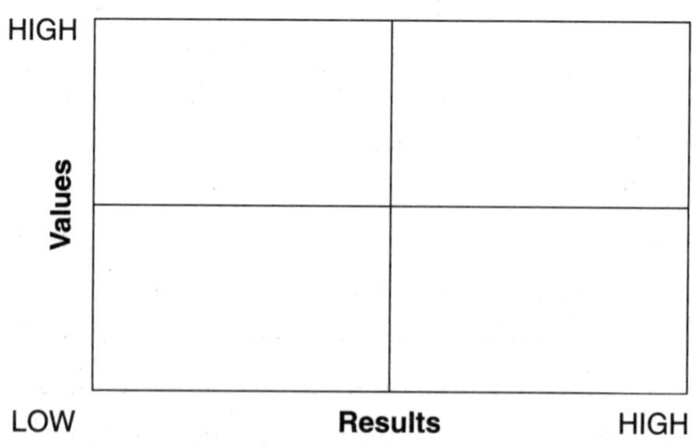

Figure 2.1. GE Leadership Matrix.

value their work as first-time managers, their acquired skills will be insufficient.

Training is also an important part of the preparation process, and it's unlikely that first-time managers have been trained in all or even many of the skills discussed here. It's even less likely that anyone has talked to them about—or helped them with—the value and time shifts that come with this passage. Specific work experiences, new manager assimilation programs, discussions with a boss or mentor, and training courses geared toward the acquisition of skills in hiring, delegation, relationship-building, job design, and the like should be made available to aspiring managers.

Monitoring: Determine whether and where someone is having difficulty with this first-level transition.

There are numerous ways you can keep tabs on whether a given manager is making a successful transition, including the following:

Observation Sit in on first-line managers' interactions with their direct reports and determine whether they're exhibiting the skills this leadership level requires.

Sampling With 360 degree feedback (that assesses for attributes discussed in this chapter), employee-attitude surveys, and other tools, assess how others view the behaviors and attitudes of first-time managers. Direct reports can provide insight about how their bosses are handling their new roles.

Gap Analysis Question first-time managers about their perceptions of their skills, time applications, and values. Contrast their answers with information received from observation and sampling, and make them aware of the gap between the two.

> Intervention: Provide regular feedback and coaching to help people make this transition; take action if they're experiencing significant difficulty in doing so.

The only way to unclog the leadership pipeline is to do something. Rather than allowing first-time managers to maintain their individual contributor attitudes and behaviors, you need to intervene in a way that catalyzes the changes you seek. Intervention can take many forms:

Coaching-Feedback There's no substitute for one-on-one coaching from the first-time manager's boss. Although written reports (based on monitoring a manager's performance) and classroom training can help, the impact is magnified when the boss delivers the news directly, is open to questions, and responds with sage advice. Scheduling of time gives many first-time managers trouble—they spend too much time doing and not enough time managing—and they're usually very responsive to coaching when it comes to these time applications. In addition, the boss must demand improvements as part of a performance appraisal process.

Peer Learning and Partnering Organized discussions with peers on specific skills can often be a useful learning experience, allowing people to exchange ideas and concerns with others who have recently undergone the same transition. Partnering is simply a more on-the-job approach for skill acquisition. Having direct reports benchmark local companies is another great learning tool.

Meetings, Readings, and Travel These techniques can all supplement more direct intervention. Staff meetings at which first-time managers talk about what they've learned during the past month (or longer period) give them a chance to articulate their understanding of the passage they're going through and express concerns. Assigned reading—articles, books, and so on—can provide an outside perspective on the leadership passage they're making. Traveling with a boss offers these managers an excellent opportunity to talk about the issues they're facing in a variety of environments outside the office.

New Work Assignment Some first-time managers simply aren't ready to take on leadership responsibilities and need to be returned to an individual contributor job and given development opportunities to better prepare them for this transition. Others simply aren't cut out for this role and should be put on an individual contributor track (that is, moved from salesperson to super-salesperson).

It's important to point out that first-time managers need to practice and perfect their skills first; mastering skills triggers the process by which these managers learn to allocate their time differently and to recognize the importance of shifting their values. When first-time managers lack the ability to delegate or coach, they'll schedule relatively little time for each activity, preferring to spend as much time as possible on what they're good at—doing analysis, designing products, creating software, and handling other individual contributor tasks. They don't want to look foolish in front of their former peers and will therefore spend time on activities that make them appear competent. They also are avoiding the monumental shift of being responsible for the productivity, output, and expansion of individual capacity that comes with a manager's job.

This is why bosses should coach them on practicing new skills, asking questions when they're confused, and seeking other assistance. Once they become proficient at a new skill, they not only spend more time doing it but eventually learn to value it. These managers require proof that a value shift is a good personal strategy that will lead to personal satisfaction. When they find that these new skills help their group achieve objectives and they receive approval for their efforts, they're likely to embrace the new value.

Who Is Responsible?

Formal training for first-line managers is relatively common, and it certainly provides them with instruction in some skills that are useful at this level. But training isn't a panacea, and the HR department isn't going to create a course that magically helps people make this passage effectively. The direct responsibility for preparing first-time managers rests with managers of managers. This latter group needs to learn how to coach their direct reports to make this transition. Unfortunately, managers of managers receive little or no training in this area.

This is especially unfortunate because first-line managers are the feeder system for all other management positions. If you're experiencing difficulty filling management slots at various levels throughout your organization, the source of the difficulty can be traced back to this first leadership transition. A simple litmus test is whether the majority of your first-time managers are being trained and measured on the skills, time applications, and values discussed here and whether they're being held accountable for the success of the individual contributors they manage. If not, your leadership pipeline is clogged at its source, and you shouldn't expect much leadership to flow to other levels. The key to resolving this problem resides with managers of managers, so let's turn our attention to the requirements for this next leadership passage.

Frequently Asked Questions

Q. Our company has so many different types of manager positions, I can't figure out if your "manage others" definition applies to all of them. How should I adjust my approach based on these differences?

A. We are aware of six different types of first-line manage others positions.

- A factory foreman responsible for many hourly employees who work on product production.
- A sales manager with eight or nine remotely located sales professionals.
- A finance manager with four highly trained analysts supplying analysis to the business.
- A call-center manager with thirty direct reports who answer phones.
- A manager in a laboratory who has responsibility for a team of Ph.D.s doing research.
- A maintenance manager with several licensed or skilled tradesmen such as electricians, plumbers, millwrights, and carpenters.

These managers of others all do the same things: plan the work, assign the work, monitor progress, give feedback, coach, measure performance, hire and fire, and so on. The work itself is the same for all six categories. What needs to be adjusted are time frames and emphasis.

For the more professionally trained populations, the planning should extend further into the future. Give them a sufficient runway to allow them to use their skills. Provide hourly workers with a sense of the future, but stress a more immediate focus and feedback. Call-center employees also need a picture of the future, and they also require help in handling difficult calls. Supply the sales force needs with more product or service training as well as skills for closing the deal. For each category of employee the objective is self-sufficiency but the method for getting there differs widely.

Q. Am I really a manager if I have two or three direct reports?

A. Probably not. At least half your time should be spent on management work for you to be considered a manager. If the majority of your time is spent doing technical or professional work then you are in the high end of the "manage self" category.

Q. What are the early signs that a new manager of others is not succeeding?

A. The first sign is failure to engage properly with direct reports: not being available, not holding meetings, not getting to know them as people and not communicating. Another indicator is failure to get clarity with their boss on things like standards for success, problem areas to be addressed, and priorities of the business. Working in isolation from their management ultimately leads to inappropriate performance.

Q. I am the head of business development reporting to the corporate head of strategy. At present I have three direct reports. Am I a manager of others?

A. No. The scope of your position and your reporting relationship make you an enterprise functional manager. Your work affects the whole company; you participate in running or advancing the enterprise. "Manager of others" is a designation for people who direct the work associated with enabling or delivering the company's products or services to customers. Their area of impact is much smaller than yours.

Observations from the Field

- The task of shifting work values required for successfully navigating this passage is more challenging than commonly assumed. We've found that many managers of others at almost every company we have worked with are stuck in "manage self" work values. They still spend most of their time doing the technical or professional work that they enjoy and value. Therefore, before promoting people to manager of others, test their ability and willingness to let go of the technical or professional work and do the managerial work. Use assignments such as team leader or project manager to test the person's ability and willingness to take responsibility for the success of other people. Prior to making any permanent appointment, determine whether the person can obtain satisfaction from helping others succeed and can value that sufficiently to sustain the effort.

- Pruning the manager of others population at least once a year is a succession planning imperative. Mistakes at this layer are costly in many ways—productivity, morale, quality, and employee engagement all suffer, and succession is defeated. It's an all-too-common practice to appoint technical or professional stars to positions where they are responsible for managing others but don't do the management work. This is the pool from which just about all future management positions will be filled. Instead of a pipeline that is full and flowing, the business has one that is clogged. The succession planning process must reach down to this level so a comprehensive review across the company can be completed at least once a year. First-line managers with six to twelve months on the job who are not performing must be reassigned. The objective should be fewer and better managers of others, with a mix of people who can move up and people who can be effective over the long term at this layer.
- There is a disturbing, emerging trend: creating many manager of others positions with only a few direct reports, as a reward for good performance. There isn't enough management work to occupy all these new managers' time. As a result, they don't really learn how to manage. They carry the manager title but don't learn to value or execute managerial work. Although they still expect to be promoted to the next layer, they aren't prepared for it. When the manager title stands for status rather than a set of work requirements, the

management culture in the business is watered down. What seems like a nice reward for a high-performing "manage self" person turns out to be a problem for the business.

- Choosing "manage self" people for manage others positions requires paying attention to both the obvious requirements and some subtleties. The obvious requirements usually include results achieved, motivation and effort, interest in more responsibility, and good relationships. The key subtleties include ability and interest in learning, ability to apply what is learned, willingness to put forward ideas in peer settings and have those ideas prevail, and a genuine interest in the success of others, not just their own success. The manager of managers (such as the hiring manager) should observe these subtleties.

3

From Managing Others to Managing Managers

Though most organizations have training programs for first-line managers, relatively few have any programs in place for managers of managers. Part of the problem is the false assumption that there's very little difference between managing others and managing managers—the logic being that if you can develop the skills of a first-line manager, you will naturally adapt to this similar but more significant role. The other aspect of the problem is psychological, in that promotion to this position is often viewed as a stepping stone rather than a major career passage. Whereas being appointed as a first-line manager is a cause for celebration, the move to a manager of managers is usually greeted with more muted enthusiasm.

Yet there is a significant difference in skills, time applications, and work values for this leadership level from the previous one, and if this transition isn't addressed, many managers skip this passage much to the detriment of their organizations. Short-term, the workforce is poorly or inadequately managed. Managers of managers are responsible for the greatest number of people in the company who do the most hands-on work; they're in charge of getting the work done that is directly related to the company's products and services. As you can imagine, quality and productivity suffer when managers of managers aren't performing their roles effectively. In fact, errors here harm the company's ability to execute and may even create a competitive disadvantage.

Long-term, the problem relates to missing skills and values that affect leaders as they are promoted to positions of increased responsibility. We've worked with very senior managers who are lacking in key leadership skills because they skipped this turn. This level offers the opportunity to embed crucial qualities into the DNA of the organization's leadership.

Let's look at a company that failed to take advantage of this opportunity, through the experiences of one individual.

A Failure to Empower First-Line Managers

Hired by a large technology corporation to be a manager of software development and conversion in the early 1990s, Vic moved from running a software application unit and managing 14 people to being responsible for 150 people, with 12 direct reports whose work units developed, purchased, and maintained existing software. Vic's new employer faced significant conversion challenges, deadlines, and competitive pressures.

As a first-line manager, Vic possessed the right stuff. Not only had he gone through a good training program but he'd also used 360 degree feedback to increase his understanding of his managerial strengths and weaknesses, working assiduously to correct flaws. In his new role, Vic spent a great deal of time learning about all the projects on his watch and getting to know his people. During this learning phase, Vic discovered that several important projects were behind schedule, that he was a better first-line manager than many of his direct reports, and that morale was low (because people were working overtime without much success).

With the decisiveness and skill that had made him a good first-line manager, Vic quickly took action. By running project reviews, reordering priorities, and reassigning applications specialists, he made some modest improvements. But these improvements weren't significant enough to satisfy Vic and his boss; furthermore, he was also drowning in people problems. A line formed at Vic's door first thing every morning as his direct reports and individual contributors sought his input and approval. Soon Vic didn't have the time he needed to address the budget and project issues that needed addressing.

The major focus of managers of managers—the area from which skills, time applications, and work values all flow—is empowering first-line managers. Instead of empowering them, Vic was disenfranchising them. By giving direct orders to individual contributors and conducting his own project reviews, Vic was taking over functions that rightly belonged to his direct reports. Individual contributors began to bypass their own bosses to talk to Vic, which resulted in his time crunch.

If Vic had properly transitioned to this leadership level, however, he would have responded much differently to this situation. Right from the start, he would have assembled his team, listened to their viewpoints, and pushed for recommendations. While Vic certainly could have exercised his veto power if recommendations were inappropriate, he also could have let first-line managers choose from the options available. By giving his people the power to make project decisions and holding them accountable for these decisions, Vic would have created a better environment in which his direct reports could hone their skills.

Vic also would have carved out time to observe how his managers managed. Rather than treat them as individual contributors doing technical work, he would have treated and assessed them as managers doing managerial work for the first time. By paying attention to his direct reports' managerial skills, time applications, and values, Vic would have gathered the information necessary for him to coach them effectively.

Vic could have done all these things if his organization had helped him traverse this leadership passage. It's important to note that his company didn't develop him in part because Vic *seemed* to be well-prepared for his new role. As a highly skilled, conscientious manager, Vic looked like he could step into his new leadership position without missing a beat. Appearances can be especially deceiving at this level. For this reason, before we identify the competencies required at this passage, let's focus on identifying the manager who looks the part but lacks appropriate beliefs and behaviors.

Five Signs of a Misplaced Manager of Managers

The one sign you generally won't find is poor technical results. Most people who are promoted into manager-of-managers positions have demonstrated the ability and desire to perform well; their promotions are often tied to their superior performance as first-line managers delivering technical or professional results. People who are struggling with this leadership passage usually are having problems with core leadership skills, as the following signs suggest:

Difficulty Delegating First-time managers often exhibit this problematic, inappropriate behavior, but they sometimes can get away with it. As people move up through leadership levels, the inability to delegate has an increasingly negative effect. If a manager of managers has seven people reporting to her who are responsible for seventy other people, she can't possibly do everything herself. First-line managers often are more frustrated and angry than individual contributors when their functions are usurped (because as managers, they believe more strongly that they should have increased decision-making responsibility). Even worse, work gets done more slowly because too many decisions have been centralized and delayed. The manager of managers, having taken too much on herself, is harried and hassled and complaining that she has too much to do and not enough competent direct reports to help her do it. Delegation problems, of course, aren't necessarily limited to being unable to delegate. Some managers delegate improperly; they lack a control system that ensures accountability for what is delegated.

Poor Performance Management To identify this problem, you need only look for someone who provides poor or little feedback to his managers, isn't a good coach, and doesn't offer clear direction; someone whose people are unsure about their goals. In other words, this manager of managers is unable to communicate productively with his direct reports.

Failure to Build a Strong Team This is someone who works with her direct reports as individuals but doesn't organize them into a productive team. Unintentionally, this behavior encourages silo mind-sets and prevents the synergy that comes when a team of managers shares information and ideas.

A Single-Minded Focus on Getting the Work Done This individual demonstrates little or no capacity for taking full advantage of his new leadership position. He is still operating with the values of a first-line manager and doesn't recognize his role as a coach and developer of managerial talent. He frequently doesn't exhibit any interest in strategic or cultural issues.

Choosing Clones over Contributors At this level, people receive many opportunities to select first-line managers. Unfortunately, they haven't been trained in this skill and often resort to choosing individuals who most closely resemble themselves. This not only causes diversity problems but also pollutes the leadership pipeline with people who lack necessary leadership qualifications. Managers at this level may also choose friends and former direct reports over people who are truly best qualified for first-line positions. This tactic can be a disaster because these friends are often unwilling to challenge their boss and don't bring fresh perspectives to the job.

What Managers of Managers Should Do

The following four skills are absolutely essential at this leadership passage:

- Selecting and training capable first-line managers
- Holding first-line managers accountable for managerial work
- Deploying and redeploying resources among units
- Managing the boundaries that separate units that report directly and with other parts of the business

Let's look at each of these skills and the values and time applications that relate to using these skills effectively.

Selecting and Training Capable First-Line Managers

Finding individual contributors who are capable of assuming a first-level leadership position is a task foreign to most neophyte managers of managers. They're not used to evaluating factors such as an individual's willingness to lead, communication and planning competencies, and ability to make decisions under pressure.

Making people decisions about leaders is often a relatively new task for them. They need to know individual contributors well enough to select them for a managerial position. This means identifying people who are likely candidates and giving them the opportunity to see whether they like and are good at managerial tasks. Giving people team- and project-leadership assignments are two ways of accomplishing this goal.

Of course, managers of managers who don't value selection responsibilities may well fall back on rewarding cronies and clones. It's only when people realize that they're not just choosing their team but also seeding the organization's leadership field that they begin to value selection. We've also found that selection is a problem for some managers of managers because they hate to differentiate among their people; they feel uncomfortable selecting one person and by inference telling the others, "You're not good enough." Managers of managers also need to make time for selection to do it effectively. It's far less time-consuming to choose a clone or a crony than it is to observe people in "test" managerial roles. But if managers of managers don't reapportion their time in this way, they can't possibility obtain the knowledge necessary to make intelligent choices.

Training first-line managers is the art of creating a supportive environment that allows mistakes but not failure. It's an environment in which there's great enthusiasm for learning interviewing techniques, performance appraisal writing, and constructive criticism. To foster this environment, managers of managers need to develop a sensitivity about power. This means they need to use their power in ways that motivate and instruct rather than demean and demoralize. More than one boss has reflexively reacted to a first-line manager's mistake by making him feel powerless, delivering a biting critique in front of the manager's direct reports. Becoming sensitive to the use and abuse of power is a requirement at this level. Recognizing the best time to deliver negative feedback (in private rather than in public) and knowing how to deliver it (focusing on the behavior rather than the person's character or intelligence) are hallmarks of this sensitivity.

Holding First-Line Managers Accountable for Managerial Work

Although they may be competent at holding people responsible for individual contributor work, managers of managers need to shift their accountability focus. They must learn to value a different type of work and develop a different framework for judging results from their direct reports. This means evaluating people based on the quality of their selection decisions, the frequency and quality of their performance feedback, their ability to team with other units, and their skill at producing results through a team. Becoming proficient at this skill requires a certain amount of experience; it takes a while to realize how to set stretch goals that allow room for growth but don't cause failure.

As part of this accountability requirement, managers of managers need to remove first-time managers who don't make the level-one grade. In many instances, this is a more difficult task than removing an individual contributor. Whereas the reason for removing an individual contributor is usually clear-cut—his performance is poor or she doesn't fit in with this company's values—the reasons for moving a first-time manager sideways or out are related to more intangible issues: failing to value management work and not spending enough time doing it. Recognizing these problems and taking people out of management roles requires a huge amount of courage, emotional fortitude, and self-confidence. Allowing underperforming managers to remain in first-level management jobs clogs the leadership pipeline at its source; it also can rob the company of high-performing individual contributors. Managers of managers therefore need to recognize when to move someone.

Deploying Resources Among Units

This is an unfamiliar responsibility for managers of managers, and it's not as simple as it might sound. Learning to reallocate money, technology, and support staff (not to mention the manager of manager's own time) to improve results is a juggling act that takes some practice. Consider some of the questions that these managers need to answer to determine whether units or teams are using resources effectively:

- Can each unit deliver the required output on time at the right quality level and for the appropriate cost? If not, what additional resources are required?
- Do we have the right mix of external and internal quality resources? How should the mixture be adjusted?
- Are any units wasting or missing resources? What should be done?
- Is this the right configuration of units, given the total output required? What resources should be redeployed?
- Which people should not be working here? How quickly can they be replaced with more productive people?

The questions don't end there. Other judgments need to be made regarding the individual and unit that require or deserve specific resources:

- Which unit is the most effective and should be given the difficult new project (the one with the most risk)?
- Which units deserve more than their fair share of support resources (because they'll use them more effectively)?
- Who, if anyone, should receive the biggest raise?
- Who needs the most coaching and the most of my time?

Managing the Boundaries

The manager of managers must be a silo buster. He must tear down the boundaries that impede the flow of work and information between different functions and other groups. This of course means transitioning from a purely functional mind-set that values a specific function to one that embraces a more egalitarian view. Just as important, the manager of managers must inculcate this egalitarian value among both his first-line managers and individual contributors so that work, information, ideas, and technology flow freely among his units.

Managing boundaries is a matter of not just values but also specific workflow management skills. This means monitoring the flow of work between the manager of manager's unit and others in the organization, asking questions, and recommending improvements. It also requires a more subtle form of boundary management: understanding and conveying functional strategies, business strategies, and the corporate mission. By conveying and testing for compliance with these larger, strategic requirements, the manager of managers helps keep her units working with other groups to achieve business goals that transcend functional goals. Effective cross-unit collaborations usually accelerate work processes, and a strong manager of managers can help her organization gain this competitive advantage.

How to Help Managers of Managers Through This Leadership Passage

To develop people at this passage, you need to make them aware of the differences between being a manager of individual contributors and a manager of managers; these two managerial levels are closely aligned in people's minds, and the differences have to be spelled out. Someone, preferably the manager's boss, must clearly communicate the new requisite skills, time applications, and values that shape how these skills are applied. Simply describing this new leadership role, however, won't be sufficient to prevent managers such as Vic from jumping in and taking over first-line work when things aren't going well. Goals and measurements must be put in place that create accountability for new managerial behaviors. Appropriate measures include the following:

- Amount of improvement in efficiency
- Degree of improvement in quality
- Frequency and impact of coaching sessions
- Number of first-line managers promoted to bigger jobs or moved laterally for broadening experiences
- Success rate of new first-line managers
- Teamwork within the assigned area
- Teamwork with other areas

Of all these measures, perhaps the most important revolves around preparing first-line managers for their roles. Inexperienced managers are tremendously impressionable, and they naturally model the actions and attitudes of bosses. If their bosses are either unable or unwilling to set a proper example and help them develop in the right direction, the leadership pipeline will become clogged at its source. In organizations where this happens, the only recourse is to recruit stars, a practice doomed to failure.

Acting the part of a manager of managers is one obvious way to communicate the right message to first-line managers. Coaching, however, is a more interactive method to help people translate this message into behaviors. In a very real sense, coaching is the hands-on art of caring; it bonds people (especially potential leaders) to each other and the organization. When you care, people know it, and this is a very important aspect of leadership at this and other levels. When coaching and caring are largely absent and pressures are intense, turnover is high and people leave to find organizations that seem to be better places to learn and grow.

All this isn't to say that you can turn every manager of managers into a great coach. Not everyone is a born coach, and some managers of managers may lack inherent talent in this area. Still, the majority possess the capacity to coach (or at the very least, to give honest, useful feedback), and it's up to functional managers (as well as other leaders) to bring it out. Training is one way for doing so, and there are professional coaches who can facilitate this process. Unfortunately, many outside coaches don't understand the business context and find it difficult to make their advice relevant. We usually recommend that coaching skills be taught through small learning groups that can support and guide themselves after an initial session with a professional coach.

Finally, it's especially important during these times of rapid change and uncertainty to involve managers of managers at a strategic level. They can play a major role in interpreting and communicating the company's evolving objectives to the workforce, either directly or through first-line managers. If you ignore engaging managers at this strategic level, however, you risk creating leaders who resist change. When Jack Welch began initiating his changes at GE, for instance, this manager-of-managers level was known as "the concrete layer." Managers at this level were primed to resist any new initiative, reflexively viewing delayering, downsizing, and workforce empowerment as a threat. GE decided to break this resistance through a training program at their Crotonville facility called "The Experienced Manager." Not only did it help participants acquire the skills needed to manage and lead at this level, but it also focused on explaining the cultural and business context for the changes reshaping the organization. Helping these managers understand the strategic impetus for change melted much of their resistance, eliminating the false rumors and misinformation about change that prevented them from managing effectively and enthusiastically.

Identifying people who are experiencing difficulty with this passage is easier than finding individuals who have gone through it and developed into outstanding managers of managers. What do effective managers of managers look like? How do their actions and attitudes reflect the type of leadership demanded at this passage?

A Role Model for Managers of Managers

Gordon runs a technical group with seven managers reporting to him at a major telecommunications company. Now in his late thirties, Gordon was intensely interested in "getting ahead" early in his career but now is more interested in stability and doing meaningful work. It's worth noting that Gordon has received some of the most positive 360 degree feedback reports from supervisors, direct reports, and peers that we've ever seen. This is not because Gordon is a "soft touch" or because he's easy to work for. In fact, Gordon is extraordinarily demanding and sets high standards both for his team and for individual performance. His people, however, believe Gordon's demands are fair and that he communicates what he wants clearly and quickly. Gordon is also very clear about the major responsibility of his job: to grow and develop managers. To do so, he provides honest feedback when people do well or poorly. In the latter instance, however, he provides feedback that is specific and constructive. Though his comments may sting at first, he doesn't turn negative feedback into a personal attack. Gordon knows his people well and tailors his interactions with them to their particular needs and sensitivities. When Gordon talks about his people, you hear the pride in his words and tone of voice. He believes that one of his most significant accomplishments is that a number of his direct reports have been promoted and done well in their new jobs. In fact, people in other parts of the organization want to work for Gordon because he excels in producing future high-level managers and leaders. Gordon also delegates well, providing people with objectives and allowing them the freedom to achieve the objectives in their own ways. He's also skilled at selection and spends a great deal of time on this issue.

For personal reasons (he doesn't want to relocate his family), Gordon may not advance much further in the organization. At the same time, he's fulfilling his manager-of-managers role to the hilt, serving as a launching pad for the careers of first-time managers.

Frequently Asked Questions

Q. I am a functional manager in a small company. We don't have manager of managers positions. What should I do to make sure I have not missed critical skills?

A. Even though you are a functional manager you will have to do much of the manager of managers tasks anyway. So, focus on helping the managers of others learn how to manage and hold them accountable for managing. Also, pay particular attention to integrating the work of the units that report to you. Unfortunately, the biggest problem will be failing to develop your functional manager skills because you will be more involved in day-to-day output than a functional manager should be. Read the chapter on functional management carefully and check your calendar to be sure you are allowing time for tackling the functional manager work properly. It is highly likely you will be spending more time as a manager of managers than as a functional manager.

Q. What are the most critical things to look for when choosing a manager of managers?

A. First, watch for a genuine enthusiasm for management work. That means the right work values have been adopted. Changing work values gets easier to do after you have done it once. Second, see whether they display systems thinking. Managers of managers are responsible for connecting their units with each other but also with units that report to their peers. The ability to see and understand how work flows and what must be connected and where to make the connection is required for real success in problem solving and organization building. Managers of managers should see the whole organization and how it should work. That ability should not be underestimated and is very hard to teach.

Q. How should we treat the manager of managers layer when doing succession planning?

A. Because this layer is the first one that truly relies on managerial skills and not technical ability, it is the best layer for cross-functional moves. In fact, cross-functional moves at this layer can accelerate the growth in managerial skills since they are key to success.

Q. Is it possible to have more than one layer of managers of managers? We are a very big business and have two layers between our functional managers and managers of others.

A. Yes, it is possible, even likely, that big businesses have two layers of managers of managers. This happens when there are multiple geographies or large numbers of employees. Both layers should be measured on similar criteria. The differences lie primarily in who is being managed. The lower layer manages the managers of others and the upper layer manages managers of managers. Both layers have integration work, allocation of resources, and training of managers as key accountabilities. The differences lie mostly in the coaching and development requirements.

Observations from the Field

- Providing role clarity made this chapter especially popular with readers. One well-known electronics manufacturer put the manager of managers definition in big letters on the factory wall. They did it to let everyone know the difference between first-line managers and managers of managers. It helps everyone know where to bring problems. Their hourly workers had been going around their direct boss to the manager of managers; managers of managers had been giving work direction to the hourly employees.

- Learning to ask the right questions is an especially tricky skill for managers of managers. Most likely they have been asking production or quality-oriented questions to their "manage self" people, such as "When will you be finished with the project?" or "Why is quality slipping?" When they ask those same questions to managers of others, these people will take personal responsibility for getting things done; they will assume from the questions that this is what their manager wants in order to speed things up or improve quality. Managers of others who were selected based on their technical prowess will frequently revert to type and become "manage self" employees. Managers of managers, therefore, should ask management and leadership questions. For example, "What should you do to your organization to assure that due dates are met?" or "How well do your people understand the quality standards and what are you doing to assure they meet then?" These questions elicit quite a different response and help the manager of others to focus on the right work. Failure to ask them the right question inhibits their development.

- Recognize the role difficulty created when managers of managers are in "no man's land." They generally don't participate in setting company direction or developing strategy. They aren't supposed to do the technical work or give directions to the "manage self" people. So they aren't leading the company and they aren't touching the product. They end up betwixt and between, causing them to overlook their true role: to link the strategy to the workers and the workers' capability to the strategy makers. If there isn't enough dialogue with their boss about strategy, company direction, priorities, and problems, the managers of managers align with the people below by default. They connect emotionally with what they already know and understand. At that point, they frequently become the "concrete layer."

- Understand that lack of sufficient management depth often is rooted in not asking enough of managers of managers. Companies don't ask them to participate in developing budgets or long-term planning. Instead, they treat them like oversized managers of others. Ask more of your managers of managers. Have them develop and obtain approval for their own budget. Making sure the right work is done at the right cost should be standard practice at this layer. Participation in long-range planning is useful stretching and offers the opportunity to demonstrate their potential for functional manager work. You should be sure you aren't artificially creating a succession gap by asking too little of managers of managers.

4

From Managing Managers to Functional Manager

This is a big promotion. At smaller companies it is often the domain of vice presidents, who become entitled to stock options, club memberships, cars, officer status, and other forms of recognition. An individual who is named functional manager is now a member of the business team and reports to a business general manager. In many instances, people who were recently his peers now report to him. His functional peers from earlier in his career report to him two or three levels removed from his current position. As a functional manager, he is going to be asked to contribute in ways that are remarkably different from how he has contributed in the past. Though his contributions will depend in part on how he uses the information he receives, he knows that he doesn't have all the information he needs and isn't sure whether all the information he has is correct. He must therefore become a skilled interpreter and seeker of information if he's going to be successful at this level.

All this requires a leadership maturity for which no one has prepared him. Mature leaders have developed empathy, timing, judgment, and sources of information; they've learned to listen and seek to absorb information from sources both inside and outside their organizations through formal and informal means. They have learned how to talk to (and correct) their people without smothering creativity and risk-taking. They recognize the importance of thinking long-term as well as short-term. In other words, they've grown up as both managers and leaders. Some functional managers never develop maturity, much to the detriment of their functions and the business. Leadership maturity is an overarching concept that describes the requirements of this passage. To develop it, the first step is to understand it. Let's begin by learning about its two essential components.

Maturing into a Functional Leader Role

To understand what we mean by *maturity*, let's look at the term first from a functional and then from a business perspective. Functionally, maturity translates into an ability to think about the function from multiple perspectives. Too often people below this level act as though their function were an island. As a functional manager, they must transition to the belief that their function exists to support the overall business objectives. This belief necessitates difficult trade-offs. It may mean that the functional head must create a new functional structure that better supports the needs of the company, changing the structure from centralized to decentralized and enduring all the travail that such a change entails.

Functional maturity also involves learning to communicate with a multilayered group. Communicating effectively becomes more difficult as additional levels are added; it also becomes difficult because people are spread out horizontally (in different offices, states, countries) as well as vertically. In earlier managerial positions, people were used to seeing their direct reports frequently and having one-on-one conversations with them. Now this communication mode isn't always possible. Sometimes other people are too geographically distant. Sometimes the functional manager simply doesn't have the time for this type of communication. As a result, the mature leader learns to delegate and trust rather than always require in-person, frequent, lengthy conversations. This leader's calendar, too, is skewed to manage upwards and horizontally.

Functional immaturity manifests itself when functions are asked to work together for the good of the organization. Too often, managers become embroiled in finger-pointing when things go wrong or in arguments about who deserves the credit when things go right. Although the company may well subscribe to a boundaryless ideal, they may not measure and compensate accordingly. As a result, the immature functional manager screams that his group should get credit for a successful project because they did the bulk of the work or accuses another functional manager of "screwing up." Rather than maturely leading his function in ways that create synergies with other functions and overcome parochial differences, he complains and makes excuses.

The other aspect of maturity involves thinking like a businessperson rather than just a functionary. For someone who has spent ten or more years working exclusively on a functional level, this is a significant leap of thinking. Being able to consider how a decision affects not only one's own "community" but also the larger society of which one is a member has not been inculcated into managers. Developing a view of the business as opposed to a view of the function takes a mature perspective.

This perspective comes with experience. Ideally, organizations will have their young, high-performing people serve on task forces, committees, and project teams and give them other assignments that force them to plan and implement ideas that transcend their functions. By developing a network of relationships that reach across functions and by practicing strategic thinking, they are more likely to grow up faster as leaders.

Leadership immaturity can be difficult to identify. When a functional manager is clearly an expert at what she does and has a solid track record as a manager within that function, her deficiencies may seem relatively minor or may even be missed. At this level, you need to know the behaviors and attitudes that indicate leadership immaturity, and fortunately we have a classic case to share with you.

A Common Flaw in New Functional Managers

From a functional perspective, Will had always been on the fast track. For most of his career, he had run production centers and had demonstrated great interest in and aptitude for state-of-the-art production processes and equipment. When Will was promoted to a position in which he was running production for the company's hottest new product, he attracted management attention with his innovative product improvement and cost-saving ideas. When he became a manager of managers, Will felt comfortable with this leadership role; he'd held leadership positions when he was in the military.

In most ways, Will excelled as a manager of managers. He empowered direct reports to test innovative production technology and coached them on how to develop their people. Though Will was generally satisfied with how things were going, he did grumble about not receiving sufficient project money to accelerate the production area's growth. During Will's two-year tenure, his operation doubled in size and he and his team were rewarded for their contributions. The best reward came when Will was named as the head of manufacturing.

Will had nine managers of managers responsible for production planning, quality control, purchasing, manufacturing engineering, and other areas. In addition, information technology, human resources, and other support people reported to Will on a dotted line. Most of these people were older than Will, who had advanced quickly.

As a functional head, Will made an effort to gain knowledge about purchasing and two other production operations, areas where he had little or no previous exposure. He "toured" these areas and reviewed their goals, plans, and budgets. After what he felt was an objective analysis, Will determined that purchasing wasn't well run and that the two other production operations were overstaffed. He decided that if he shifted some money that was going to these areas in favor of projects in his former new-product production area, the manufacturing group would be well served.

After Will cut their budgets, the direct reports responsible for these areas were incensed. When Will told them about his observed inefficiencies, the purchasing head resigned then and there. When Will's boss was informed of what had taken place, he was even more angry than the direct reports. Will's surface analysis didn't reveal that the two production operations played a critical role in maintaining strong customer relationships; it also didn't reveal that purchasing had been working long and hard to replace vendors whose quality was slipping and that the purchasing head was highly skilled at finding and establishing relationships with the best quality suppliers. Will had jumped to conclusions based on his limited knowledge and expertise and had used his findings as an excuse to fund his long-standing pet projects. In short, Will had not yet developed the leadership maturity necessary to be an effective functional head.

Playing favorites is a sign that someone is having difficulty with this passage. Typically, new functional managers are asked to supervise multifaceted areas in which they have little or no experience. Without a good frame of reference, they react by overvaluing their former, well-known area of responsibility and undervaluing the unknown. Will needed to transition from an operational orientation focused on a few projects to a strategic orientation focused on all the function's projects. Unfortunately, no one told Will about this need or developed him in this direction.

A Strategic Mind-Set, a Holistic Approach

The best functional managers are the ones who think strategically and manage with the whole function in mind. To do both of these things takes a level of maturity most functional managers don't come by naturally. The nature of working within a function is to think tactically and be responsible for one or two aspects of that function. Most functional managers have come up by performing well in one or perhaps two areas. For instance, the head of marketing will have excelled in one of the following: advertising, communications, brand management, product management, direct marketing, and so on. As good as he is in one of these areas, he's probably only marginally competent in most of the others. It's rare to find someone who understands state-of-the-art concepts for all areas in the function, who can balance current functional needs with future business goals, who understands the roles and contributions of all the other functions and how they impact and are impacted by his function.

To make sure the leadership pipeline is open and free-flowing at this level, functional managers must learn to value, develop necessary skills, and spend time on functional strategy and managing the whole function. They must also be ready and able to recruit externally if they lack sufficient talent to meet immediate needs. Let's examine the strategic requirements first.

Functional Strategy

Up to this leadership level, managers have spent their time creating supporting operating plans in a given area of their function for the functional strategy. Now they must shift to creating functional strategy. The five requirements at this level are as follows:

Longer-Term Thinking (Three to Five Years) The business general manager must produce a long-range strategy, and the functional manager has to follow suit with a dovetailing plan. Matching the functional strategy time frame with the business strategy time frame is an unfamiliar task for a manager who has spent his work life thinking in annual terms. Again, the notion of maturity is a useful concept here.

State-of-the-Art Awareness Staying ahead of the state-of-the-art curve is a challenge for functional managers. Keeping abreast with what's possible technically, operationally, and professionally is essential; it will directly affect their function's capacity to contribute to the business's competitive advantage. In our current environment, a strategy that is anything less than state-of-the-art is woefully behind the times. In an Internet society, information about new technologies is easily acquired, and people can find and bid for new opportunities electronically. Functional managers need to capitalize on the Internet and other tools to keep informed about new developments that will maintain or achieve cutting-edge status for their function. Companies such as Dell and Toyota have achieved competitive advantage through state-of-the-art functional strategies. A customer can order either a computer or a car customized to their specifications and receive it with unprecedented speed. Demand-flow technology has produced a competitive advantage for these organizations, and functional managers who master new processes and technologies will be able to help their companies gain a similar edge.

Complete Understanding of the Business Model in Detail and Long-Term Strategic Direction and Goals This might seem obvious and easy to achieve, but it's not. Partial understanding or even misunderstanding is often the norm for new functional managers, simply because they've been isolated in their operational frame of reference for so long. Mature leaders recognize that they must grasp the large picture rather than the small piece with which they're comfortable. A functional manager possesses good understanding if she can answer questions such as these:

- What is this business trying to accomplish?
- How does it want to position itself in the market?
- Has the strategy changed recently or is it likely to change soon?
- Does my function contribute to our competitive advantage?
- What must each function contribute to that strategy?
- How does my function's effort impact the strategy?
- How does my function impact the other functions' ability to contribute?
- How is the money made in this business?

Factoring All Aspects of the Function into Strategic Thinking This is a place where functional managers need to shift their time applications. In the past, they probably spent little time learning about functional areas for which they weren't responsible. Now it's mandatory, and it requires a significant amount of time. No matter how competent a functional manager's direct reports are, he is responsible for integrating all the pieces into a viable strategy. Without sufficient knowledge, he can't do this effectively.

Ability to Make Trade-offs Within the Function That Support Business Strategy, Profitability, and Competitive Advantage (Rather Than Just Supporting Functional Success) This requirement involves recognizing the connections among various functional groups. The sometimes complex linkages aren't apparent unless continuous dialogue is taking place. Again, functional managers should take the time to talk to their direct reports and learn how each of their groups works best with other groups. Functional managers must also understand strategy and systems thinking so they can link what's going on under their watch to the larger business issues and goals.

Managing the Whole Function

While there are many responsibilities attached to whole function management, perhaps the most significant involves communication. Certainly managers have developed some communications skills over the years, but the shift here is from talking to listening. Leadership at this level is information-intensive, and nothing clogs the pipeline faster than a manager who makes decisions and policy pronouncements without all the facts and ideas at his disposal. Soliciting ideas and information from the outside world of customers, vendors, and industry analysts as well as the inside world of colleagues is required. Within that inside world, listening must be an equal opportunity endeavor. Scheduling regular listening sessions with people at all levels of the function is absolutely necessary; it's the only way to establish "sonar capability" and detect dangers and opportunities before they surface for all to see. During these listening sessions, managers should keep their ears and minds open so they can answer the following questions:

- What are people working on?
- Are they being managed, developed, rewarded, and coached properly?

- Do they understand enough of the business strategy, profit model, functional strategy, business challenges, competitive conditions, and short-term priorities to do the job right?
- What problems are they encountering?
- What are the obstacles?
- What ideas do they have for improving their contribution, the function, or the company?
- What innovation is taking place?
- Is there sufficient speed in decision cycle times?

Listening (as opposed to talking without listening) is a hallmark of a mature leader, and it's one that requires patience, empathy, and approachability. Obviously, functional managers also have to communicate with their people. At this leadership level, there's no room for inarticulate or isolated managers or ones who can communicate only with their direct reports. With more levels to penetrate, functional managers must engage in dialogue with people up and down the line and in all subfunctions. Some of this dialogue can be facilitated by the Internet, intranet, faxes, and so on, but there's no substitute for face-to-face conversations and the emotional engagement that results from them. Again, this means making more time for this activity and taking away time from a less important one.

Functional managers must master a variety of listening skills. For instance, they must be able to listen to not only what is being said but what is not being said. They must be alert for topics that are avoided, for hesitancy about addressing a particular problem. They also must be able to cross-check frames of reference. By this we mean that each individual in a conversation has a particular set of assumptions and experiences that shape his words. This is particularly true when it comes to measurement. One person may say the results are outstanding, while another views these same results as mediocre; it all depends on the frame of reference. Functional managers learn to take these frames of reference into consideration during conversations to avoid misinterpretation.

Valuing What You Don't Know

Because functional managers have to deal with so many new and unfamiliar issues, the challenge is twofold:

- How do they learn to manage what's new?
- How do they learn to value it?

Valuing what's new and unfamiliar is a particular challenge for young, aggressive, ambitious functional managers. Immature, they often fall into the trap of having to know all the answers. Feeling they must "justify" their promotion, they start clogging the leadership pipeline the first day on the job. They're resolutely unwilling to ask questions or say "I don't know" for fear of being thought undeserving of their leadership status.

Ideally, functional leaders love to learn what they don't know. Their subordinates will accept questions and uncertainties early in their tenure and are eager to fill them in. Customers and end users, too, will be more than willing to provide them with knowledge and ideas. The key is for functional managers to engage others in dialogue, listen carefully and reflect on what they're told. Functional managers truly value their work only when they truly understand it, and an eagerness to learn will help them adjust their values appropriately. The following story illustrates this point.

Ron's Story

Ron was appointed as head of sales for a midsized transportation company. He came to his new company with

> a sterling reputation and carte blanche to revive a moribund sales group. Though this was his first position as a functional manager, Ron was clearly an expert in his field and had helped the sales group he ran at his previous employer do extraordinarily well. It would have been easy for Ron to attempt a massive overhaul of the sales department, firing a significant percentage of employees, bringing in his own people, and instituting methods that had worked for him in the past.

Fortunately, Ron had been developed properly; he had gone through each previous leadership passage and recognized that he needed to shift what he valued as well as learn new skills and time applications as he went through this passage. As a result, he didn't do what he had done in the past (focusing his energy and time on improving sales performance). Instead, he made a concerted effort to have one-on-one conversations not only with his direct reports but also with young salespeople, customer service representatives, and the fulfillment people. Though the company's CEO had brought Ron in, Ron didn't concentrate all his attention on this relationship; he made an effort to understand the concerns of other functional managers. When Ron had gathered sufficient information, he crafted a strategy that took the complexities of the company into consideration as well as the interrelationships of subfunctions in his department. Much to the surprise of many in management, Ron chose to focus on customer service improvements. It surprised people because everyone assumed he would concentrate on bringing in top salespeople from the outside or reorganize the structure of the sales group so it resembled the effective team he had enjoyed at his previous company. Ron, however, had listened carefully and thought strategically and in holistic terms about his function. Poor service was the main reason for slow sales growth, not a weak sales force. New customers were being added but existing customers were bailing out.

As a result of Ron's insights, the organization's performance improved dramatically and he was promoted to a position that gave him significantly broader responsibilities.

Identifying Dysfunctional Signs

Like leaders at lower levels, functional managers often rely on the same skills and time applications and maintain the same values that they relied on in their previous positions. Though this should be a clear warning sign that they're not handling this transition properly, it's often masked by their high competence in a specific subfunction; they *look* as though they're doing a terrific job because they continue to come up with great ideas and generate results in one area. But they're clogging up the pipeline because they haven't embraced what really counts at this leadership level. Functions run by managers who haven't made this passage don't move the business toward strategic goals. They create anger, resentment, and turnover within the function because of favoritism, and they end up hurting the function's performance in the long run.

To identify managers who are having trouble with this passage, look for symptoms in the following three areas:

- Failure to make the transition from an operational-project orientation to a strategic one
  - Demonstrates a poor sense of how the business operates

  - Lacks long-term thinking (much more focused on the short-term)
  - Lacks a functional strategy that ties functional activity to business goals
  - Ignores corporate functional standards, needs, policies, and programs
- Inability to manage and value work that is unfamiliar or of relatively little interest
  - Spends little or no time with people and problems in unfamiliar areas and a great deal of time with people and opportunities in familiar areas
  - Shows a bias toward a familiar area in terms of salaries, bonuses, budgets
  - Loses people in his function at a higher-than-normal rate (though this attrition can also be due to necessary housecleaning)
- Immaturity as a leader-manager
  - Isn't particularly interested in taking on the responsibilities of a leader; much more interested in being a hands-on manager and performer
  - Doesn't trust others, especially subordinates in unfamiliar functions
  - Can't let go of work and must control everything
  - Has poor communication skills, in terms of both listening and speaking; isolates himself except for a few subfunctional cronies
  - Delegates too much and lacks a control system (or vice versa)

Though leadership immaturity also manifests itself in the first two areas, the third group of symptoms particularly will tip you off that someone is having trouble with this passage.

Developing Mature, Strategic, Whole-Functional Managers

Maturity is a result of learning from success and from mistakes—in other words, learning from experience. Ideally, people will have had the opportunity to see the business broadly and become immersed in diverse situations where they succeed as well as err. They will have had the occasions to exhibit immature behavior and learn from their mistakes through mentoring, coaching, feedback, and so on. Given that many relatively young, high-performing people are being promoted to functional manager positions, however, the odds are that this maturity isn't always fully developed. To help these managers grow, place them on task forces, teams, and committees of managers from different functions or subfunctions with different backgrounds, skills, and experience. Having to work effectively with people who are different is a growth experience. Not only will functional managers learn about new areas of work but they'll also establish relationships with new people who use different methods and skills. It will take them out of the cocoon of the familiar function and help them see a wider range of choices.

Developing strategic competencies can be a more formal process. After three to six months on the job, training in these skills can be done through university classes, consultants, or in-house resources. The best method of training, however, involves hands-on learning activities in which the manager uses the function's own data, challenges, and resources in a strategy-related assignment. After completing the assignment, the manager should be evaluated and receive feedback.

Development aimed at helping people become whole-functional managers can involve a variety of activities, but one of the best is meeting with other functional managers who can share their assessment of this particular manager's function. Where do they see a need for improvement? Where do they see opportunities for synergy? The perspectives of peers can provide a new functional manager with an appreciation of her function that is much more wide-ranging than she would ordinarily possess.

Development progress can be measured with a calendar check. Functional managers have to make significant shifts in how they spend their time if they're going to transition to this new leadership level successfully. Time has to be blocked out for strategy sessions, communication meetings with a variety of subfunctional representatives, and so on. Functional managers should note on their calendars the time they've devoted to these activities. In addition, they should be spending time benchmarking cross-industry and be involved in local networks such as YPO groups. A regular review of their calendars will tell you whether they're really devoting the time necessary to develop as functional managers.

Perhaps the best way to measure developmental progress, however, is to watch for signs of maturity. We've noted many likely signs. But maturity can also be measured in development of traits such as humility. A mature leader doesn't have to be the expert in every functional area (and in fact, can't be); he's willing to admit that others know more than he does and is willing to learn from them. Similarly, mature leaders recognize that if they're going to succeed, they need to get cooperation from others. To do so, they'll delegate, communicate, and ensure that information flows smoothly and quickly.

Finally, a clear sign of maturity is letting go of old silo behaviors. When silos were the rule, functions and subfunctions worked apart rather than together. Although management has attempted to tear down these silos, the old attitudes persist. Mature leaders will turn away from a narrow dedication to their function and embrace a more integrated, total business philosophy.

Frequently Asked Questions

Q. What is the central purpose of a functional manager besides running the function?

A. Functional managers are supposed to deliver competitive advantage to a business or company. They determine how to beat competition in the delivery of service to customers. They must know what competitors are doing and figure out a way to gain distinction. For example, "Our business has better people than the competition because we recruit, assimilate, and train better than anyone in our industry." Or "We are more innovative in solving customer problems or serving customer needs because we have better market research and customer communication." The functional manager must see her- or himself as the first line of competition with others who are trying to win in the marketplace.

Q. Why are functional managers often more competitive than collaborative with their peers, the other functional managers?

A. Two common misconceptions about functional leadership seem to account for this problem. First, these managers often assume a zero sum game when pursuing company resources. They believe that every dollar other managers receive is one they don't get because the total pot of money is a fixed size for the business. Second, they compete rather than collaborate because of the succession overhang—they see themselves competing with peers for appointment as the next business manager.

Both of these assumptions are false. In the first case, business success is not a zero sum game. The better the whole does, the more resources are available for each part. Therefore, functional managers must recognize that if they fail to help other functions, this lack of collaborative effort will adversely impact first, the business, and second, their allocation of resources. From a positive standpoint, they should understand that if they help another function achieve a business goal, this will generate both profit and good feelings, both of which will result in more access to corporate resources. Likewise, personal success and advancement is more likely when the business succeeds. Personal success at the expense of one's peers leads nowhere for the business or for the person.

Q. What is the best way to develop highly effective functional managers? Should they have cross-functional assignments before or after they reach this level?

A. Major assignments in several subfunctions seem to have the biggest developmental effect. For example, assignments in production, manufacturing, engineering, quality control, purchasing, and production planning or at least three of these helps prepare people for manufacturing functional manager positions. The other functions all have multiple subfunctions to be mastered. Moving up through a single subfunction doesn't produce the desired breadth of achievement, experience, and knowledge. In addition, provide a cross-functional assignment before reaching functional manager positions. A different view of the business and firsthand knowledge of the workings of other functions is invaluable preparation for participating on the business manager's team.

Observations from the Field

- Transitioning to functional manager is trickier than we originally portrayed it to be. New functional managers must grasp that they are no longer a member of the function. Instead, they have become the function's leader. Performing functional work, such as solving the most difficult technical or professional problems, is no longer their responsibility, despite the importance of these tough tasks. That work should be done at the manager of managers layer or lower. Being the functional problem solver ties functional managers to day-to-day or near-term work when they should be more focused on the future. When they solve the toughest technical or professional problems, others don't learn how to solve them.

- Let's clear up the confusion regarding how functional managers are defined in certain settings. Some companies are really just one business and the CEO is both business manager and CEO. Therefore the functional managers lead corporate functional work as well as business functional work. Corporate functional work perpetuates enterprise as well as positions the enterprise in the world.

- Business functional work is focused on serving customers or enabling the service of customers. In this single business configuration, the corporate functional work usually suffers and long-term growth is compromised. The functional manager must organize to get both kinds of work accomplished.

- Another example comes from companies where product managers report to the business manager and have profit-and-loss responsibility. They think they are business managers. That P&L responsibility is frequently a misnomer. They don't really have accountability for cost and revenue and may have neither. Much of the cost is in manufacturing, which reports elsewhere, and revenue is generated by a sales force, which also reports elsewhere. So these product managers have *influence* over what is made and sold, but not direct management. *Functional manager* is a better definition for these positions than *business manager*. Strategy and competitive positioning are central requirements, but they aren't sufficient for a business manager designation.

- Failing to uphold the interests of the business or corporation within the function is a common and serious problem. When the functional manager works in isolation from the business manager and her or his peers who run the other functions, the function's value is greatly diminished. The work being produced may meet excellent functional standards—for example, scientifically exact research or high-quality recruiting programs—but fail to support the business strategy. In many instances, the loyalty or commitment of the functional manager is to the profession and not to the business, or the functional manager may not agree with the business strategy. Whatever the cause, make sure functional managers understand and accept the business strategy and all members of the function do the same.

- Racing to the functional manager layer isn't healthy for the individual or the organization. Don't yield to the temptation to place bright, ambitious people in these key roles as soon as possible. We've learned that these positions are too important to trust to underprepared people, no matter how bright they are. This chapter emphasized emotional maturity as a prime requirement; it takes years for most people to develop this. If young people seem to have mastered the subfunctions quickly, give them a cross-functional assignment as a manager of managers before moving them to functional manager. The broader view of the business and learning about the new function will provide a great base for pursuing competitive advantage as a functional manager. Changing the setting will help them gain maturity.

5

From Functional Manager to Business Manager

Many top executives look back at their experiences as heads of businesses as the most enjoyable in their careers. As business managers, they have accountability for both making a product or creating a service and for selling it. They manage cost and revenue. There is a tremendous sense of ownership. At the same time, this first business manager position represents a huge challenge—probably the biggest challenge of all six leadership passages. It's not simply a question of learning new skills or reallocating time. Business managers actually have to change the way they think.

Anyone transitioning from functional management to business management is in for "leadership shock." A business manager is in a much more visible position and is closely watched by all his functional heads as well as senior management, Wall Street, and other constituencies. Many business heads also feel that they're "going it alone"—they're receiving much less guidance from their boss than they did when they were functional managers. In addition, there's enormous complexity at this leadership level. Building business strategy and integrating functional work requires connecting lots of dots. And of course, there's a huge value shift: from valuing one's own function to valuing all functions appropriately.

Ratcheting the challenge up another notch, e-commerce is changing the way businesses compete and is impacting this leadership level even more than the other levels.

We'll examine each of these challenging shifts in skills, time applications, and values and why this leadership passage bedevils so many highly successful functional managers. Let's begin by examining how a very bright, accomplished functional manager responded to her first business manager position.

Super Performance Does Not Require Superwoman

As a functional manager, Katarina was a star. She worked for a large financial services company, and as the operations functional head she had helped turn the company's credit card division around. Her financial acumen combined with her grasp of the credit card group's operating nuances enabled her to deliver results that captured everyone's attention. When Katarina was appointed to head a newly acquired bank in South America, no one was surprised. Katarina had lived and worked in several countries, and she was comfortable with international assignments. The bank was losing money because it had too many branches, lacked an articulated strategy, and suffered from poor controls, among other problems. Katarina was excited about the chance to be in total charge of a turnaround situation.

Katarina was confident that she could reverse the bank's fortunes. With the high degree of control that came with the position, she was sure she could meet senior management's expectations. But Katarina was wrong. Though Katarina grasped the cost issues involved better than just about anyone could, her turnaround strategy was all operational. She focused exclusively on her technical strengths to make everything work. Just as she had significantly increased credit card profits by implementing more efficient processes, she tried to do the same thing on a larger scale with the bank. And while some of her new processes were effective, they weren't enough. The portfolio of products was too broad, and some products were obsolete. She should have eliminated the products rather than deliver them more efficiently. Her thinking was based on "doing it better" rather than "should we do it?"

Katarina realized process improvements weren't enough and began working nonstop and micromanaging every area of the bank. As a functional manager earlier in her career, she had pulled the equivalent of all-nighters in order to achieve goals, and she had been successful. Now her superhuman efforts failed. She found herself paralyzed by the complexity of the issues she faced. Katarina debated long and hard about closing unprofitable branches, stymied by the seemingly equal pros and cons. The team she inherited representing the bank's various disciplines was offended by her micromanaging. They were not interested in being told what to do daily by someone with no experience in their disciplines. After a short time, they stopped trying to help and did only what they were told.

Katarina wanted to request help from senior management, but she didn't feel comfortable doing so. She knew she was in the spotlight. Great things were expected from her, and the last thing she wanted to do was demonstrate her weaknesses in front of her new boss. In addition, her boss was removed both geographically and emotionally from Katarina's bank. Previously Katarina had enjoyed a close working relationship with her bosses. Her new boss, however, had pretty much told her she was on her own when he gave her the assignment, explaining that at this level "you're expected to solve your own problems." She literally tried to do that. She worked at a fever pitch, but she only succeeded in burning herself out. Katarina left not only the bank but the financial services company, unable to understand how an apparently great opportunity had turned into a great fiasco. Katarina, her colleagues, and the financial services company all lost.

Thinking Differently

The first requirement—learning how to think differently about the business—is more difficult than it might seem. Though all leadership transitions require some thought shifts, this one is monumental. It is qualitatively different from previous levels in terms of scope, trade-offs, time frames, and external and internal decisions. Functional leadership focuses on what can be done: Can we get the order? Can we design an optimal compensation plan? Can we get the product out in time? Business managers, however, must focus on a different set of questions: How are we going to grow? How will we earn better than the cost of capital? Is profit level sustainable? How will we increase our competitive advantage?

Up to this point, managers have been turned on and driven by achieving new capability levels. Now they must temper their capability focus with a new set of measurements. They have to think in terms of profitability and sustainable competitive advantage in a global context, and that's not easy to do if you've spent years thinking tactically about short-term, functional goals or in a domestic context.

Functional strategic thinking is very different from business strategic thinking. Obviously, the latter requires a broader frame of reference. Business managers must consider myriad external factors, such as customers, competitors, demographics, macroeconomic drivers, and other external constituencies, such as governments and communities. Events taking place in one's industry and the world at large must be incorporated into strategic thinking.

Don't underestimate the difficulty of making this thought shift. As much as you tell a new business manager that she must change her thinking, she's going to fall back on her old mental model reflexively. For ten or twenty years, she's been drilled in pragmatic, short-term thinking. Like Katarina, she's going to revert to that thinking under stress, even if she knows that it's the wrong way to approach this leadership position.

Managing the Complexity

To grasp the complexity of a business manager position today, look at Table 5.1.

Few people are prepared for this avalanche of accountability. Not only are many of them unfamiliar but the sheer volume of unfamiliarity is also daunting. Though some functional managers are given cross-functional assignments to prepare them for deeper and broader accountability, this often doesn't suffice. As a result, learning new functions—what they do and how they do it—is an early and time-consuming priority for business managers.

If this were only linear learning, it would be more manageable. Functional managers need to learn about unfamiliar activities within functions, so the process isn't foreign. But the learning here is both three-dimensional and linear. Conceptually, the challenge is to make connections among diverse people, functions, and processes. This "connecting-the-dots" responsibility is much more than child's play. It requires business managers to make connections for both the short term and the long term. For instance, entry-level recruiting must not only fill jobs now but also eventually produce function and business managers. Sales can't simply

Table 5.1. One Hundred Elements Found in Most Businesses.

Advertising	Affiliates	Assets	Authority	Automobiles
Bad debts	Benefits	Bills	Blueprints	Bonds
Brand	Cash	Checks	Commitments	Communication
Community involvement	Competitors	Computers	Consumers	Contractors
Copyrights	Costs	Credit	Credits	Culture
Customers	Data	Energy	Ethics	Experience
Expertise	Factories	Furnishings	Furniture	Goals
Goodwill	Ideas	Individual contributors	Innovation	Insurance
Intellectual capital	Intranet	Inventory	Job descriptions	Jobs
Knowledge	Laboratories	Leaders	Ledgers	Liabilities
Licenses	Licensees	Logistics	Logo	Market position
Measurements	Memberships	Mission	Mortgages	Networks
Notes	Offices	Organization	Owners	Partners
Patents	Pensions	Plans	Processes	Products
Profit	Programs	Projects	Prospective customers	Raw materials
Real estate	Receivables	Reports	Reputation	Research
Revenue	Rewards	Risk	Rules	Services
Stock	Stock options	Strategy	Suppliers	Supplies
Systems	Technology	Threats	Titles	Trademarks
Training	Unions	Vision	Warehouses	Warranties

Source: Drotter Human Resources, Inc.

build a profitable customer base now but must also find customers who will succeed for years to come.

The complexities are such that no business manager can connect all the dots by herself. Some functional managers may have succeeded at being a lone ranger, but it won't work at this leadership level. To attempt to go it alone is to risk the burnout that Katarina experienced. Business managers are reliant on the teams of functional managers they assemble, but this reliance isn't so much on individual managers as it is on the team itself. There is so much complexity in any business that it requires a multidisciplined approach to solve it. A human resources problem can also be a strategic planning and budget problem. Only by assembling a strong team and leading it so its members work efficiently and effectively together will a business manager be able to cope with the complexity.

Learning to Value All Functions

As managers step out of their traditional functional role and become responsible for a full spectrum of activities, they need to take the time to learn about the key ingredients of individual disciplines and how they integrate from a total business viewpoint to produce results. On the surface, this isn't a particularly difficult task; it just takes some time, intelligence, and perseverance. What becomes difficult is learning to value all functions appropriately. From this leadership point on, functional prejudice becomes a serious problem. It can result in everything from overreliance on a particular function to failing to maximize the contribution of one or more functions.

Although unvalued functions can include the major ones, unvalued support functions are a particularly destructive problem. A new business manager once said, "I've spent my career avoiding human resources people and now I own a bunch." Typically, this type of attitude comes from a bad experience in the past (HR blocked the promotion of a favorite subordinate) or from ignorance. It's astonishing that business managers can arrive at their leadership positions with relatively little understanding of HR, finance, legal, audit, credit, and actuarial.

Without this understanding, they often ignore or reject these functions, much to their detriment as leaders. Good support people serve as an early warning system for problems in a business. They're the ones who are first to identify a sudden change in sales, morale problems, or an emerging pattern of lawsuits. Often support people can also fix or contain a problem before it explodes. In addition, support people can be the eyes and ears of a business manager. Because of their support roles, they're more likely to have been involved in the total business and can keep a business manager abreast of developments that his other direct reports may miss or choose not to communicate upward. Unfortunately, we've found that, in a disproportionately high number of instances, business managers have failed to use support functions to make the business more effective.

Being Highly Visible

Every leadership position has some degree of visibility; everyone has a boss who is watching to see how he performs in a new managerial role. The visibility at this level, however, is much more intense from above and especially from below. Senior management certainly has a great deal riding on how well a general manager can run the business.

What is more significant, when a business manager takes over, every person downstream is watching and waiting. Just about everyone has questions like these:

- Will the business manager make it?
- Will he change strategy?

- Can he get the resources we need?
- Will he keep the team in place?
- Will he change now that he has all this power?
- Will he favor his old function?
- Will he be too hands-on or not hands-on enough?
- Will he be externally or internally focused?

Business managers possess great power over projects, plans, and people, and this power makes their every move subject to scrutiny. Paradoxically, they must use this power to take risks and learn. Business managers typically have a million of their own questions, and to get them answered they sometimes need to take risks and make mistakes for the sake of learning. These mistakes are magnified because everyone is watching and judging business managers.

The contrast with their visibility as a functional manager is significant. Functional managers' visibility exists primarily within their function. Though their people also hang on their every word and observe every action, a common functional purpose and shared language moderates the effect of that visibility. Of course, people in other functional roles as well as the business manager keep their eyes on this functional manager, but in general, the heat of being in the spotlight is more intense for business managers.

Addressing the Challenge of E-Commerce

It's estimated that e-commerce will be the fastest-growing segment of the U.S. economy and that several hundred million people around the world will use the Internet by 2010. Even now, however, business is booming on the Internet for Old Economy and New Economy companies alike. Many general managers are facing the challenge of adding an e-commerce business.

Although e-commerce impacts every leadership level, business managers bear the brunt of it. The time, work values, and skill shifts they need to make are dizzying. Many of their assumptions and much of their knowledge about the very nature of a business must be reassessed. Here are some of the common shocks to the system that leaders at this level feel:

- Margin compression is a reality, requiring internal infrastructure reduction (cost reduction and speed) to precede price reductions.
- Business models can become obsolete overnight; they can shift from vertical to horizontal in the blink of a cursor.
- Every business is immediately global.
- Infrastructure must lead growth; prospects and customers will move elsewhere if they can't move through a site quickly and easily.
- Costs escalate rapidly, and it's easy to be surprised; spending on skilled techies and technology is necessary, but both can become outdated any minute.
- Brand is more important than ever before; it helps users sort through what seems like an infinite number of choices.
- The balance of power is shifting to the customer.
- People planning must be given top priority, not just by HR but by all leaders.
- Intellectual capital can be used to run businesses differently and to greater advantage; intranets, idea banks, online global business reviews, and the like can focus multiple, diverse minds on problems and opportunities.

Warning Signs of Leadership Transition Troubles

Identifying people who are experiencing difficulty with this leadership passage requires informed observation. The signs and symptoms aren't obvious. People who have trouble managing the complexity of a business, for instance, don't go around complaining about how complicated everything is. And no business leader in his right mind would denigrate e-commerce. The warning signs are more closely related to the stretch that business managers are being asked to make—a stretch that is longer and harder than at any other leadership level.

Here are some of the most common signs of struggle with this leadership transition:

Uninspired Communication It is as though the complexity of this new leadership level has rendered them tongue-tied. People who communicated powerfully and convincingly as functional leaders find it difficult to inspire and energize their teams. They may be having trouble with the "language," as they're used to speaking in a shared functional language rather than an omnifunctional one. The root of the problem is that they haven't learned to think differently about the business; therefore they haven't learned to talk about it in new and exciting ways. In group settings and one-on-one, they haven't found an appropriate strategic frame of reference to get their message across.

Inability to Assemble a Strong Team Building the right team is crucial at this level because of the complexity, unfamiliarity, and volume of work. Nonetheless, some business managers persist in being a one-man gang. A common symptom of this mentality is an ineffectual team of direct reports. Typically the business manager exhibits favoritism toward a function (usually the one he came up through), and this alienates other team members. It's also possible that this business manager just doesn't provide the encouragement and understanding necessary for functional managers to work well together; there's an undercurrent of distrust when these managers meet. In some instances, there's open warfare among managers. When teams of functional managers are contentious, distrustful, and ineffectual, it's a sign that the business manager is not transitioning well. Finally, some managers simply don't know how to recruit outside their function to secure the people necessary for a strong team.

Another related sign is running the business through products or technology rather than through people. Rather than relying on his team to handle the product and technology sides, the business manager steps in and takes "personal responsibility." Not only does this undermine those responsible for these functions but it also detracts from his integrator and strategist roles. Any business manager who has problems in this area is not likely to become an effective CEO. Nonetheless, some business managers who run their businesses through products or technology may make their way to the top of a company, though usually it's via the headhunter route.

Failure to Grasp How the Business Can Make Money Here accountability is for delivering profit and doing so with high capital efficiency, and many managers just don't get what the profit improvement requirements are. Though they may understand them on a certain level, they aren't able to translate that understanding into appropriate behaviors. For instance, new business managers from operations or finance sometimes are obsessed about customer calls, falsely assuming that this is the key to profit. Rather than see the entire profit chain, they focus only on this piece, thus undermining the sales function.

Just as significantly, this failure to recognize where profit comes from shows up in a lack of understanding of the core business processes. Understanding takes work; it means asking a lot of questions and admitting ignorance; it requires finding trusted advisors who can fill in the blanks. Transitioning from a function that a manager knew like the back of his hand to a cross-functional position with many unfamiliar aspects is highly challenging. It's tempting for some business managers to bluff their way through rather than invest the effort and sacrifice their ego in order to know what core processes are needed to win. Business managers possess sufficient self-confidence to admit there are areas where they lack knowledge; they should demonstrate a willingness to shift assignments to people who possess the necessary knowledge.

Problems with Time Management When you see a frenetic business manager who rockets from project to project and never has enough time to spend with any of his key people, you're observing a clear sign of trouble at this leadership level. Business managers often have problems with their time management and can't find the appropriate balance between spending time working upward in the organization, externally, visiting customers, and so on. Because they're still stuck in the functional mentality of the previous leadership level, they're trying to do too much. Rather than create a strong team and trust them to do much of the tactical work, business managers become intent on solving problems themselves. Prioritizing from the "whole business" point of view and delivering results on an appropriate short-term and long-term basis is a key for success.

Neglect of the Soft Issues Managers who ignore cultural issues haven't learned to value culture, feedback, organizational beliefs, and so on. As a result, they studiously avoid spending time, emotional energy, or money on assessing or reshaping their business's cultures or defining what it is their units stand for. Being the custodian of the culture is a new responsibility for these leaders, and their reaction is to ignore it or to assign it a low priority.

Development Options: Self-Learning, New Experiences, and Reflection

At this leadership level, development is often self-directed, with an assist now and then from the business manager's boss. There are many challenges people face as they attempt to make this leadership transition, and perhaps the toughest one is handling the complexity. The alignment triangle is a good tool for framing that complexity (see Figure 5.1).

As you can see, the alignment triangle is designed to shape and connect the diverse responsibilities and requirements of a business manager's position. At the very least, this triangle will remind business managers of the knowledge they must acquire and the balance they must achieve between diverse knowledge areas. Translating this knowledge into meaningful plans and actions is the best way for business managers to deal with the complexity at this level.

For example, if market share is dropping or the business isn't meeting its market share goals, the business manager, using the

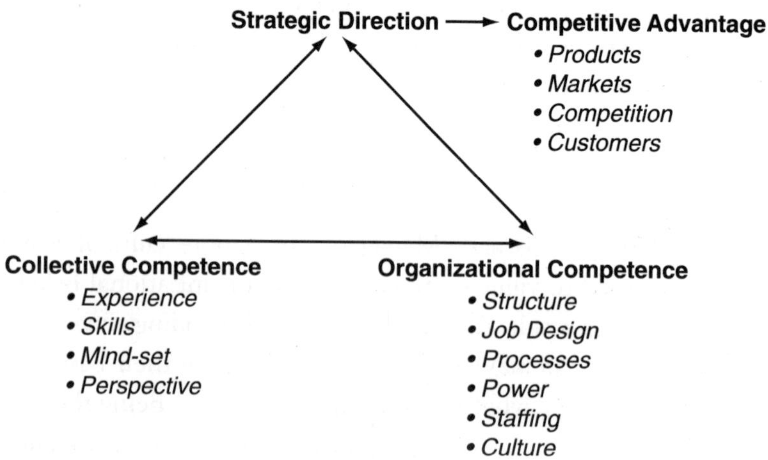

Figure 5.1. The Alignment Triangle.
Source: Drotter Human Resources, Inc.

triangle, can ask himself some questions about the elements at each corner (see Exhibit 5.1). The answers to these questions then guide the actions that the business manager must take. This method of analysis helps avoid knee-jerk reactions such as immediately cutting price to gain share.

Helping business managers learn to value all functions and to assemble and rely on strong teams of direct reports requires a number of actions. Ideally, all the functional heads will have the experience and expertise necessary to facilitate appropriate treatment and total trust on the part of the business manager. In reality,

Exhibit 5.1. Sample Questions Based on the Alignment Triangle.

Strategic direction	• Do I have the right products? • Are we in the right markets? • Is my competitive advantage viable? • Is the positioning of my business differentiated and sustainable? • Are we reaching the right customer segments?
Organization	• Do I have the right process for defining customer needs? Market potential? • Is my product development organization empowered to do the research required? • Are my costs too high and forcing prices up? • Are we organized appropriately for the challenge we face?
People	• Are my people innovative enough? • Are we skillful at designing products that respond to customer needs? • Do we have a customer mind-set? • Do we understand where we are versus competition and versus goals?

Source: Drotter Human Resources, Inc.

this is rarely the case. Therefore the business manager's boss should consider doing the following:

- Encourage the business manager to spend time with each of the functional heads and to ask questions, listen to the answers, and reflect on what he's heard.
- Set specific goals for the business manager for each of the functions, linking these goals to the support functions so they serve as an early warning system for problems.
- Suggest that the business manager make it a habit to take an appropriate functional head along on trips; this will help the manager become more attuned to the value of each function in real-life situations.

Though changing the way a business manager thinks isn't easy for any boss, it can be made easier if this issue is addressed on the first day on the job. We've found that people are most open and responsive to advice in the earliest stages of a new assignment or when they're in trouble. The boss should schedule a series of meetings from day one that illuminate this leadership transition and the different work values, time requirements, and skills at this leadership level.

As part of these early discussions, bosses should focus on the balance between short-term operating results and longer-term business positioning. This transition in thinking is tough, and business managers need to learn how to achieve both, rather than one at the expense of the other. By framing the issues and helping a business manager think and talk about the time and resources he will allocate to each, a boss can facilitate balanced thinking.

Dealing with the high visibility this leadership level necessitates is an ongoing process. In some cases, managers will have developed a degree of maturity at the previous level that will help them handle the spotlight. Some managers' natural reaction to being closely and widely scrutinized is defensiveness and rigidity. To encourage openness and flexibility instead, business managers should try the following tactics:

- Pretest ideas, decisions, and proposals with a trusted associate so that they're not placed in the position of becoming locked in when their positions are questioned in public.
- Resolve to say "I don't know" when uncertain about answers or decisions and then make a commitment to find the answers by a certain date.
- Collect many opinions—both for and against—before making decisions; look for external inputs as well.
- Use the *Wall Street Journal* test: ask yourself how you would feel about an idea or transaction if it were on the front page of the paper tomorrow.

The final issue—the e-commerce challenge—demands constant questioning of both oneself and others to develop an informed viewpoint and be able to implement e-commerce into the mix effectively. Here are just a few of the questions that business managers should be asking about their e-commerce knowledge and capabilities:

- Do I get it? Do I *really* get it? Am I willing to challenge the non-e-commerce paradigm that governs my business?
- Does the information technology department get it? If they're separated from the business (as is often the case), are they hurting rather than helping our e-commerce agenda?

- Given the importance of the individual, are we sufficiently human-centered? Are we attracting and keeping the right people?
- Am I moving fast enough?

A Successful Transition: Letting Go of the Functional Mind-Set

In many organizations, leadership pipelines are clogged with business managers who retreat from the complexity of their new positions. Rather than take the time and expend the mental energy necessary to grasp the situations confronting them, they fall back on familiar leadership approaches.

Gary is an example of someone who embraced rather than retreated from complexity when he was named a business manager by his giant financial services organization. For ten years Gary had moved through a series of increasingly difficult assignments in the company's commodity trading business. He had done well, and when his boss was promoted, Gary replaced him as business manager. It was an expected promotion, as Gary's business was considered one of the best in the world and he had a great deal to do with its success.

Gary's boss had also been very successful in running that business, and when Gary took over he could have easily maintained the strategy of his predecessor. Revenue was about $500 million, and the business enjoyed an excellent 23.8-percent operating margin. Gary, however, was not about to assume anything about the business. He used the alignment triangle as a tool to evaluate, understand, and connect strategic direction, collective individual competence, and organizational competence. He also was willing to ask his direct reports and customers questions that betrayed his ignorance in areas new to him.

What he discovered was that the industry was in an overcapacity position, the value of traditional products was declining, and the European Monetary Union was about to become a reality and would reduce the demand for his products. His global business was strong in Europe, but the talent in the business wasn't distributed evenly, and goals were poorly integrated. Working closely with his team, Gary came to the conclusion that the current business model was not in line with current realities and customer needs.

This was an alarming discovery, but one that helped Gary change his thinking about the business. This wasn't easy for many reasons, not the least of which was the fact that he owed his job to his former boss, and he was about to embark on a new strategy that moved away from the successful strategy his former boss had formulated. Gary had made the effort to grapple with a very complex environment, however, and he trusted his team sufficiently to let them help him take action in the midst of this complexity. The result was a transition plan that moved the business away from product transactions and toward professional advice. This meant reducing the number of traders in the business and increasing the number of specialists who could provide clients with advice on a range of trading issues. It also meant changing the basic processes for acquiring new customers and servicing existing ones.

The strategy panned out perfectly. Gary and his team had astutely figured out how to increase the business's profitability. The fee-for-service advice reduced the business's risk position and capitalized on a number of significant market trends. All this took guts. Even more visible than most new business managers, Gary did not wilt in the glare of the spotlight. Instead, he did his homework, worked with his team, unraveled the complexity, made the connections, and embarked on a strategy that was exactly what the business needed.

Frequently Asked Questions

Q. What are the best actions for helping a functional manager quickly become an effective business manager?

A. Walking away from the function that has been "home" for fifteen or so years is the biggest challenge. Habits, thought processes, daily interactions, memberships in functional organizations, and so on all have to be changed. Tight control of the calendar is the first step. The new business manager's boss or human resources advisor should spend a good amount of time shaping the calendar to include strategic thinking and planning time; meetings with the senior executives at customer companies (not their contact for sales); one-on-one time with new direct reports, particularly if they were peers; and reviews of key processes across the business and listening sessions at lower levels. New business managers may feel fully versed in these tasks. However, their perspective on them needs to change from functional participant to business owner and from functional effectiveness to integrated business.

A second critical action: Develop their own assessment of key people individually and all employees collectively. Developing and conveying standards for judgment is part of this action. To the extent possible, old judgments based on functional experiences should be pushed aside in favor of new judgments based on contribution to business success.

A third critical action: Define the contribution they want to make. When their tenure as business manager ends, what do they want said about them? The answers might include *rapid growth, great leadership, market leadership, great coach.* When business managers commit to this newly defined contribution, they are motivated to obtain skills that can help break the functional skill patterns.

Q. You mentioned "connecting the dots" as a key responsibility. What does that mean exactly?

A. Connecting the dots means seeing how all the elements in the business fit together and impact each other. Many business managers have been successful functional managers who connected their own function dots and some of the dots from the other functions. Now they must understand and connect all the dots in the business, particularly when making a decision. For example, if we give this customer a bigger discount, what does that do to other customers, our market position, our profitability, our supply chain, our vendor relationships, our R&D budget, sales commissions, and the like? Plans, decisions, and actions (or inactions) must be viewed in terms of their effect on everything. This requires the business manager to be familiar with all aspects of the business (that is, to see all the dots)—particularly those avoided in the past.

Q. What is the hardest part of becoming a business manager?

A. Many business managers have told us that they've struggled with revising their judgments about people. Friends from previous assignments may not measure up when viewed from the viewpoint of the business manager's requirements. Those "friends" may have to be reassigned—or worse. New business managers may feel they owe them out of loyalty or based on their past performance, but what they really owe them is candid feedback on their job performance now. All eyes are on these business managers, so they must work at being fair and consistent, no matter how personally painful it may be.

Observations from the Field

- Adopting a true business perspective on e-commerce is even more important now than when we wrote the first edition. E-commerce has become even more critical to organizations than it was ten years ago, but they don't always do a good job of integrating e-commerce into the business. Many Web sites are hard to navigate, have inappropriate explanations of terms and conditions, feature bad photography, and contain obsolete information. Business managers must pay more attention to e-commerce rather than delegating the responsibility to their tech people. Getting the right look and feel for the Web site, rethinking terms and conditions for electronic businesses, developing e-commerce partnerships, and accepting and responding to electronic feedback all should be an important part of the business manager's agenda.

- More often than not, business managers are consumed by short-term profit requirements. Although strategy development and strategic thinking are accepted parts of this role, the work and time applied are minimal or left to others. Delivering this month's numbers appears to be the business manager's single-minded focus. The shift in work values from functional capability to a profitability focus seems to be happening, but near-term profit dominates. Delegating work on the future to the strategy officer or the business development manager may temporarily clear the harried business manager's conscience. Yet business managers must devote time to the future so that they can internalize a clear sense of where their markets are headed and what will be needed to compete. Short-term profit and long-term profit should be valued equally.

- A key mistake business managers often make is failing to recognize their key role in creating a business-oriented team. We have observed many business managers supporting training and development in general terms, but we haven't seen enough one-on-one coaching of their direct reports: the functional managers. They view their direct reports as functional experts, not as sources of competitive advantage. Because they don't really know most of the functions (it is likely that they have worked in only one or two of them), they avoid coaching these functional managers. But it's critical that the business manager help each of them to completely understand the strategy and its implications for their functional work; this is the foundation for sustainable business success. Additionally, each functional manager should have a business mind-set, not a functional mind-set. Business managers can and must coach their direct reports to be sure they understand and accept the strategy and to view their work with a business mind-set. Allowing the functional manager to work in isolation or only against functional standards is a serious mistake.

- Facilitating alignment is crucial, and the alignment triangle helps achieve this goal. The alignment triangle provides a framework for tracking the progress of the business effort to get all elements in sync. Business managers who use it have talked to us about its value and utility. We have observed human resources leaders engaging more effectively with their business manager using this framework. All functions should use this tool to be sure they are moving toward or achieving alignment within their functions. Business managers should require their direct reports to rely on this tool or something similar. Certainly the framework can be tailored to be specific skills, mind-sets, processes, customers, and so on. Business managers must orchestrate this alignment, sharing responsibility with their functional managers to tighten the interface between the business and the functions.

6

From Business Manager to Group Manager

This leadership passage can be a major letdown. As we've emphasized, business managers usually love their jobs because running one's own business is enormously fun and rewarding. But as a group executive, they're no longer running a business. Sometimes they lack a staff and must borrow staff from a business unit or the corporation. The skills required at this level are more subtle and indirect. Group executives must engage in the sometimes frustrating business of allocating limited corporate resources among competing businesses, developing business managers without stepping on their toes, and developing an appropriate portfolio strategy that creates horizontal synergy among various business units and enters new businesses as appropriate. They must also assess business managers, their teams, and their cultures, behaving as though they were the sole owners of the business units, requiring externally driven goals and demanding performance. In other words, they're going from the leadership position that they found the most fun to the one they find the least fun. Some group executives tell us that they're slogging their way through this transition only because they view it as a stepping stone to a CEO position. Some even view it as a figurehead position.

There is no denying that in some large companies this layer is viewed simply as a span-breaker. In other words, the group executive is helping the CEO by reducing the number of people who report directly to the CEO. This is a necessary but demeaning definition of this role. Companies that truly understand the potential of this level require a group strategy to be developed, usually global in scope, that encompasses issues such as unserved markets, unaddressed customer segments, and likely increases in required capacity. Many of these savvy companies also make group executives responsible for driving critical initiatives down through the organization, and they test their ability to build external relationships for the whole enterprise by assigning them government, Wall Street, industry, or key customer responsibilities. When group executive responsibilities are broadened in this manner, the span-breaker role includes more than just supervision of business managers. It also involves being tested for CEO potential by doing some CEO work. Done correctly, it provides experience leading multiple and often diverse business units.

Although group management is a crucial development experience for future CEOs, it is also a pivotal level for any organization. Leadership pipelines often become clogged because group executives aren't prepared for or supported in making this leadership passage. As a result, they usurp the functions of their business managers, their business managers usurp the role of their functional managers, and so on down the line. In effect, they start a chain reaction in which everyone pushes their direct reports down one leadership level.

There are some parallels here with the leadership transition to a first-time manager. In both cases, people have to give up work they really enjoyed doing and that defined their previous success. They must relinquish their hands-on responsibilities for more ephemeral and less immediately satisfying tasks. In some instances, this can even mean tearing down something they've built; they may have to reduce resources for a business they grew or even shut it down because of changing market conditions or overall portfolio strategy objectives.

Before going into the specific requirements for this leadership level, we'd like to emphasize the work value that's crucial here.

Succeeding Indirectly

Valuing the success of other people and their businesses is absolutely essential. Group executives' effectiveness depends to a significant extent on their ability to help their people and their businesses succeed. Cognitively, this may be a foreign concept to highly ambitious, results-oriented people who become group executives. As much as they've learned to delegate and coach at earlier leadership levels, this is the first time they've had to cede just about all direct involvement in running an entity to others. This is also the first time that they must think about a collection of businesses and their relationship to the larger corporation (rather than just a singular business). As one discontented group executive said, "I just can't *do* anything. Hands-on business is what I get a kick out of, and it's why my last job was great. Now the fun is gone."

Success, therefore, comes through a path different from what they're used to. Judging the strategic skills of business managers and using their power and influence to approve projects are just two requirements that are different from those they've met at earlier leadership levels. The following three questions will help you determine whether a new group manager has made this value transition:

> Can the group manager make good decisions that differentiate between businesses on the basis of likely results?

The goal is no longer to grow one's own business but rather to create the right mix of investment in a number of businesses. Resource allocation is a crucial CEO skill, and group managers need to start valuing it. This means weighing the pros and cons of growing one business through investment versus harvesting another business for cash that can generate growth dollars for other businesses. It may also mean looking at different countries and customer groups in terms of growth prospects and making investment decisions accordingly. Determining how Wall Street might assess a move is also crucial here. As you can guess, this is a much more complex, ambiguous process than investing resources in one business. It requires the ability not only to develop strategy but also to critique it.

> Can the group manager work with his direct reports to grow them as business leaders?

As we'll discuss later in this chapter, this role is quite difficult for many group managers because it is primarily a nurturing, hands-off role. The biggest mistake group managers can make is to assume some or all of a business manager's responsibilities or to dictate a strategy for a business rather than letting a business manager learn on his own. Again, the problem relates to what group executives value. Most come into the job valuing a more involved, interactive relationship with direct reports. Now they need to step back and be more Socratic in their supervisory style.

> Can the group manager prioritize a portfolio of strategies over individual strategies?

Many group executives reflexively focus on individual strategies for individual businesses. In the past they valued the performance of one business, and this perspective often is an obstacle for the portfolio strategy necessary at this level. What's required is multidimensional thinking, integrating a variety of business needs and issues into a holistic plan. Again, this is a much more indirect way of viewing strategic planning than most managers are used to.

Let's see how these values—or the lack of them—shape skill and time requirements during this leadership passage.

Managing and Developing Business Managers

Group executives run their business managers and approve their strategies, but they do not run their businesses. This isn't just semantics. Group executives are strongly tempted to change a business strategy, challenge pricing, consolidate factories, and do all the "fun" things they used to do as business managers. Although it's critical for them to ask questions and evaluate whether business managers are carrying out these tasks effectively, they do tremendous damage to the leadership pipeline if they do these things themselves. Similar to the transition that a manager of managers goes through, group executives must exhibit restraint. In even the largest, most complex organizations, there are usually no more than two hundred to three hundred business managers. These are the best and the brightest, the talent pool from which an organization's top leadership positions will be filled. Not developing them effectively virtually ensures that a company will have to look outside to fill its top positions. As crucial as it is to develop direct reports at all levels, developing them at this level is of paramount importance to the future of the enterprise.

To help develop business managers properly, therefore, group executives need to stop creating individual business strategy themselves and learn how to critique the business managers' strategies. They must resist the impulse to impose an effective strategy on a direct report's business and instead ask the questions and provide coaching that allows that direct report to forge his own strategy. The best group executives are astute about their business managers' strategic planning ability. Through their questions and observations, they can determine whether their direct reports have made their own leadership passage successfully or whether their thinking is stuck at the functional manager level. Strategy review skills are honed here and are crucial to success.

Group executives must also learn to measure business managers on more than financial results. As you can well imagine, it's difficult to see beyond this major measure. But as we discussed in the previous chapter, business managers succeed in large part because they learn how to connect the dots and integrate functions. When a group executive makes a request that requires thinking in broad, multiple-level terms about an issue, how does the business manager respond? Is she unable to make the connections between the diverse elements of a business, including customers and suppliers? Is she stymied when she must pull functions together and help them work toward an ambitious goal? Paying attention to business managers' performance in these areas and recognizing when an individual is having problems are perceptual skills that group executives must concentrate on. They must also communicate to direct reports that *everything counts*; that they're accountable for more than solid financial performance.

In terms of time, group executives must spend a significant amount of time with functional managers. Becoming proficient at selecting functional managers who can handle a business manager position is key. Group executives who are good at making these assessments don't have any intuitive magic. They simply spend the time necessary observing functional managers' patterns of achievement, skills, and motivation. They also test them in cross-functional or cross-business assignments, observe the performance, and talk with the candidates. Because of their willingness to invest this time in evaluation, they become good judges of business manager talent. The payoff is that they have a team of direct reports who don't require a group executive to violate his leadership level and start running his people's businesses.

Connecting the Business to the Corporation

No business unit is an island. Despite some business managers' Lone Ranger mentality, they must plug into corporate goals and strategies, and it's up to group executives to monitor and enforce this connectivity. The actions of a business impact the larger corporation in many ways. When a business pollutes the environment or breaks a law, the public doesn't differentiate between that business and its corporate parent. If a brand name is tarnished, the entire organization suffers.

Group executives must make sure their business units obey the law, adhere to company policy, and maintain or enhance the brand while pursuing profit. Their task is not just the *what* but the *how*—how profit is made. To monitor compliance with corporate values and policies, group executives need to rely on the eyes and ears of their support staff. If they attempt to tackle this enormous job by themselves, they'll miss the compliance problems.

Another connective responsibility involves capital allocation. The group executive holds various businesses accountable for delivering the agreed-upon profit and strategically allocates the corporation's capital among these businesses. Again, this requires a significant shift in thinking at this leadership level. A business manager has a narrower focus and often is an advocate for a particular product, customer segment, and so forth. Group executives have to maintain a broader and more objective perspective. They need to assess the probability of success for each proposed venture before making capital allocation decisions. They must also determine which products have the most growth potential and become sophisticated about financial analysis. Their capital allocation decisions are tough, because ultimately some business managers won't accept them well and will challenge group executives every step of the way.

Which brings us to our third connective skill: strategic differentiation. This involves deciding which business has the best strategy, which one is aligned tightest with corporate strategy, and which one should therefore be fully funded. For the first time at this leadership level, managers must walk a tightrope between doing what's best for the corporation and supporting the businesses in their group. This can be a tricky position, given that what's best for the corporation isn't always what's best for the business. For this reason, group executives have to develop the knowledge, analytical skills, and personal credibility to maintain good relationships with both their direct reports and the corporation. Group executives who are respected for their fair-mindedness and business acumen are best able to pull off this high-wire act.

Managing the Uncovered

Before they reach this leadership level, managers focus primarily on what's "visible." At this new level they must become comfortable thinking and strategizing about what's invisible. Consider that most group executives are responsible for businesses within a certain category, united by a common market, technology, and so on. Within any given category, there are all sorts of potential opportunities. Group executives need to uncover and analyze these opportunities. If they uncover an opportunity, they must decide whether to extend a business to cover it, start a new business, or make an acquisition. Being able to effectively anticipate where a category of businesses is headed and project who the new players might be and where innovation might occur demands a high level of strategic thinking.

The most significant uncovered opportunities today may be those that involve e-commerce. Given the various businesses a group executive supervises, it's likely that there are myriad uncovered niches that e-commerce operations could target. To assess these uncovered possibilities, group executives must answer questions such as these:

- Should each business have its own e-commerce capability, or should there be just one for the entire group? Or should there be just one for the entire corporation?
- What e-commerce strategy will be best for customers?
- What strategy gives the group its greatest market clout?
- What are the long-term benefits versus the short-term benefits?
- What are the e-commerce threats and how do I protect against them?

On top of all this, uncovered opportunities may be capitalized on in untraditional e-commerce ways rather than through traditional business launches. It may be that an investment in bricks and mortar is unnecessary and an online business will be just as effective (if not more effective). To make this and other decisions, group executives must be willing to put in a tremendous amount of time thinking, learning, and strategizing.

A Business Manager Mentality in a Group Executive Body

David is a good example of someone who struggled mightily with this leadership transition and ended up contributing to his company's clogged pipeline. A country manager for a large multinational corporation, David was an American who was highly successful in building his company's business in Poland. To no one's surprise, he was rewarded with a group executive position, supervising the company's operations throughout Eastern Europe, which includes six country-level business managers. They were his peers when he ran operations in Poland.

Despite his superior performance in Poland, David really struggled in his new role. His direct reports complained that he was competing with them rather than offering help or advice. He would say things like, "This strategy isn't as complete or data-driven as mine was in Poland." When they called him to discuss a critical problem or a new business deal, his response was always the same: "I'll be there in a few hours." He raced around the region putting out fires and closing deals. The majority of his time was spent in that way, visiting countries, dictating solutions for problems, and making business-level decisions on prices and products.

His subordinates became reluctant to call him for any reason. The region was growing, and they needed resources to take advantage of the opportunities. They soon learned they were better off going through the finance functional chain—having their finance function manager call his counterpart at the global level, who in turn called the enterprise-level financial people for resources or budget relief. When David heard about this practice, he became incensed.

One of us had worked with David in Poland, so that person called to ask David for advice. When we arrived at his office, one of his country business managers had just resigned to join a local competitor. David said he was shocked to hear the news. After discussing the issues with David and meeting with some of the country managers, the issues became clear. David felt he was accountable for the success of each business but not for the success of the business managers. In addition, he had never really liked coaching and therefore avoided it. He liked doing deals, and most of all, he liked action.

Most of the country business managers were bright and energetic. Their businesses were growing, and they had to grow with them. David felt that some were capable of extraordinary success, but he took no accountability for helping them because he believed people were responsible for their own success.

David wasn't making the values shift that comes with the passage to group executive. In fact, his inability to make this shift was why he failed to support his direct reports appropriately. David still valued his own success to the exclusion of others, and because of this "old" value, he never bothered learning how to coach.

Warning Signs

Though group executives can exhibit a variety of behaviors that indicate they don't "get it," they most often commit the following four sins:

Acting Like Business General Managers Rather Than Group Executives Most commonly, they develop strategy for one or all of the existing businesses, provide work direction to functional managers, and make changes in products and services. Any of these behaviors indicates that someone is having difficulty with this leadership passage. Another giveaway is business managers who feel as though they're still functional managers; they complain that they're not being allowed to do their jobs. Perhaps the most obvious and disturbing sign is when entire leadership layers are pushed down one level. This may not be limited to group executives and business managers: functional managers may be leading like managers of managers, and managers of managers, like first-time managers.

Maintaining an Adversarial Relationship with the Corporation Some group executives avoid corporate work as though it involved the most odious tasks imaginable. Many of them spent the early part of their careers working in field locations far removed from corporate headquarters. As a result, they view the corporation unfavorably, using terms such as *ivory tower* and *Fort Fumble* to communicate their disdain. When a group executive says, "This is no place for an operating executive," you know the executive is having trouble with this transition. Group executives should be spending a significant amount of their time—about one-third of it—on corporate matters. If they're spending only 5 or 10 percent of their time on corporate work, there's something wrong. They need to value the corporation's needs, and if they're not making an effort to understand and respond to these, it's a bad sign.

Ignoring the Uncovered It takes a while for a group executive to possess the knowledge necessary to deal with this challenging responsibility, so don't jump to conclusions if a group executive doesn't address uncovered areas of his business category immediately. It usually takes several months to do the exploration, research, and analysis necessary to grasp a given business sector or category. After that, however, the group executive must work on uncovered issues, starting new businesses, or extending existing ones in order to develop a new niche. People who complain about how unnecessary this type of work is or shy away from the hard work involved are not fulfilling this level's leadership responsibilities. Those who focus entirely on the existing businesses will probably fail.

Passing Up Business Manager Development Opportunities Management development is a crucial responsibility for group executives. It's a sure sign that they're not carrying this out when they don't spend time with their direct reports and when their words and actions suggest they don't value their development role.

Business managers are the primary drivers of profit in organizations as well as the pool from which the top leaders are drawn. When group executives order them about or treat them paternalistically (telling them what to do and how to do it), they are exhibiting behaviors characteristic of first-level managers rather than group executives.

Developing Group Executives: A Mix of Training, Measures, and Experience

At this level, the best companies consider development a corporate responsibility and take this task seriously. At General Electric and Citibank, succession planning focused on group executive candidates and provided them with a series of assignments designed to develop their ability to run multiple businesses.

> When Jose was running a country and was considered a prime candidate for a group executive position at Global Jewelry Corp., he was given two other country manager assignments in Latin America. The first was a medium-sized country with a broad range of products, several of which were new to him. The second was a large country with complex markets. As Jose went from country to country, his progress was monitored and coached. Consistent feedback on his performance as well as special appointments to develop weak or missing skills (for instance, Jose was assigned to a task force to work on a distribution issue relevant to the entire region) groomed Jose for his eventual group executive position.

Perhaps the most important developmental experience for group managers, therefore, is managing more than one business. Ideally, they will have the opportunity Jose had to manage very diverse businesses. This will help them make the shift from knowing one business model to experiencing different business models and will enable them to move beyond the belief that the known model is the only model. Although some executives make this leadership transition successfully even though they've grown up in one business, most will have difficulty unless they are exposed to multiple businesses and learn to adapt accordingly.

Through experience and coaching, group executives can also learn the art of critiquing strategy. Essentially, the skill they really need to master is helping their business managers produce a better strategy by asking the right questions and by examining the underlying data. This means knowing what questions to ask these managers, evaluating the strategic options they have presented, assessing the risks, and telling these managers to go forward or go back to the drawing board. To a certain extent, some of these strategic skills can be acquired through training. An organization's strategic planning unit has people who can critique strategy and who can transfer much of this knowledge. We've found most group executives are eager to obtain this knowledge, especially when portfolio management and acquisitions are the subjects.

Selecting functional managers for business manager positions is another group executive skill that can be developed. Selection is an important skill at all levels, but it's especially important here from a pipeline perspective because many functional managers fail to make this difficult leadership transition. Even if a group executive has had training in assessment and selection earlier in his career, it's important to receive additional training from qualified human resources people. An individual's readiness to assume a business manager position can be difficult to determine. CEOs are frequently involved in helping select business managers, and group executives who recommend the wrong individual can suffer negative career consequences. The purpose of this training should be to help group executives define job and candidate specifications, know what questions to ask during interviews with candidates, and know how to interpret the answers. An interview and selection process that will help them identify the right person for the right job is the desired outcome.

The CEO is in charge of developing the group executive's skill at connecting the businesses to the corporation (and vice versa). Some chief executives take this requirement for granted, but they should not. A savvy CEO will indoctrinate his group executives, making sure they understand and value corporate direction and needs as well as understand the corporate identity programs and the images they're trying to project. At the same time, however, the CEO must avoid "smothering" his group executive and give him the chance to use corporate staff appropriately.

Finally, the most powerful tool to develop group executives is the set of measurements used to judge their performance. Purely financial measures are insufficient; they send the message that squeezing profit out of the businesses is the only imperative at this level. As a result, group executives measured this way often feel compelled to run the businesses themselves, driving business and functional managers down a level as they attempt to take control of the drive for more profitability. To avoid this situation, measures must include choosing and growing business managers, strategic differentiation capabilities, corporate citizenship, and ability to assess and plan for the uncovered part of the businesses, as well as the financials.

The Quintessential Group Executive

We'd like to leave you with the story of one of the best group executives we've ever encountered. In many ways, Bob embodies the skills, time applications, and work values that we've described, qualities that are crucial for traversing this leadership passage successfully.

When Bob took over his organization's energy group, it included businesses that built equipment for generating and distributing electric power as well as for storing and moving petroleum. Each business was based on a set of products and also included a small parts and service department. Though the group viewed itself as the world leader in their industry, the overall business had been in decline for several years. Morale was low, and the outlook was bleak. Faced with industry deregulation, a changing sales process, product quality problems, and a low demand for the company's products in the United States, Bob recognized and accepted the challenges. He also was aware that there was little sense of direction in his group and that his senior staff were pursuing individual agendas rather than collaborating as a true team. Strategies proposed by business managers were shallow, and a promising new product that was recently launched was failing in the field. Bob's assessment told him that his top people were "running in place" and belonged to a previous era when the group was so dominant in the markets that it was relatively easy to meet its goals.

From the very start, Bob was sure the key to success was the selection of people for business manager roles. After conducting in-depth assessments on the team he inherited, he quickly reassigned some people, replaced others, and redefined the roles of two others. Two people who were outstanding performers were given expanded responsibilities. He did all this with a perceptive eye for business manager requirements that he had developed in his previous job running a much smaller group. Once Bob had the right people in place, he didn't meddle in the existing businesses, and he provided his managers with great freedom to run them within the strategic framework he had developed.

But Bob also took the time to coach and grow them so that their efforts were also aligned with corporate requirements for business leaders.

In terms of the larger business issues, Bob circled the globe to meet customers, made calls on potential customers, and obtained a bird's-eye view of the market. Because Bob had been developed in such a way that he understood a wide variety of business models, he quickly perceived global opportunities the group had not taken advantage of in the past. As a result of what he learned, Bob made the strategic decision for the group to tackle the global market, a decision that dovetailed with corporate initiatives and direction. Again, he didn't foist specific strategies on his business managers; he merely provided them with an overall direction and framework. They made their own strategies within the framework.

Bob also identified and helped fill uncovered market segments with products and services. Because this strategy required significant technologies that the group lacked, Bob initiated a number of acquisitions that brought in new businesses with the required technological capabilities and some new products.

We should also note that Bob was brilliant at redistributing investments in various businesses and creating an effective portfolio strategy. He reframed the business with a much greater emphasis on the service component. The service market potential was five times larger than the product market, and Bob correctly reasoned that offering more services could lower customer costs as well as increase revenues. Because their own people knew the products best, they could deliver service more inexpensively and handle the entire installed base of their business's products and not just those recently sold.

As a result of Bob's efforts, a demoralized, underperforming group became a growth engine for the company. The group doubled sales, tripled profits, and built a new avenue for growth in four years. Besides all these business accomplishments, Bob opened up the leadership pipeline, helping functional managers make the transition to business managers. He pushed the whole organization to add new talent at every level in this large, complex business. Performance standards were raised and met at every level in his organization.

Frequently Asked Questions

Q. How should group managers spend their time in order to make the best contributions?

A. We've found that the most successful group managers spend 50 percent or more of their time coaching and developing people. They treat most interactions with business managers as learning events, and ask the right questions more than they give the right answers. Their effort is not limited to business managers. The best group managers also extend their coaching to functional managers. As a result, they make the effort to understand the capability of the functions in total and the potential of the functional managers. Functional managers are the hiring pool for business managers and for the group support staff positions (see Chapter Twelve). If there isn't sufficient potential, then new talent must be acquired or promoted. The best group managers also pay attention to the capability and potential of managers of managers. That is why the most successful group managers drive the succession planning process.

In addition, the group managers should devote at least 25 percent of their time to strategy and strategy-related work: developing portfolio strategy, critiquing business strategy, evaluating potential partners, and attending customer meetings at the highest levels.

Between 10 percent and 20 percent must be spent on enterprise needs. Helping the CEO run the company, tackling company-wide problems, meeting with key external groups on behalf of the company, and working with peers on any required redistribution of resources are all part of this. The remainder varies greatly from company to company and industry to industry.

Q. How can you tell if a business manager is a good candidate for group manager?

A. Since the first edition was published, we've worked with many companies that have struggled with group manager selection. There are many similarities between this selection challenge and the selection of the enterprise CEO. The obvious criteria apply, such as exceptional results, strong strategic skills, effective people development, passion for satisfying customers, and well-developed business acumen. The more subtle indicators are demonstrating concern for the success of the corporation by supporting corporate initiatives, willingness to share resources, living the corporate values, and making time available for corporate events. Running a business successfully but ignoring the corporation is a danger sign.

Breadth of thought and learning is another key indicator. Can the manager come up with big ideas that business managers will respect? Can she see gaps between the businesses that must be filled? Does she have interest in and learn from businesses other than her own? The portfolio strategy requirements for group managers requires thinking and learning well outside the boundaries of existing business.

A third indicator is peer influence. Group manager candidates should be able to convince their peers that a certain course of action or a new program is worth pursuing. They must build credibility and trust with business managers. Thought leadership is also an important part of being the leader at these levels of the organization.

Observations from the Field

- Working with the enterprise CEO to run the company is a crucial but neglected requirement. In fact, we neglected to emphasize it in the first edition. When the CEO gathers his direct reports, including the group managers, he needs them to put aside their specific accountabilities and participate in enterprise thinking and decision making. Three different enterprise CEOs, all in the same week, asked us how to get their direct reports to come to the staff meetings and participate like they were responsible for the entire enterprise. When the enterprise CEO's team is together, the CEO must see the enterprise as one thing, like a basketball, not as many different things, like golf balls in a bag. This "basketball" perspective requires everyone in the room to understand that if the basketball is leaking air, it is everyone's problem, and everyone must be willing to participate in the solution. The world has become very small, and business has become too complex for one person (like the enterprise CEO) to have all the answers. The entire team must weigh in on the problem to be sure a broad range of expertise is applied.

- Valuing long-term results, not just short-term ones, is even more essential for group managers than for business managers. In fact, the most common point of discomfort for new group managers is the absence of short-term gratification. They say it is hard to go home each night and not be able to feel the satisfaction they used to feel from accomplishments completed that day. Most of the success now comes from long-term effort. So relishing delayed gratification is the norm and a sign of executive maturity. Group managers need this maturity to function in the role. Otherwise they will reach into the businesses and meddle!
- Being a group manager provides invaluable training for enterprise CEO positions. Though this point may seem

obvious, we've found that many companies don't select group managers with CEO succession in mind. Working with the CEO to run the company and learning to live with delayed gratification are two ways group managers prepare to take on CEO responsibilities. A third way is detaching from running a business. This separation is a must for being effective as a CEO. Group managers should also master evaluating several businesses for the purpose of capital allocation; this is a CEO requirement that must be learned at group manager level. Although not all enterprises can or should have group manager positions, these have great training value, especially because the leap from business manager to enterprise CEO is too big for most people. Group managers should be selected with CEO potential in mind.

- Building group manager positions in companies that didn't have them previously has many benefits. This effort frees up the enterprise CEO's time, provides more coaching for business managers, and directs more energy toward improving the portfolio of businesses. These benefits are immediate, though to realize them certain challenges must be met. Careful delineation of duties for both the enterprise CEO and the business managers is the first and biggest challenge. Both the enterprise CEO and the business manager must let go of some prized work in order to get the benefits from the new group manager. Relationships with corporate staff must be redefined before a power struggle erupts between them. Most group managers want and get their own finance officer, human resource officer, legal counsel, etc. That raises questions about corporate access to the business CFOs, HROs, and the like. We discuss this in Chapter Twelve, The Functional Career Passage.

- We would add one caveat: no kids! Staff positions supporting group managers must have people with both business savvy and emotional maturity to make the right contribution while building and maintaining a complex set of relationships. Group managers need their own support. If they don't get it, they will use up the time of the business managers' staff.

7

From Group Manager to Enterprise Manager

A great deal of recognition surrounds this leadership passage—as well as a great deal of failure. When new CEOs are named, *Wall Street Journal* articles are written about them, their appointment is hailed by friends and colleagues, and their social calendars fill up quickly. Within a few years of their appointment, however, many chief executives are gone or on their way out, and recently the turnover has accelerated almost beyond belief. These aren't stupid people. In fact, many failed CEOs were brilliant strategists and visionaries. Nonetheless, they lacked the skills, time applications, and work values demanded at this leadership level.

Successful CEOs exhibit sound judgment on people matters and execute well deep into the organization. Though strategic ability, vision, and other factors are important skills at this level of leadership, they won't rescue a CEO who can't get things done or who lacks the ability to put the right person in the right job.

What makes the transition to enterprise manager so difficult is that the executive is managing an enterprise in its totality, not a business. CEOs are responsible to multiple constituencies—boards, Wall Street analysts, investors, alliance partners, the workforce, shareholders, direct reports, local communities, and so on. More than any other leader, they're under the microscope of all these constituencies.

There is also less room for error at this level. The price of making errors in this day and age is very high for most CEOs. CEOs who miss three or four quarters of earning expectations usually pay a significant penalty. For some people, especially those who have not experienced much failure in their work lives, this can be a shock.

More so than in the past, we've seen people become CEOs quickly, and they have failed to obtain the appropriate experience. They've skipped some of the passages that prepare people to be successful CEOs and thus display a lack of judgment when faced with new issues or uncertain conditions.

Lack of experience isn't necessarily linked to age. Forty-five-year-old Jack Welch, as newly elected CEO of GE, went through some rigorous passages and experiences to be prepared for this job. John Reed took over Citi in his early forties and had little corporate banking experience. Both held their CEO positions for about twenty years, despite bumps in the road, because they were incessant learners.

At the same time, we are seeing more forty-five-year-old CEOs than ever before. Especially in knowledge worker industries, people are moving to the top at unprecedented speed. As a result, they must transition from one leadership level to the next very quickly. The dot.com companies are not exempt from this rule. Bright young twenty-four-year-olds can create dot.com companies, attract the best people, and hype their stock, but lack of experience through the leadership passages eventually catches up with them because they too must meet the demands of Wall Street. Getting there first without training and sufficient experience is highly risky for the enterprise and the individual. In addition, some business managers bypass the group executive level and go directly to CEO. The group executive level can provide a great interim step toward the top spot, making the adjustment to CEO less of an intellectual and emotional jump.

As you can see, this passage confronts even highly successful and talented executives with serious challenges. Let's look at the five most significant leadership challenges enterprise managers face.

Challenge One: Delivering Consistent, Predictable Top- and Bottom-Line Results

In any publicly held company, most CEOs are evaluated by investors and security analysts. The scorecards are posted hourly on stock exchanges. Every quarter, Wall Street publishes expectations of both top- and bottom-line growth. Any slip in expectations and delivery of results detracts from a CEO's credibility—his most important asset. The heads of Honeywell, Boeing, and Amazon .com all experienced this credibility loss as they moved into the twenty-first century. To survive, CEOs must learn to value short-term and long-term results, develop the skill to balance both, and invest the time required to achieve this balance.

This passage isn't made overnight. In most instances, people who make the transition successfully have gone through all the earlier leadership pipeline passages. They've learned how to make trade-offs at each level. They've developed the ability to anticipate long-term ramifications and adjust short-term tactics with the long term in mind. Over time, they've become adept at seeing the larger picture, dealing with multiple constituencies, and communicating. At some point, they've acquired the emotional fortitude necessary to make unpleasant decisions. The distinguished club of CEOs who have run organizations for twenty years and met this long-term, short-term challenge include Jack Welch of GE, Reuben Mark of Colgate, Chuck Knight of Emerson, and Andy Grove of Intel.

Challenge Two: Setting Enterprise Direction

To understand the enormity of this challenge, imagine trying to keep a company steady in a geologically volatile area. With the tectonic plates shifting frequently, it requires knowledge and instinct to keep the enterprise on solid ground. Vision, strategic acumen, and positioning know-how are all crucial skills in that regard. This challenge has bedeviled many CEOs despite liberal use of expensive consulting firms. The enterprise manager must decide where to take the company, what his assumptions are about the changing industry or field, what recipes or business models will make money, and what competitive patterns to heed. No question, the CEOs of companies such as Sears, Sprint, Motorola, and IBM have all encountered this positioning challenge. To meet this challenge requires more than a vision statement. Many companies have such statements and hang them on their walls. Most of these visions are so broad and unfocused that they are meaningless. As an experiment, collect the statements of fifty companies; you'll find that they're remarkably similar. The real challenge for the CEO is to craft a concrete definition of where he wants to take the enterprise. At the very least, this demands that a CEO display real courage. Such courage has been displayed by the CEOs who reinvented Intel and spurred the comeback of Compaq.

In a very real sense, this leadership passage requires CEOs to value tasks that they've never done before, and that can be scary. More than one CEO has told us that this is the first time they felt a lack of confidence in their ability to set strategic direction. Valuing the risk taking, deep thinking, and complexities at this level all are crucial if CEOs are to be successful.

Challenge Three: Shaping the Soft Side of the Enterprise

Every company is a social organization. When two or more people work together, they invariably develop positive or negative relationships. Managing the social relationships as well as the environment in which such relationships evolve is a crucial responsibility of the CEO. Focusing on these soft issues while also striving for hard business results is a juggling act not every CEO can handle.

More so than ever before, CEOs must energize people, releasing this energy at all levels and particularly at the lowest level, where the action is. For example, the CEO of Electronic Data Systems (EDS) regularly sent e-mails to 145,000 employees across the globe, informing his people about wins and losses and keeping them "personally" aware of events that impacted the company and their jobs. In turn, the employees responded with feedback and tough questions for the CEO. This was a job that the CEO did not delegate but took on as his own responsibility, and as a result he forged a bond with his people. Communicating in ways that energize large and diverse groups of employees is a soft skill that CEOs must learn to value and master.

No company can prosper without having the right people in the right jobs, especially at a time when a high-grade skill person can become a low-grade skill person in the wink of an eye (or a change in technology). Selecting the right people and continuously upgrading their skills and knowledge is a responsibility that ultimately falls on the CEO. While others may carry out the technical aspects of selection and development, the CEO must initiate, maintain, and manage the process. He must continuously ask questions such as these:

- How good are we at selecting the right people?
- How candid are we about giving the right feedback?
- How willing are we to end mismatches between jobs and people in a timely fashion?
- How vigilant are we in retaining high performers, moving them faster, rewarding them appropriately, and giving them unprecedented opportunities to test themselves?

Challenge Four: Maintaining an Edge in Execution

Contrary to popular belief, CEOs don't need to be strategic wizards or brilliant visionaries to succeed. They do, however, need to get things done. CEOs who are indecisive or don't deliver on commitments are the ones whose organizations suffer; they're also the ones who are asked by their boards to leave.

Execution is more critical for CEOs now than in years past. Just about every industry is more competitive because of the global marketplace and e-commerce. Information technology has empowered customers in ways that make it even more important for organizations to sell the steak rather than the sizzle. As a result, CEOs can't simply talk a good game. At other leadership levels, they may have been able to get by with flawed execution. At this level, the flaws will kill a CEO.

Valuing execution isn't always easy for CEOs. The nitty-gritty details of getting things done aren't the most glamorous aspects of the job. The best CEOs, however, recognize that this is where the payoff is for themselves as enterprise leaders and for their organizations. Those who maintain an execution edge continually ask themselves the following questions:

- *How's my performance?* To answer this question positively, CEOs develop performance forecasts for the next eight quarters (not just the usual four). Early on, they start thinking about performance-focused changes they may need to make down the line.
- *Do I know what's going on?* Execution requires the latest information from the most important sources. CEOs should be directly connected to customers and frontline employees and be well informed about how the company and the markets are doing. Sam Walton, for instance, instituted the daily practice of store visits, making sure he was always where the action was. Bill

Marriott visits hotels as part of his regular routine—well over three hundred in a typical year. He has learned to tell very quickly whether things are going well or poorly. CEOs should also be aware of whether direct reports are following through on their commitments. What is most important, they should heed their observations about whether the company is doing well or poorly and act on these observations.

- *Are people telling me the bad news?* At some organizations, people are afraid to give the CEO bad news. At others, CEOs are unwilling to hear the bad news, rationalizing every negative report. CEOs can't execute properly if they let bad news build to the crisis point. By the time they're willing to act, it's too late.
- *Is the board fulfilling its mandate?* If they're just a rubber stamp, they're hampering the CEO's ability to achieve results. When they hold the CEO and his direct reports accountable and ask for information about succession and the company's markets, they're enhancing the CEO's capacity to execute.
- *Is my team productive and enthusiastic?* When a CEO's team is divisive and inconsistent, it is often a sign that the CEO is in trouble. When the team can't achieve consensus and accomplish a relatively simple goal, it's likely that the CEO is having trouble producing acceptable results.

To complete this leadership passage successfully, CEOs must shift their skills, time applications, and work values in the direction of execution. This means they must develop an insatiable appetite for accomplishment and results. It means they must understand the business deeply, acquiring an almost instinctive sense of how the company makes money. It means they must spend a great deal of time diagnosing whether the organization is performing at full potential. And it means they must become skilled at converting learning into practice, identifying the best ideas, and translating them into tools and programs that benefit the organization.

Challenge Five: Managing the Enterprise in a Broader, Global Context

No company can survive without paying attention to the community around it. Just as every organization takes from the community, it must also give back to the community. Organizations must be aware and active in solving the global problems that confront them. They must pay attention to and take positions on environmental, safety, and health issues. Ford and Du Pont, for instance, have taken a strong leadership position in the Green movement. Every CEO must know his constituency, be they environmentalists or other special interest groups.

Many CEOs come to their jobs lacking knowledge or experience in these areas. They may never have thought much about how their organization is impacting global warming or whether they are in some way harming the economy of a Third World country. In fact, many CEOs have told us that they don't have a handle on how to deal with various community groups whose modus operandi and base of power are very different from their own. In attempting to lead the company in a broader, global context, they find the experience foreign in both figurative and literal senses. Yet to make an effective transition to this leadership level, CEOs must adapt their thinking and values to this broader context.

A Significant Value Shift

Given the five major challenges CEOs face as they make this leadership transition, they must adapt their values accordingly. As we've suggested, enterprise leadership demands a system of beliefs substantially different from what is required at other leadership levels. Though we've discussed some of the values that prove helpful to CEOs, we'd like to focus here on the larger value shift that must take place.

Up until this point, most managers have learned to value short-term and medium-term operating results and regular, measurable achievements. Though they may recognize the need for long-term planning and goals if they've successfully navigated previous leadership levels, they often find it difficult to accept the pace at which enterprise results happen. To achieve a cultural change or implement a new quality program can take a long time to implement fully. For managers who have built their careers achieving results faster and more effectively than their peers, valuing slow, evolutionary results can be a struggle. Giving up on long-cycle programs (such as quality-based ones) before they're fully implemented and producing measurable results is a common CEO failing.

Similarly, many CEOs experience difficulty valuing only three or four key objectives. Business managers and even group executives frequently have long lists of goals. They derive satisfaction by checking off one item after the next. The enterprise manager, however, should derive satisfaction from a short list of long time-cycle initiatives. Changing brand identity, for example, can take years. In a very real sense, the shift in values is from immediate gratification to sustained progress. Enterprise managers recognize that the most ambitious, significant objectives take time to achieve, and they learn to do without the quick fix of immediate achievement that characterizes other leadership levels in favor of slowly but surely working toward a major success. The confounding paradox, of course, is that side by side with this patience is the need to deliver quarter-by-quarter commitments. They resolve this paradox by learning to get certain things done fast and others slowly, and they make sure they don't confuse the two (getting things done slowly that need to be done fast, for instance). Finding the balance between the short term and the long term and executing it is what makes CEOs successful.

Another problematic value shift involves taking advice from boards. For people who are accustomed to running their own businesses, this value can be an obstacle. In the past, managers may have received advice from peers, coaches, or bosses, but boards are a different breed of advice giver. Board members' opinions may seem superficial or less informed than an insider's perspective. Also, directors as individuals may provide conflicting advice, and some CEOs will devalue that advice simply because they're perplexed by it. We've found, however, that enterprise managers who are open with their boards and make an effort to listen and learn from them ultimately benefit in their decision making. If the board is unable to provide informed advice, the CEO's responsibility is to educate them until they're able to do so.

Finally, the best CEOs come to value asking questions and listening to a broad spectrum of people. This is almost a counterintuitive value, given the power that comes with the CEO position and the ego that's required to obtain it. In fact, a significant percentage of chief executives have risen from one leadership level to the next based on their strong, aggressive style and their ability to wield power. Power, however, becomes dysfunctional when enterprise managers don't exercise restraint. Although CEOs possess ultimate position power, true leaders at this level don't rely exclusively on position power to get things done. They recognize that influence can get things done with energy and innovation rather than just with grudging compliance. Influential enterprise managers share their vision with a variety of people in order to capture their interest and motivate them to perform.

The dictatorial, ego-driven CEO tends to ask few questions and not listen to the answers. He values his own opinion above all others and as a result tunes out ideas and perspectives that clash with his own. Although most new CEOs don't fit the dictatorial stereotype, many do not fully value listening to multiple perspectives. Too often, a new CEO relies on one trusted advisor rather than soliciting a broader range of opinions and ideas.

Signs That a CEO Is Struggling

The most obvious sign is a downward financial spiral that occurs under the new CEO's watch. Although a financial crisis may not be caused specifically by an enterprise manager experiencing difficulties with this leadership transition, his response (or lack thereof) to the crisis may signal transition problems. In many instances, however, the signs are a bit more subtle. The following four behaviors and attitudes suggest that this passage is giving a CEO trouble:

Ignorance of How the Company Gets Things Done This goes back to Challenge Four: maintaining an edge in execution. Sometimes new CEOs just don't get it—*it* being how the place works. In conversations and by their actions, they demonstrate their ignorance of what is required to get the right people in the right jobs or to implement a new program or policy. They don't understand how to use their influence to pull the right levers to overcome inertia or fight through other obstacles to get results. Either they're not interested in learning how the enterprise executes or they're content with their false assumptions. In either case, they make little or no effort to examine and review operations in all businesses, listen to people at every level, and obtain the customer's view of service and quality.

Signs of disinterest in these issues are relatively subtle. Overt signs are financial, and deterioration in earnings signals that a CEO is walking toward the brink. We know of at least four CEOs who didn't have the faintest idea about how their enterprise executes, and the result was at least a $1 billion loss in each instance. When a new CEO is blindsided with significant operating shortfalls, it's often a sign that he doesn't understand how things get done.

Although the CEO of a company with less than two hundred employees may understand enterprise execution if he's been there a few years, in a bigger company, a rapidly growing organization, or one in a complex industry the learning curve is steeper. A CEO who isolates himself from a range of people and information or leaves execution to others is not making this leadership turn.

The Majority of the CEO's Time Is Spent on External Relationships It's not that customer functions, government meetings, community events, celebrity golf tournaments, and the like are unimportant. Part of the CEO's role is interacting with external groups and projecting a positive public image for both himself and the enterprise. This is a seductive role, however, and some CEOs lose sight of the larger leadership responsibilities at this level. Specifically, they fail to see that no one's minding the store. CEOs should spend their time in a balanced way on external and internal issues. If the balance tips in one direction—and usually it's in the external direction—then something is wrong. CEOs who get caught up in acting the part rather than being the chief executive often land their company (and themselves) in hot water.

The CEO Is Not Devoting Enough Time to the Soft Side of the Business This challenge goes back to Challenge Three: shaping the soft side of the enterprise. The people issues can be terribly complex from a CEO's perspective, and some enterprise managers find it easier to deal with product issues instead. For instance, CEOs are in charge of the leadership pipeline, and if they show no interest in selecting and developing leadership at all levels, this is a sure sign that the soft side of the business is going unattended. Similarly, some people reach CEO positions and immediately appoint their "buddies" to key jobs, surrounding themselves with friends. Though a chief executive certainly is entitled to select a team of people he knows and trusts, any form of corporate nepotism sends the wrong message throughout the organization. It demotivates strong performers and encourages noncritical responses to superiors instead of honest dialogue. CEOs should establish a process and requirements for key positions, and if they don't, they're demonstrating an aversion to soft-side matters.

Board Members Keep Asking the CEO the Same Questions When results are below expectations and shareholders are scrutinizing a company closely, board members feel the pressure and begin to ask hard questions of the CEO. If the CEO isn't answering the questions satisfactorily and the same questions are asked at several board meetings, it's a sign of trouble. Even if boards are generally not the rubber stamps of the past, they're rarely adversarial. A disharmonious relationship with the board often means that the chief executive lacks a key CEO skill or doesn't possess appropriate values for this leadership position.

CEO Development: No Skipping Levels Allowed

There are many paths to the chief executive spot, but all of them should allow managers to make leadership transitions at each level. People who become enterprise managers and have skipped levels are burdened by a gap in their leadership experience. They may never learn how to value the success of other managers or become proficient at managing more than one business. All the skills, time applications, and values learned at earlier levels have a cumulative effect that facilitates the transition from group manager to enterprise manager.

The ideal development path for future CEOs begins early in their careers with a diversity of functional experience around the core competencies of the business. Too many CEOs still labor under a functional bias, having skipped this transition early on. As their careers progress, they should have at least one international assignment as well as a sequence of progressively larger profit and loss (P&L) jobs in different business sectors. Growing different businesses is key, and the businesses ideally will include a start-up as well as a turnaround. All along the way, these people should be exposed to formal and informal coaching and feedback as part of the learning process.

To help develop group managers into enterprise managers, one of the keys is to have them run a group that is different in market position, product, or customers from what they're used to. They need to learn how to deal with a new business model. This is good preparation for a CEO position, because running the company is much more challenging than grasping a new business model. If they can't master new business models, they won't master their role as enterprise leader.

Another development step is to have them take on a staff position with companywide responsibilities. Expect operating executives to dismiss this assignment: "I'm not a staff guy," they often say disdainfully. The more disdainful they are, the more they need this experience. Research, deep analysis, long-term planning, and measurement are necessary for CEO success, and staff positions can provide opportunities to develop these skills. It will also give them an appreciation of staff work and help them value and use staff more effectively when they're managing the enterprise.

It's also a good idea to expose group executives and even business managers to the board of directors and Wall Street analysts. Exposure means more than letting them sit in on a meeting. Ideally, they'll be given real projects and asked to produce results in order to develop an appreciation for how boards and analysts function. In the middle 1990s, for instance, Jack Welch began to expose his managers to security analysts, and this practice helped build Wall Street's confidence in GE's leadership genes, particularly when it comes to succession issues. At the same time, GE's leaders gained insights about what Wall Street expects.

Certainly CEOs can develop themselves on the job, and the best ones are open to development opportunities. They participate in different forums and networks where they exchange best practices with other CEOs. In addition, they make an effort to arrange meetings with and attend talks by academics and other thought leaders. They also read a great deal and draw ideas from their reading, staying informed about social, economic, and business trends.

Perhaps the best development method for CEOs is having a coach or some other "peer" who can give them feedback. In an ideal situation, boards will fulfill this role. In some instances, a particular board member will take on this coaching assignment and mentor new CEOs as they learn the ropes.

Though no specific course or training method grooms managers to become CEOs, a diversity of experience, coaching, and feedback all along the way and a willingness to listen and learn go a long way toward preparing people for this challenging leadership position.

Don't Set Up a CEO for Failure

Organizations sometimes choose CEOs based on their intellect or strategic capabilities. For these reasons, many consultants are being moved into senior operating and even CEO positions. We've found, however, that consultants often tend to make poor CEOs because they've failed to go through all the passages of leading people.

Leading an enterprise requires intelligence, but it isn't a paper-and-pencil exercise. Making dazzling PowerPoint presentations to boards isn't what the job is all about. It's really about ensuring successful execution, choosing the right people, valuing enterprise results, and building relationships inside and out. CEOs who aren't adept at these tasks—who don't have a clue about how to select and nurture leaders or build relationships in all directions—will probably fail no matter how skilled they are at mapping strategy.

Typically, consultants have skipped passages, and the result is that they often lack appreciation for and skill in mid-level and lower-level work requirements. They also frequently have difficulty motivating first-line workers, integrating diverse functions, coaching, knowing what questions to ask, and accepting advice from support functions.

To guarantee success for a CEO, organizations simply need to make sure that this individual has successfully navigated the most critical passages of the pipeline.

Frequently Asked Questions

Q. How long does it take new enterprise managers to get their arms around the job?

A. The transition is formidable because the job is complex. Our best guess is two years to get comfortable with the altitude, put the right team together, and develop a strategy they can believe in and sell to the organization. It will take longer, possibly three to four years, if the company was in trouble. The current practice of measuring new enterprise managers solely on quarterly earnings and removing them in eighteen months denies the realities of the transition. The bigger the mess, the more short-sighted this eighteen-month timetable becomes.

Q. Are there two or three key characteristics that we can use to select an enterprise manager?

A. We wish it were that easy. It isn't unusual to have fifteen to twenty significant results that must be achieved in the first year. Twenty to thirty attributes—experience, skills, and personal characteristics—are needed. There aren't any shortcuts. Preparing future enterprise managers is a long and deliberate process. Selecting them requires a thorough assessment by many people. Focusing on two or three characteristics is a mistake we have seen boards make frequently. A comprehensive picture of the work to be done and the required skills, experiences, and personal characteristics provides the best opportunity for success. That being said, there are three characteristics that stand out: (1) a sense of purpose beyond the numbers, (2) a clear roadmap, and (3) the ability to communicate purpose and roadmap to large groups of people the CEO will never see.

Q. How do I think about my career relative to this leadership pipeline if I don't aspire to be CEO?

A. Very few people get the chance to navigate the entire pipeline. Most people don't want to be CEO. The best way to think about your career and the Leadership Pipeline is to take it one passage at a time. If the passage you are assigned to provides you with sufficient rewards and challenge in relation to your skills, don't pursue the next passage until you fully understand what will be expected of you. Avoid spending the back end of your career doing work you don't like just because it offered more status, money, or power. A good match between challenge and skills offers the best opportunity for happiness as well as on-the-job success.

Observations from the Field

- Enterprise managers are not as powerful as the company's employees or those outside the company believe. In fact, it isn't unusual for a CEO's strategies, edicts, or desires to be ignored at lower levels. This isn't necessarily malicious behavior or even benign neglect. It is just very difficult to have any plan or edict carried out through all layers of the company. The message gets garbled very quickly. Each layer interprets the strategy from its own vantage point, so key ideas are lost. Supporting actions needed for implementation—such as additional resources, training, or removal of obstacles—may not get done. A CEO can't do it alone. It takes both a team and the will to execute at each layer in the organization. Most CEOs would be more powerful if they paid attention to what actually goes on at each layer and spent more time convincing everyone to sign up for the agenda.

- The enterprise manager is the biggest beneficiary of a full and flowing leadership pipeline. Filling senior executive positions quickly with high confidence is possible if leaders at every level make the proper transition, build the right skills, adopt the right work values, and work with the appropriate time horizon. A full and flowing leadership pipeline also enables exceptional performance. We have observed many enterprise managers who refuse to spend the time needed to get the leadership pipeline right because they lack appropriate work values; they prefer devoting time and energy to more glamorous external events than to the human side of the business. The enterprise managers who have put the time in get the results. Those who come around and start investing the time see benefits quickly—without exception. Those who don't wonder why the company isn't doing better.

- Valuing the corporate staff based on old criteria causes new CEOs considerable pain. Enterprise managers suffer when their human resources officer can't judge talent; when the CFO isn't strategic; when the chief information officer is a techie, not a businessperson; and so on. Choosing the right corporate staff heads makes life much more enjoyable and success more likely for the CEO and the company. Enterprise managers who set out to gain competitive advantage through a new emphasis on innovating to accelerate growth or to enter new businesses or to make major cultural change must take a hard look at their top staff officers and be sure they are up to the new requirements. Just because they served the predecessor well doesn't mean they will serve their successor well in a new game. In addition to different skills, enterprise managers may also want a different kind of relationship—perhaps one with more initiative or more willingness to challenge their thinking.

- Failing to address performance problems soon enough is the number one reason enterprise managers fail. Even the toughest enterprise managers have trouble moving quickly to address direct reports who do not deliver expected results or deliver them in inappropriate ways. The performance shortfall is usually visible to anyone who cares to notice and clear to the other direct reports. Teamwork is impaired, morale is lowered, and the enterprise manager's capability comes into question. The longer it goes on, the worse things get for the enterprise manager. Enterprise managers must establish an open and honest communication environment with frequent and candid feedback, preferably on a monthly basis. Their reports must feel free to raise concerns regarding the way problems, particularly performance problems, are handled with direct reports.

8

Diagnostics

Identifying Pipeline Problems and Possibilities

As you'll see here and in the following chapters, you can use the Leadership Pipeline model in a variety of ways. Performance management, leadership development, coaching, and succession planning are all facilitated by familiarity with the six leadership passages we've described. First, however, we'd like to show you how this model can be used to diagnose and troubleshoot problems that are preventing organizations from building and maintaining a leadership pipeline.

Certainly there are other models out there designed to help companies diagnose leadership shortcomings, such as balanced scorecards and competency models. The former help increase the range or categories of expected results (such as people results), whereas the latter list targeted skills and capabilities. Although these and other approaches can be useful, they're limited by their exclusive skill focus and failure to differentiate among the six leadership passages (leadership is viewed as basically the same thing at all levels of the organization). Value shifts and time reapplications are absolutely critical if people are going to develop at each leadership level, and we'll concentrate on diagnosing problems in these areas even more than in skill areas (which are more easily identifiable).

The Leadership Pipeline model provides a diagnostic specificity that other models lack. Instead of vague determinations that a company is lacking a talent pool of young leaders, the Pipeline approach enables you to pinpoint the precise level where problems are occurring and the skills, time applications, and values at that level where people are coming up short.

Three Good Reasons to Diagnose Early and Often

We've found that just about every organization has people working at the wrong leadership levels. This problem can occur at any of the six levels, but it's most common among these:

- First-line managers who are spending most of their time doing individual contributor work
- Business managers who are doing functional work
- Group executives who are focusing on business manager work

As we'll see by way of example, many of these level-inappropriate people are high-potential individuals who have been allowed to skip certain experiences because of their talent. In the rush to move them up, they often end up missing or hurrying through the passages that would have helped them build the foundation of skills, time applications, and work values demanded at higher levels.

Why is it important to diagnose these problems? Why can a company still thrive if its leaders are working at the wrong levels but still delivering results? Here are three compelling reasons:

> Important work isn't getting done even though there is a significant amount of output.

For example, when a sales manager spends all his time selling, he isn't managing salespeople. No matter how hard the salespeople work or how well the sales manager sells, the odds are that some needed work isn't getting done. Salespeople may not be focusing on adding new customers or may be failing to sell more difficult products. Though short-term results may look great, no one is laying the groundwork for sustainable results.

We know of a CEO who designed the waiting room for a new factory while his company plunged into bankruptcy. We know of the head of HR at a major bank who spent his time designing forms for succession planning while senior executives were desperate for his help in reducing turnover. These are obvious examples of leaders operating at the wrong levels, but these leaders are also working hard and producing. Although bankruptcy communicated that the CEO just mentioned was coming up short, we often miss the signs that a leader is performing below capacity. Without a good diagnostic tool, we often mistake output for leadership effectiveness.

The cost of each business transaction is increased.

To recall the previous example, the sales manager is being paid to manage but is actually working at an individual contributor level. But the cost doesn't end there. In all likelihood, the sales manager's boss—a manager of managers—is probably doing what the sales manager should be doing. So he, too, is working below the level his company is paying him for. Typically, people at higher levels are pulled down to fill the void. The mismatch of work and pay may be endemic to the company, and this mismatch becomes "how we get things done in this culture." When companies accept and even institutionalize these mismatches, true effectiveness becomes difficult to achieve. How can you determine whether leaders are at the wrong levels when they're just doing what the culture deems acceptable? This is a very big challenge to diagnose and remedy.

People don't develop properly.

If your boss is doing your work, you end up doing whatever is left to do. Typically, people revert to doing what was most important at their previous leadership level, usurping the most important responsibilities from their direct reports. This insidious chain reaction can't be stopped without proper diagnosis. Only when the cause of the problem is located and spelled out can a solution be implemented.

A Tool to Look Beyond What Got Done

It's tricky to identify people who are working at the wrong level, because the organizational focus is usually on what got done. No one is noticing the financial cost or the failure to develop people. Instead, if objectives are met, it seems as though a given leader is performing effectively. Here's an example that illustrates this point.

Mary and Charlie's Story

Mary, a professional recruiter, was promoted to manager of technical and professional recruiting at a large defense contractor. A superb recruiter herself, Mary now supervises nine other recruiters. During her first week on the new job, Mary's boss, Charlie, asks her for a status report on several jobs that are unfilled, holding up a crucial company project. Mary talks to each of her direct reports about the status of candidates, offers, and acceptances, then reports back to Charlie. He is getting a lot of pressure from management, and he tells Mary that there are too many openings and the stream of candidates is too thin. He asks her to "get personally involved" in generating more and better candidates. Because she's going to be busy recruiting, Charlie will come up with a plan to realign resources she was managing in order to address other needs.

In this instance, Mary and Charlie solved the problem and filled the critical positions. As a result, Charlie and Mary received special performance bonuses. In fact, Charlie told his boss that Mary was his most likely successor because of her great work during this crisis.

On the surface, it looks like Mary and Charlie fulfilled their leadership roles. In reality, they subverted them. Charlie has set the precedent that when there's a crisis, Charlie will do all the thinking and Mary can revert to her old role as a recruiter. As a result, Mary learns to value the wrong things and never learns how to reallocate resources (among other things). Charlie is a manager of managers in name only, though he is being paid as one. Rather than working with the company's project managers so that they have alternatives for getting the work done when candidates for key jobs can't be found quickly, he's working at a lower level, and important work at his level isn't getting done. When Charlie eventually names Mary as his successor, she will be woefully unprepared for leadership at this next level.

The best way to diagnose these leadership problems is by looking at whether managers are meeting the skill, time, and work value requirements at their particular levels. Using the Pipeline model as a diagnostic tool during crises is especially effective, because this is when weaknesses in each of the three areas are most likely to emerge.

Let's apply this diagnostic to Charlie and Mary. Assume you're their boss and you want to determine whether they're working at the appropriate leadership level. At first, you don't need to do a complete analysis of how they're doing relative to all the skills, time applications, and work values at their leadership level. You can diagnose leadership problems relative to a specific crisis situation and get a quick read of whether they're fulfilling their roles.

Start by focusing on *leadership skills* for Charlie's level (manager of managers) and ask the following questions to determine whether he displayed the skills during this crisis:

Leadership Skills

- Did Charlie ask Mary to do work appropriate to her level?
- Did Charlie know how to develop a first-line manager? Did he have the skills to do it?
- Did Charlie know how to build the right connection to project teams or others in the company so he could receive an early warning of problems or timely information about critical needs?

Answering these questions involves some subjectivity, and it's quite possible that Charlie's lack of demonstrable skills in this instance may not be indicative of what he might do in other situations. Perhaps he is a good developer of first-line managers, only he's not so good when he's in a crisis situation. Therefore you need to test your assessment by expanding your inquiry outward. If Charlie is a good developer of managers, his direct reports (first-line managers) should be skilled at choosing the right people for jobs, clarifying their roles, and coaching them. Talking to some of Charlie's past and present direct reports can confirm or negate the initial assessment. Talking to individual contributors about who really manages them—Mary or Charlie—would give you evidence about whether he has developed his managers effectively. If the individual contributors respond that Charlie is really their manager, he has usurped Mary's role (as well as the role of other managers).

Here are *time application* and *work value* questions that you might ask regarding the Mary and Charlie scenario:

Time Application

- How much time has Charlie spent helping Mary understand the role of a first-line manager?
- How much time has Charlie spent coaching Mary on how to be a first-line manager?
- How much time has Charlie spent communicating with the key internal customers for his recruiting and staffing services?
- How far into the future has Charlie planned? Does he have an annual plan that accounts for the peaks and valleys of demand for people?

Work Values

- What work does Charlie think is really important, as demonstrated by his behavior toward Mary and others during this crisis?
- During this crisis, what was the first thing Charlie did when he came in to work? With whom did he have a meaningful discussion as soon as he arrived in the morning?

Time applications and work values are naturally linked. People decide how to fill their work hours based on their own value systems as well as the company's values. Contrary to popular belief, time isn't allocated based on a boss's directives but on what the individual views as valuable work. You'll find that if you think and talk about time applications and values in relation to each other, a clear picture will emerge as to whether someone is meeting their requirements for a given leadership level.

Diagnostic Steps

As you asked the preceding questions, it probably occurred to you that Charlie may have acted the way he did because of formal and informal organizational values. For instance, transaction-oriented companies in fields such as banking, transportation, and retailing often espouse short-term thinking. This emphasis turns leaders at all levels into individual contributors who value immediate, measurable results above all else. The six leadership levels lose their essential distinctiveness, and it becomes difficult if not impossible to keep the leadership pipeline flowing in this environment.

You should also keep in mind another organizational factor in your diagnosis: the reward system. Charlie and Mary received bonuses for obtaining the right results in the wrong way from the wrong people; therefore the reward system and the leadership development needs are misaligned. The misalignment can reach to the highest levels, and we've seen organizations where top executives are fixated on short-term output in order to meet performance goals. These situations will impact your diagnosis, and it's important not to jump to conclusions about individuals when organizational cultures and systems are at fault.

We'll talk more about organizational issues in later chapters. For now, let's look at how you can diagnose problems in the leadership pipeline from individual and group perspectives:

Individual Perspective

You should establish a process by which you use the Pipeline model to assess your people. This is important not only because it formalizes what can be a highly undisciplined procedure but also because it gives you a basis for comparison; you can compare the assessment for one individual with another at the same level and draw interesting conclusions about who's better able to assume a leadership position later or who is doing a better leadership job now.

The following steps will help you assess an individual quickly and accurately:

1. Identify the individual's behaviors and work production through observing and talking to the individual. Look at his calendar to determine how he's spending his time. Find out what work he's producing and the major focus of his efforts. Figure out what this person does the first thing each day. Who he meets with and what type of work he turns to first often reveal what his priorities are.
2. Discover his impact on others—direct reports, both past and present, as well as people in other units. Has he developed direct reports effectively for their current leadership levels? Does he interact well and frequently with people from other units?
3. Overlay this information on the Pipeline model. Analyze how an individual's actions and attitudes align or misalign with a given level's skills, time applications, and values.
4. Determine the level at which someone is actually working versus the level at which he should be working. Although someone may not fit perfectly into any leadership level, he may lack only some of the skills at his assigned level, or he may use his time as befits his level some of the time. You can usually fit an individual into one of the six levels with a reasonable degree of accuracy. When you do so, be specific

in identifying the gaps between his operating level and his assigned level.

5. Create a development plan that is value-focused. Though we'll talk more about this in the following chapters, keep in mind that if people learn the right values, the right time applications and skills usually follow.

Group Perspective

Many times, the Pipeline diagnostic is useful for different groups within an organization. Business teams can use it to figure out whether they're working at the proper level, given their assignment and goals. Human resources can use it to analyze whether a specific group of people (first-line managers at one specific business unit, for instance) are at the right level or whether there's sufficient leadership depth in that group. And organizations can use it to examine the entire leadership pipeline, discovering whether there are problems at a particular level or at all levels.

The following steps will help groups use the Pipeline diagnostic effectively:

1. Conduct individual assessments of leaders who are part of the group being assessed.
2. Look at the individual assessments cumulatively and determine whether the skills, time applications, and work values match what is appropriate for the level across the group.
3. If they're not appropriate, what are the specific gaps? Spell out what the misalignment consists of (for example, the majority of leaders at this level value doing technical work rather than developing others).
4. If you're looking at the entire pipeline, analyze each level's strengths and weaknesses. For instance, is the business manager level in good shape (there's alignment among the skills, time applications, and values) but the functional

manager level in bad shape? Put another way, where is the pipeline clogged? Can you pinpoint a particular level or levels where appropriate leadership is lacking?

Skipping Levels: The Brightest Aren't Always the Best

One of the most significant contributions this six-level diagnostic makes to strengthening the leadership pipeline is "tagging" people who have skipped one or more crucial leadership passages. Certainly it's important to spot leaders who have gone through all the training and had all the requisite experiences but still lack the appropriate skills, time applications, and values. But it's more difficult to spot the alleged stars of the organization who fall short as leaders. These are the "high-potentials," and people usually give them the benefit of the doubt because they're rising stars and usually highly skilled in important areas. As a result, they are promoted quickly and allowed to zoom through or bypass crucial leadership experiences. Without the Pipeline diagnostic, organizations routinely allow these people to slip through passages and into important leadership positions quickly—positions in which they ultimately fail and catalyze failure in others.

At one large corporation, this problem became dramatically apparent during a large-scale executive coaching program. Over a thousand managers went through this program, and 360 degree feedback was an integral aspect of the coaching process. The functional managers being coached fell into two distinct groups. The first group had gone through the leadership passages described in this book, receiving a mixture of training and experience that qualified them for each leadership position. The second group moved up to functional managers faster than the first, and they were the high-potentials. Many of them were MBA recruits from the top schools, and they often entered the company in a staff role, working on business development and other important projects. In this capacity, most of them skipped the first-time manager level, spending their time instead working with a team of consultants on these projects. As a result, they missed out on the training and experiences that would have helped them value and become skilled at performance management—setting objectives, coaching, selecting team members, handling conflict, and so on.

A significant percentage of these high-potentials were promoted to functional manager jobs. After the results of 360 degree feedback were in, it was clear that these rising stars were coming up short in values and skills for their leadership levels. Although some of these people excelled in certain areas such as strategy, innovation, and risk-taking, they were uniformly poor in the performance management area. Many of them still wanted to work as though they were individual contributors. In fact, their direct reports complained that these managers treated them like "worker bees" who could help them complete a series of projects. There was very little inclination to develop talent or coach. They didn't value developing other people, and in some instances seemed as though they were competing against their direct reports to do projects faster and better.

Time and again, we've seen high-potential people fail as leaders even though they work hard and display obvious talent. When you're cognizant of the six leadership levels and accompanying skills, time applications, and values, however, you're less likely to be blinded by an individual's personal brilliance. When you use these leadership levels as a diagnostic for assessing whether managers truly value the work at their given level, you stand a much better chance of identifying leaders who will damage your organization's pipeline and those who can flow upward.

Frequently Asked Questions

Q. How should we coach leaders who are working at the wrong level or are concerned that they might be?

A. It can be quite difficult to convince leaders that they are not working at the right level or on the right things. Talking with their boss is the first step, but be aware that the boss may be part of the problem as well as part of the solution. Be sure the boss understands the problem and is working at the right level. If he isn't, go up one level to obtain support for delivering better results. In addition, consult direct reports and ask them whether they're receiving adequate support, guidance, coaching, role clarity, priorities, and so on. Lay out the specifics of what a leader's team needs and what this person's boss expects. Communicate the essence of what is required at this level as well as the consequences for failing to meet these requirements. Finally, monitor this leader's agenda and use of time.

Q. How do I identify the appropriate layer for a given individual if we don't have all the layers listed in the model?

A. It is easiest to work from the top down rather than the bottom up. Start with your enterprise manager (CEO) and her or his direct reports. If there is only one business, then the CEO is also the business manager and the direct reports are functional managers. If there are multiple businesses, the CEO is also a group manager, some direct reports are business managers, and some are corporate functional managers. Direct reports to the business managers are functional managers. Under functional manager, in each of these two cases, the direct reports could be managers of managers, managers of others, or "manage self" depending on what the structure under them looks like.

Q. I am an HR business partner. How do I improve my diagnostic skills?

A. Diagnostics are best performed by looking at the work before looking at the person. Find out what tasks are being accomplished as well as the key ones that are being ignored or done poorly. Assess what goals are being achieved as well as those where groups are falling short. Determine the leaders who have people who are earning promotions as well as other leaders whose people rarely if ever are considered for jobs. With this knowledge, you can connect the missing work to the Pipeline passage to see where the problems lie. To diagnose properly, you must learn the details of the business.

Observations from the Field

- Working at the wrong level is a problem that exists in almost every company. The phrase "working at the wrong level" is now part of the management lexicon, though before this book was published it was not a common term. Now we hear it everywhere we go. Although the problem existed before, the Leadership Pipeline framework helped create the language necessary to begin a dialogue. We encourage all leaders to bring this language into their business if it isn't there already.

- Understanding the results leaders are delivering and how they are being delivered helps us assess level appropriateness. At functional manager and above levels, the diagnosis gets harder because of the breadth of the position and the complexity of the work. The time horizon and the calendar provide the best insight for judging the level at which they work. A short time horizon, one year or less, almost always means they are too involved in technical work or today's problem. Today's results will probably be pretty good but the future is not being addressed. Also, a calendar full of operational meetings without any time set aside for strategic thinking, analysis, and planning also means the future isn't being addressed even though today's problems are being solved. Some business crises require a short-term focus but if this focus is extended over a long period of time, it represents a lower-level approach.

- Relying on the alignment triangle (Figure 5.1) facilitates diagnosis. This tool reveals whether leaders are tackling their full range of responsibilities. What shows up most often as a shortfall is improvement of organizational competence (the lower right corner). Unfortunately, organizational shortfalls reduce individual effectiveness. Poorly defined jobs, missing or broken processes, power held up high, and so on all contribute to individual and organization failure. A bad organization will defeat a good person every time. So one way to tell if a leader is working at the right level and doing her or his whole job is to examine the problems that the leader's direct reports and the rest of the organization are having.

- Struggling with boss-catalyzed issues is common for leaders in smaller businesses. Typical problems are bosses who provide unclear direction, are overly slow to make decisions, allocate resources inappropriately, and offer insufficient one-on-one time. The diagnosis shouldn't surprise you if you understand the Leadership Pipeline model. The enterprise manager (CEO) is working at too low a level and needs to make a turn. Because the layer above doesn't exist, it has to be created. The greatest need appears to be changing the CEO from a functional manager to a business manager. Heavy involvement with all aspects of the business at the start-up stage influences the evolution of the CEO/ founder's job. These individuals tend to stay involved in everything but add layers under them. When they replace themselves they give the same advice to their successor. When the organization reaches a certain size, support functions have to get stronger and take over the work the CEO was doing—such as budgets, cash management, financial planning, reward programs, new employee screening, new business development, and quality control. So the CEO needs good functional managers and needs to learn how to be a great business manager and CEO. Many of the direct reports can't make this transition to functional manager and should not be pulled up just because the CEO moves up. Careful selection of the functional manager is as important as the CEO making the turn.

9

Performance Improvement

Clarifying Roles and Creating Performance Standards

Once you've diagnosed that an individual or a group of people is working at inappropriate leadership levels, you have some major pipeline repair work to do. Specifically, you must develop your managers so that they possess the appropriate skills, time applications, and work values for their particular levels in order to ensure appropriate job performance.

This is a challenging task for two reasons. First, in most organizations, role clarity for leadership positions is frequently absent. Although organizations may do a good job of defining financial and operational requirements, they often do a poor job of defining leadership requirements and differentiating them by leadership level. As a result, even individuals who want to improve their leadership performance have difficulty doing so because they aren't clear what their targets should be.

Second, most companies fail to create performance standards that are differentiated by leadership level. In fact, performance standards tend to be nonexistent. They tend to be financial outputs rather than a complete set of performance requirements. Consequently, it's difficult if not impossible to measure leadership results at any of the levels. As important as it is to possess appropriate skills, time applications, and work values, they must produce results. When someone is performing exceptionally, that's when he's ready to move to the next leadership level.

As we'll see, our Leadership Pipeline model is useful in both defining leadership roles and evaluating leadership performance.

The Relevance of Role Clarity

Most leaders think about their work in terms of goals and tasks. As important as these factors are, they don't encompass the totality of a leader's role. For instance, the following requirements of mid-level leaders are frequently overlooked:

- Enabling others to be successful
- Engaging a team emotionally as well as physically or intellectually in order to unleash their energy
- Providing specific guidance in the form of standards
- Working horizontally (crucial in an e-commerce context) to ensure a smooth work flow

In addition, few organizations position a leader's work in relation to other leaders above, below, and on the same level. This is a crucial aspect of role clarity today, in that the downsizing and delayering of the last two decades has caused disconnects throughout companies, and some roles have become free-floating. What are a person's leadership responsibilities relative to his direct reports and his boss? Is anyone assessing whether their roles overlap or whether there is a gap between the roles?

The Leadership Pipeline provides a fast and effective way to establish role clarity. By comparing what a leader *does* versus what is *required* at a given leadership level, as well as what his boss and subordinates do versus the model, you can sharpen role clarity. Because most development occurs on the job, it's important to establish the right role requirements so a leader understands them and develops in the right direction. This process can best be understood graphically. Let's assume that a job is represented by a circle. Now let's look at where circles fall on a graphic of our Pipeline model (Figure 9.1).

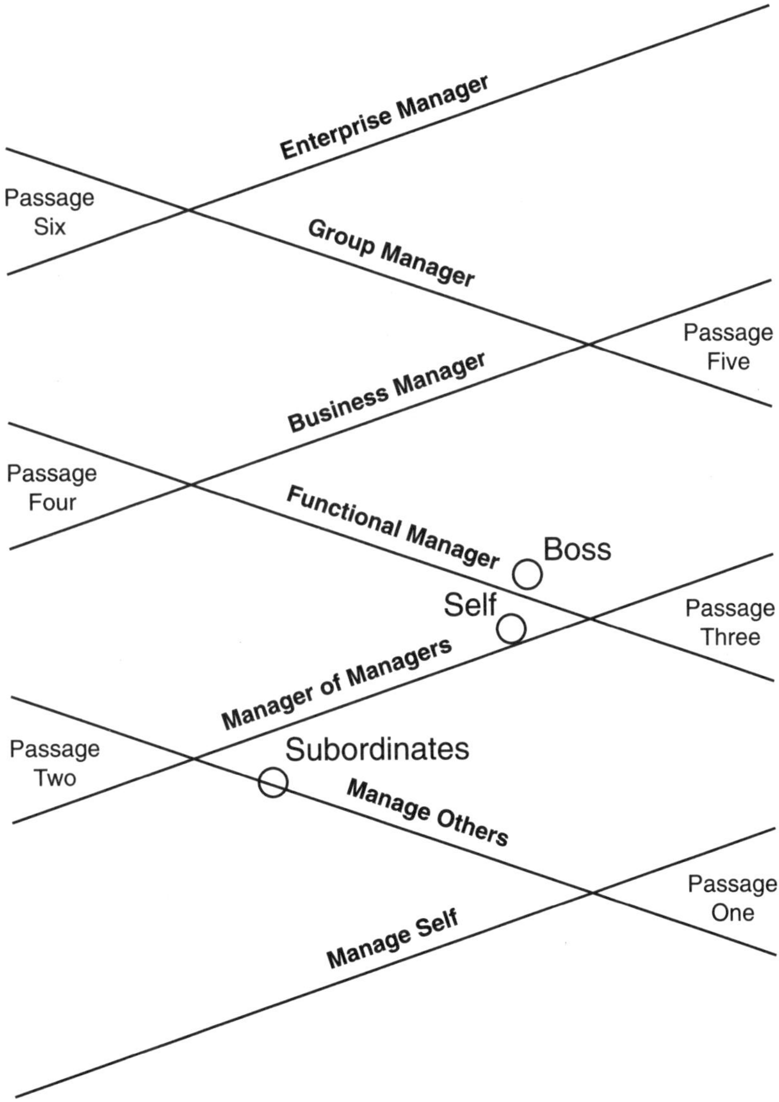

Figure 9.1. Using the Leadership Pipeline Model to Clarify Roles.

Simply being able to plot where a particular job falls relative to the six leadership passages can be eye-opening. Instead of viewing a job within the narrow range of tasks and responsibilities, you can now simultaneously broaden and sharpen the view so that the job is seen within a leadership framework. Do the same for the boss and the subordinates. Both the organization and its individual managers can visualize exactly what the role requirements are and the boundaries between leaders and their direct reports. It is common in large organizations for several organizational layers to exist on the same pipeline level for managers of managers and group executives. A functional manager, for instance, can become aware that both his direct reports and their direct reports are managers of managers. It becomes obvious that considerable work will be required to clarify the specific differences—and that he has to spend time on this.

Be alert for the following common gaps and overlaps:

Gaps

- A lack of performance feedback from one level to the level below it, resulting in a recurring problem.
- Inability to execute a plan because of missing resources; the plan was made at one level and the level below was supposed to execute, but neither felt responsible for obtaining or assessing the resource needs.

Overlaps

- Both the functional manager and the manager of managers give instruction to a first-line manager.
- Both the business manager and the marketing functional manager feel prime responsibility for developing the product plan.

Role clarity, therefore, can be achieved with the following steps:

1. Using the pipeline model to identify the leadership level at which a given job is located.
2. Communicating to managers what this level is and the skills, time applications, and work values demanded by this level.
3. Making everyone up and down the pipeline aware of the potential gaps and overlaps between "adjacent" levels and taking action to correct the gaps and overlaps.

Defining Performance Standards

As important as role clarity is for developing leaders at all levels, it isn't the complete answer. The problem: performance tends to be in the eyes of the beholder. If you take six managers of managers at six companies, they may all provide convincing arguments about what constitutes "doing a good job." As sincere as they may be in wanting to do this job well, they probably all have very different ideas about what a good job is. Even if their roles have been clarified in terms of skills, time applications, and values, they may translate these responsibilities into very different behaviors and results.

Well-defined performance standards therefore are crucial. Without them, it's virtually impossible to convey leadership expectations and requirements. As useful as balanced scorecards and business strategies are, they are focused on organizational rather than individual results. They typically do not cover a complete set of requirements for sustaining long-term success. For this reason, companies must establish performance standards that achieve the following three objectives:

Standards cover a complete set of performance requirements.

It is no longer possible for leaders to direct their efforts exclusively toward sales or profits or product or any singular subject. Leadership at all levels of the company needs to be multidimensional. Traditional one-dimensional performance—even if it involves producing a great product or setting sales records—is not enough. A broad range of results must be the goal of all leaders, and they should revolve around the following:

- Operating results (revenues, costs, profit)
- Customer results (acquisition, retention, penetration, satisfaction)
- Leadership results (setting direction, communicating, developing people, setting standards)
- Management results (control, quality, timeliness)
- Relationships (working relationships, team play, internal and external, business and government)
- Social responsibility (doing right by the community, governments, and environment)
- Individual technical competence (those parts of the work that only you should do)

> Standards involve both long and short terms.

Wall Street's emphasis on quarter-to-quarter returns can't be the only performance standard. Longer-term issues such as people development, research and development, and brand identity must be considered. To get a sense of a good mix of short-term and long-term standards, examine Exhibit 9.1.

Exhibit 9.1. Standards for Judging Performance.

Many different gradations are possible; the following three are considered to be workable in a large company. It is critically important to define exceptional performance to prevent effective performance from being viewed as exceptional.

Exceptional Performance

- Consistently exceeds operating, technical, and professional output requirements.
- Consistently exceeds requirements for managerial tasks, such as planning, organizing, and controlling the work; communicating with peers and others; and developing staff.
- Demonstrates excellent leadership ability, including establishing and communicating strategic direction and enabling staff to perform at the highest standards.
- Achieves results in a way that *always* builds and maintains constructive working relationships with many constituencies including subordinates.
- Consistently active in the community and enhances the reputation of the company.
- Is usually given the toughest assignments; the boss would fight to keep this person.

Please note: These results must have been achieved for a significant period, usually three years.

Effective Performance

- Consistently meets or exceeds all operating, technical, and professional output requirements.
- Consistently meets or exceeds requirements for managerial tasks.
- Demonstrates effectiveness in leadership.
- Achieves results in a way that usually builds and maintains constructive working relationships.
- Is occasionally active in the community and reflects favorably on the company's reputation.
- Is occasionally assigned extra work.

Exhibit 9.1. Standards for Judging Performance, Cont'd.

- Is considered a good performer, but equivalent talent could be found, if needed.

Please note: An individual in this category can be an exceptional performer for a short period but is usually an effective performer on a sustained basis.

Not Yet Full Performance

- Is below standard execution of most operating, technical, and professional output requirements and of managerial tasks.
- Occasionally demonstrates necessary leadership ability but usually demonstrates insufficient leadership ability.
- Achieves results in a way that does not always build and maintain constructive working relationships.
- Has infrequent community involvement.
- Requires a lot of the boss's time in management.
- Would not elicit boss's concern if this person left the organization.

Please note: An individual in this category can be an effective performer for a short period but usually performs at a level below standard.

Source: Drotter Human Resources Inc.

As you can see, we've categorized these standards as exceptional, effective, and not yet full performance. A bit later in the chapter, we'll demonstrate the importance of using these three categories as a leadership development tool.

> Standards are differentiated by leadership level.

This final area brings us back to our pipeline levels. It's critical that standards be tailored to each level's skills, time applications, and values. Here's an example of how one company tailored its standards. After a number of people had been let go and new people brought in to replace them, this company decided to refill their leadership pipeline in part by developing subordinates. Because the newly hired leaders were raised in different companies, management wanted to make sure that everyone was working from the same set of performance standards. It would be impossible to develop subordinates into truly effective leaders without universal standards and ones that differentiated by level. Here is how the "strategy" full performance standards looked for three levels:

Group manager: Creates a vision and translates it into long-term strategic framework for groups; builds contingencies; allocates resources to assure long-term and short-term success.

Business manager: Within the group strategic framework, establishes and gets approval for long-term business strategy; builds contingencies.

Functional manager: Understands and supports the business strategy and the group strategy; revises functional plans as needed to support strategy changes.

These standards link the levels without creating gaps or overlaps. As you can see, each standard is crystallized from the skills, time applications, and values of the three leadership levels involved.

Using Performance Standards to Develop Leaders

Performance standards aren't theoretical concepts that are nice to think about but difficult to apply. The standards we've defined and used in conjunction with the leadership pipeline have enabled organizations to develop leaders at all levels with great speed and effectiveness. To facilitate your use of these standards, review the circles we describe in Figure 9.2 as a symbol for a given job.

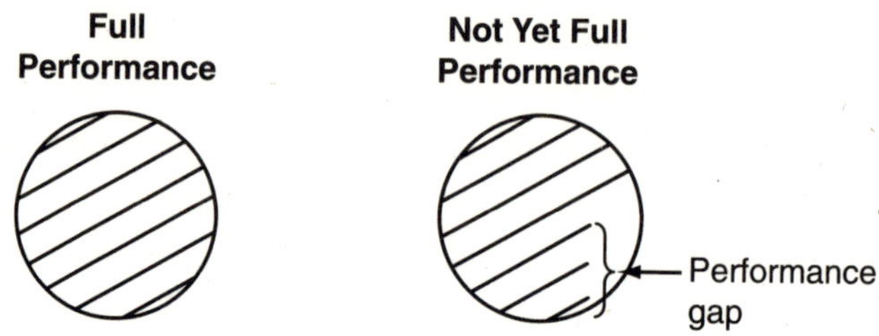

Figure 9.2. Portraits of Performance: Full Performance and Not Yet Full Performance.

Source: Drotter Human Resources, Inc.

Everything inside this circle is the responsibility of the individual who holds this job, and everything outside the circle is someone else's responsibility. To develop the notion further, there are seven lines within the circle that represent the seven performance dimensions we noted earlier: operating results, customer results, leadership results, management results, relationships, social responsibility, and individual technical competence. A full performer would therefore have a circle that looks like the left circle in Figure 9.2. This full-performance circle is the goal of leadership pipeline and development activities. The most common circle indicates that although some performance dimensions are being met, others are not (Figure 9.2, right).

The left circle in Figure 9.3 represents exceptional performance, but it is performance that comes at a price. In these situations, people feel as though they've outgrown their leadership level, and their ability to exceed the position requirements makes them restless and vulnerable to headhunters' calls. The final profile is the most troubling, as the individual profiled here clearly has the potential to do more (Figure 9.3, right). He is not doing the work he should be doing and is often sidetracked on things that he feels like doing but that are inappropriate to his specific job.

These four circles can be used to convey performance problems to leaders at all levels, helping them see where they're coming up short (as well as where they're performing well). Figure 9.4

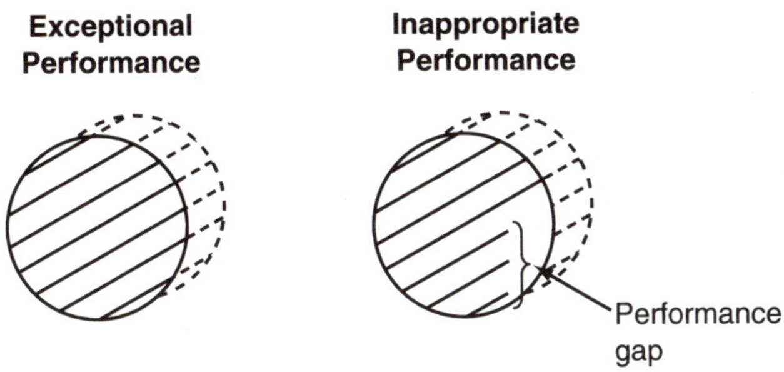

Figure 9.3. Portraits of Performance: Exceptional Performance and Inappropriate Performance.
Source: Drotter Human Resources, Inc.

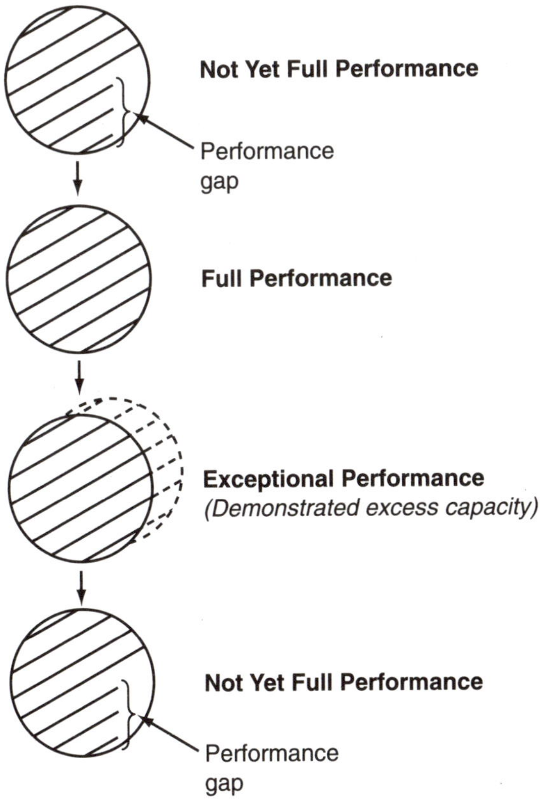

Figure 9.4. Using Performance Portraits to Define Development Needs.
Source: Drotter Human Resources, Inc.

illustrates how to fill the leadership pipeline by using these circles as a developmental guide.

1. As you appoint individuals to new leadership passages, you immediately create a performance gap because they can't possibly possess all the skills, time applications, and values required for success at the new level. Consequently, they are not immediately capable of delivering strong results in each of the seven key areas.
2. Develop individuals through coaching, training, and other means to close the gap and achieve full performance.
3. Once people reach full performance, test them to see whether they can handle additional responsibilities and demonstrate excess capacity.
4. Move exceptional performers to more challenging assignments or to the next leadership level. When you move them to the next leadership level, expect another performance gap, which takes you back to step one.

This four-step process won't work unless you accept the following underlying premises:

Performance Gaps Will Always Emerge When Someone Is Appointed to a New Leadership Level No matter how skilled managers may be or how successful at the previous level, gaps are inevitable because they're entering a new leadership passage. Once you accept these gaps, you can start closing them from the very moment someone is appointed to a new position. Using the pipeline model, you can provide guidance and training and track the results with each level's skills, time applications, and work values in mind. At the same time, the managers being developed must be informed and willing participants. This means they must be open to giving up work methods and beliefs that may have made them successful in the past but aren't appropriate now.

Development Must Go On Until They Reach Full Performance Incremental improvements aren't sufficient. Everyone must accept full performance as the target. This acceptance is easier when organizations see full performance as a competitive advantage rather than some technical human resources concept. In effect, a company must be willing to make a strategic investment in developing leaders to the point of full performance.

Full Performers Should Be Rewarded for Their Performance Full performance should not be taken for granted, as it is the prime objective of leadership development. Full performers not only should receive rewards but also should be given important new assignments and sought out for opinions on key issues. Yet it is common for leaders to spend most of their time working with poor performers and undoing their mistakes.

Full Performers Should Be Tested for Excess Capacity and Promoted If They Demonstrate It Excess capacity is a sign that someone is ready to move up a leadership level, and it should catalyze promotions. People can be tested by assigning them work from the desk of someone on the leadership level above them and seeing which of the circles in Figure 9.5 emerge. Moving full performers too far or too fast is a major mistake. It turns a full performer into someone less valuable, and it is almost impossible to reverse the process.

Strategies for Getting to Full Performance

A fully performing pipeline of leaders isn't possible if you simply rely on standard development approaches. Identifying the root causes of performance breakdowns is crucial. By spotting these problems, you can pinpoint and eliminate pipeline clogs. Finding root causes requires considerable communication between the boss and the subordinates as well as situational analysis.

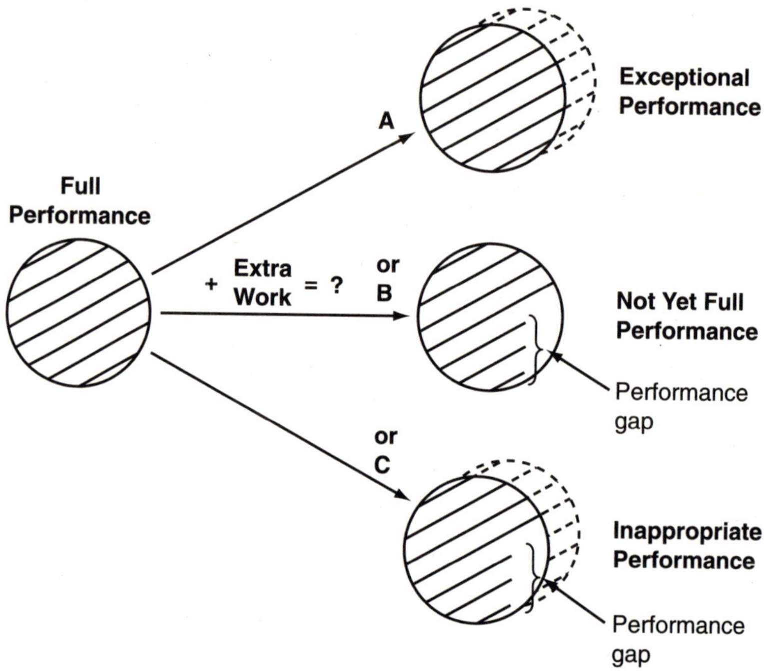

Figure 9.5. Testing Full Performers to Assess Future Capability.
Source: Drotter Human Resources, Inc.

This isn't a job just for human resources. Every leader in the business should be involved in finding and fixing performance problems. If this seems like overkill, consider the analogy to a high-performance factory. In such a factory, input and output are tightly measured, and performance is high because machine operators are trained and measured with great precision. Perfect operation is the goal. Technical support and training are used freely. Obviously, this analogy is somewhat flawed because the causes and effects of leadership problems can be much less visible than input and output in a factory. Still, exact training and measurement can greatly benefit any organization's leadership development, especially if full performance is the goal.

We've found that certain leadership development strategies have proven to be very effective for companies attempting to improve the flow in their leadership pipeline. Here are four that you should find useful.

Strategy One: Start with the Boss and Not the Subordinate

When we run succession-planning training programs, we ask the people enrolled in these programs to draw performance circles for their direct reports. We then ask them to list the reasons for performance gaps. An incredible 75 percent of the reasons listed relate to the boss. Bosses may be working at the wrong leadership level, for instance. Or they may be micromanaging or undercommunicating. We're not saying the boss is the cause of all leadership and performance problems. What we are saying is that the boss is the place to start if you want to increase full performance throughout the leadership pipeline.

Bosses must ask themselves what they're doing (or not doing) that's impeding leadership development and performance of their subordinates. They must also ask themselves how they might change in order to promote better performance. You'll find the performance circles useful in illustrating boss-caused performance problems (Figure 9.6).

Other common performance problems caused by bosses include the following:

- Failure to fix broken equipment
- Poor job definition
- Poor communication
- Inadequate resources
- Lack of performance standards
- Favoritism

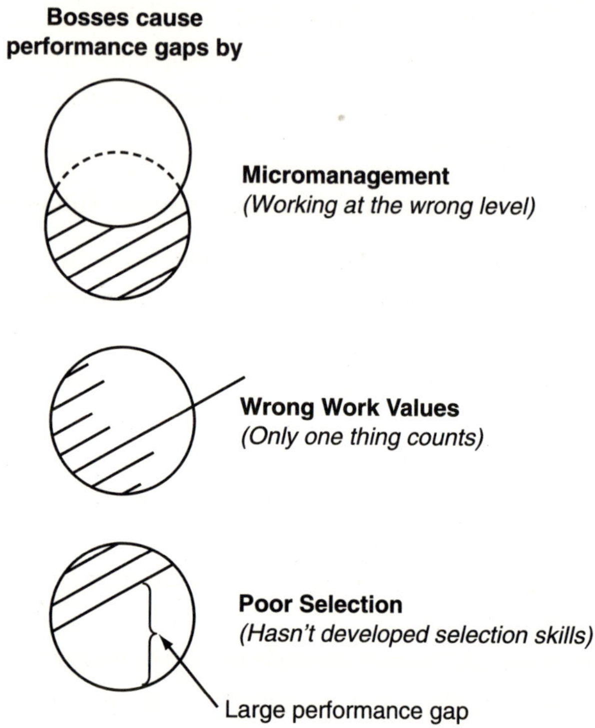

Figure 9.6. How Bosses Cause Performance Gaps and Clog the Leadership Pipeline.
Source: Drotter Human Resources, Inc.

At the same time, you should also be aware that organizational factors—factors over which the boss often has some control—can result in performance gaps. The most commonly cited factors are

- Inappropriate organizational structure. This is often due to unnecessary overlap (a matrix structure often produces this overlap).
- Poor job design. Though a set of responsibilities has been identified and assigned, they may not be doable or even necessary.

- Broken or nonexistent processes. Full performance is rare when work doesn't flow or key people are left out of the processes that impact them.
- Misallocation of power or authority. The age-old issue here is responsibility without authority.
- Improper staffing. Staffing occurs without astute analysis of job requirements and candidate specifications.

Strategy Two: Search for Evidence of an Appropriate Values Shift

Most people make some short-term adjustments in their operating style when a job is new and not well understood. If you go simply by initial appearances, it may seem as though there has been a values shift. Don't rely on initial appearances. The leadership pipeline's viability is riding on a real value shift among many leaders. Behavior won't shift on a sustained basis without a real shift, and people won't take their leadership turns successfully.

The evidence of a values shift entails people willing to see their roles differently. They must be willing to reallocate their time, change the way they attack problems or change which aspect of the problem they tackle personally, and accept new skill-building requirements. Verbalization of new values is insufficient. People can talk all they want to about being willing to give their direct reports more autonomy or becoming more of an integrator rather than an implementer, but unless there is tangible evidence of a sustained shift in behaviors, the values probably haven't changed. To gather this evidence, do the following:

Conduct a "Lessons Learned" Discussion After Both Successes and Failures As we've emphasized, verbalizing values is insufficient; nevertheless, what people say about their actions and behaviors can be telling. Ask questions after both successes and failures. For instance, after a failure to complete a project on time, ask, "What have we learned about our ability to meet the deadline?" If people start talking about how they didn't have the time—and their leadership level demands that they give their people authority to achieve assignments on their own—it's clear that a value shift hasn't taken place.

Examine Managers' Calendars Values drive priorities and time allocation. If the calendar is filled with meetings, determine the purpose for which these meetings were convened, what decisions were made, and who made them. Were the types of meetings and decisions appropriate to the leadership level? Or were they spending their time on activities better left to subordinates?

Listen Carefully to How Managers Evaluate Subordinates If someone is fixated on one performance dimension—operating results, for instance—then it's clear what this leader values. Though all leaders should value all performance dimensions, there are particular value shifts that must be made at each leadership level, and when managers focus exclusively on a particular dimension, it can indicate that they're stuck on a certain value.

Look at Plans Managers Submit from a Values Standpoint Plans often reveal what managers value most. Look for what is most thoughtfully discussed in the plan or where the greatest amount of space and effort has been devoted. These points of emphasis are clues to values. In some cases, the plans themselves are inadequate—they demonstrate unclear thinking or erroneous assumptions—thus indicating this person doesn't value planning, an important aspect of leadership at all levels. It could be a skill problem, but if the person valued planning she or he would get help to ensure that a plan was produced.

Strategy Three: Use Action Learning as a Primary Vehicle for Development

Action learning is a tool for both changing behaviors and shifting values. It's been used in organizations as diverse as General Electric and Johnson & Johnson. From a leadership development perspective, its strength is that it often results in more than just skill acquisition (though that is also a benefit of action learning). When managers are placed in challenging situations where they can learn and do things that have applications to their business, they grow as leaders because the experience affects them on cognitive as well as emotional levels.

In a nutshell, action learning involves setting up teams of leaders who are all on the same leadership level and assigning them a highly challenging task related to a significant business objective. These are stretch assignments that demand that participants develop new skills, time applications, and values in order to complete the assignments successfully. They are also broad assignments that encompass most if not all of the seven performance dimensions.

On the surface, this may sound somewhat similar to other team-based development activities. The differences are as follows:

- The goals and structure of action learning programs are broad-based. A significant amount of team and individual time is given to learning (guest speakers, research), team-building exercises (outdoor challenges), coaching (360 degree feedback), and reflection.
- The real business challenges integrate with personal growth and team activities so that participants take action learning seriously. The end of the process often involves a presentation to a top executive, and careers are impacted by leadership performance within the program.

- A coach facilitates the process, guiding teams and providing individuals with feedback and opportunities for learning and reflection.

In essence, action learning creates a "parallel world" environment that accelerates the acquisition of new skills and values. If there is a performance gap, individuals can close this gap faster by participating in this type of program. If they need to give up old values and develop new ones, they can do so because the process reaches deep, causing people to reconsider who they are as managers and how this self-definition may be limiting their leadership abilities.

Strategy Four: Address Inappropriate Performance Immediately

Leadership pipelines clog when performance gaps are allowed to exist for lengthy periods (Figure 9.7). Not addressing these gaps immediately (when someone is promoted to a new leadership position) lets everyone know that the organization doesn't deem leadership passages particularly important. When managers are allowed to operate below their appropriate leadership levels with impunity, no one takes leadership development seriously.

The four sure signs that this is happening are when managers

- Fall back on old, familiar behaviors and skills
- Tell their bosses what the strategy really should be

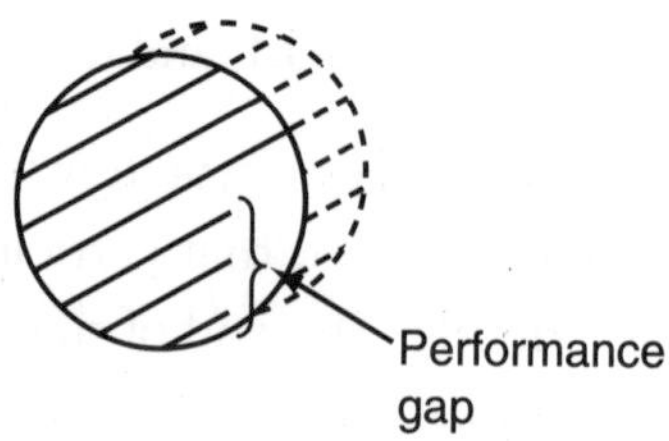

Figure 9.7. Inappropriate Performance.
Source: Drotter Human Resources, Inc.

- Try to convince the rest of the world that their boss is a jerk
- Are intent on showing everyone how smart they are

In other words, leaders are allowed to do what they like and skip the rest of their responsibilities. On any leadership level, this behavior should be unacceptable, identified early, and remedied. The goal of the remedy should be to eliminate performance outside the defined leadership role and to encourage acceptance of the required leadership role. Then performance improvement should be pursued.

The Retention-Development Connection

The war for talent is not just a recruiting problem. Retention is becoming an increasingly significant concern of just about every organization as new economy companies lure talent and as technical skills are in increasingly short supply. Retention can be a salary and career-advancement issue, but it also can be closely linked to an organization's leadership development efforts. We've found that a strong development program that prepares people for full performance at all levels is often an incentive for staying with an organization. People tend to stay where they can learn and grow. Here are some reasons why:

- Development is a very personal matter. It demonstrates that an organization cares for individual managers and their success, regardless of whether they're first-time managers or group managers.
- Learning and growth are rewarding, desired feelings. In today's organization, most people don't want to plateau and stagnate; they realize that feeling comfortable and secure is no longer the goal. Learning and growth engage ambitious, talented managers.

- Development is the ultimate perk. It can't be taken back once given, and it leads to other benefits.

Conversely, the lack of a sound development program can create retention problems. Poorly developed leaders invariably impede the development of their subordinates by doing their work for them, modeling the wrong values, and so on. Frustrated, many of these subordinates leave the organization—especially the most talented among them, who are anxious to develop new leadership skills.

Of course, not just any leadership development program will be a good retention tool. In fact, any program that ignores these six leadership passages will drive people from the company because their development expectations won't be met. When organizations help managers move from performance gaps at a given level to full or exceptional performance, they increase the odds that these managers will stay in the pipeline.

Frequently Asked Questions

Q. How does the Leadership Pipeline model help improve performance?

A. First, it spotlights differentials between the layers. This means that the Pipeline creates clarity around the difference between what the boss's job is and what the subordinate's job is, sets both of them on the right path, and removes some ambiguity. Second, the skills, time application, and work values provide a framework for getting at root causes for any problems. Work values, especially, are crucial for improving performance, and these values are often overlooked. The Pipeline model makes sure they're front and center. Third, this model raises managerial consciousness about the importance of coaching, providing the motivation and framework for leaders to coach and raise their people's performance. Fourth, we've found that the model helps leaders understand the changes in skills, time application, and work values required for success in a new job. This knowledge helps them facilitate their own transitions. Fifth, the model gives leaders a guide to foster organizational as well as individual success; it's not just for managers to help their direct reports but also for leaders who seek a vision and framework for enabling the organization to make a quantum leap in performance. Sixth, it enables the right leadership capability to be matched with the right work content. It also helps focus on how the leader's capability must change as work requirements change. That movement is a driver of performance improvement. (Note: Our next book, *The Performance Pipeline*, will go deeply into how to use the pipeline concept to drive performance success throughout the organization.)

Q. What are the most common performance problems you have seen when working with companies to build their leadership pipeline?

A. Organizations sometimes accept a narrow performance measure. Leaders who are identified to us as high performers frequently are delivering results in only one work dimension, usually technical or professional. In many cases, other work dimensions—such as leadership, management, relationships, innovation, or social responsibility—are not being addressed. What we often hear said about high performers are statements like "Charlie has done a great job for a long time, but we can't move him because he doesn't have a successor" or "Mary leads her peers in getting functional results, but her team really needs a lot of work." The human side of the business is frequently unaddressed. There should be consequences to the person, but too often there aren't any. Success will be temporary at best.

The bottom two layers frequently focus on doing the work rather than focusing on getting the work done by others and helping them grow as a result. As long as this condition exists, the Pipeline can't be built.

Q. How frequently should performance discussions take place if we want to keep our pipeline full and flowing?

A. Regular discussions are crucial; let us explain the logic. Performance across all work dimensions is more important than potential in keeping a pipeline full and flowing. Performance that includes leadership work, management work, and relationship work means people are being developed, the organization is being improved, and business performance is being addressed. Therefore, frequent performance discussions ensure that attention is paid to all the dimensions. We recommend monthly reviews of all aspects of performance. Leaders who use the circle diagram found in this chapter for performance discussion tell us it really works. The most important performance discussion in any year is the one held at the end of the first month, when there is still plenty of time for correction or catch-up. The next most important comes at the end of the second month.

Observations from the Field

- Getting the most from the Leadership Pipeline model requires you to define your company's actual passages rather than rely on the generic model in this book. You should use the generic model as a guide to identify your work dimensions and performance standards differentiated by layer. We've found that companies that address both performance and development (rather than just development) also receive the greatest benefit. This tailored approach—that is, defining your own pipeline—enables you to use your own business terminology, facilitating understanding of concepts and embedding them in everyday communications.

- Broadening perspective on performance is another key advantage of the Leadership Pipeline model. Typically, performance is concerned with operating results, such as the financials, KPIs, strategies, and projects. Understanding the Leadership Pipeline model stretches that definition to include measurement of leadership work, management work, relationship work, innovation, and even social responsibility. Defining these requirements in concrete terms is easy; it just takes some concentrated thinking. We have observed how this broader perspective helps organizations shift leaders from primarily operational work to leadership and management work as well as operational work. They are benefiting from more complete performance discussions with their boss and have more role clarity from the measurements. Complaints about people in leadership positions who don't lead or manage are common. Making the requirements clear by measuring leadership, management, and relationships helps those who want to do a good job to achieve that goal. We've found that most people will take advantage of these transparent requirements and improve their performance.

- Using the circle diagrams for conveying performance measurement overcomes the obstacles of mind-numbing forms and complex, hard-to-implement tools. We've found that companies love the circle diagrams, in no small part because they are simple and clear. When we've taught leaders how to use these circle diagrams, they've connected with them intuitively. Busy leaders know an impactful but simple tool when they see it. When asked whether the circle diagrams were clear, a Nike business manager proclaimed, "A ten-year-old could understand this!"
- Improving employee participation in the performance discussion is another circles-related benefit. Most companies that are using the circles have employees draw their own circles and bring them to the discussion. A given employee's circle is compared to or overlaid on the boss's version. Gaps in perception or facts are immediately evident. Meaningful discussion is now possible and necessary, because both employee

and boss can see any problems or gaps. Expectations and standards can now be clarified, which helps improve performance and makes future discussion easier. Both parties have a vested interest in a good performance discussion. Methods for the employees to convey their views should be as clear and simple as possible so that they feel part of the process, not just victims.

10

Succession Planning

Leadership pipelines often clog when top executives leave organizations and their replacements are not prepared to work at a high leadership level. Though they may possess the requisite experience and sterling track records, they lack the skills, time applications, and work values for their new level.

Every day the U.S. business press contains stories about how various CEOs are leaving their organizations. It's likely that most of these companies lacked a properly developed back-up capable of achieving full performance standards at the enterprise leadership level. This is especially true if the CEO's departure was abrupt. Typically, companies bring in an outsider who doesn't know the company well, or they turn to an insider who isn't ready to take on the company's top position. It may seem as though these people are qualified for the CEO positions, and they may well possess some solid traits. But if they haven't been assessed within the framework of the Leadership Pipeline model, it's impossible to know whether they're ready for this leadership challenge. If they haven't been developed within the Pipeline framework, it's unlikely that they can deliver exceptional performance at this level. Every day brings us a new story about a CEO selected by the company with great expectations, only to see him depart after a relatively short time, having failed to meet these expectations.

If organizations have so much trouble bringing in qualified candidates at the top, it stands to reason that they're having even more trouble one or two leadership levels down. The incumbent CEO, the board of directors, the head of human resources, and occasionally outside advisors (headhunters) are often involved in CEO selection. Though these groups spend a great deal of time and energy in choosing a CEO, they don't seem to be able to make the right choice with any degree of consistency. Less time and energy is spent on lower-level leadership positions, making it even more probable that poor decisions are made there.

A new approach to succession planning is needed. The Pipeline model is useful in this regard, providing organizations with a tool for selecting and preparing the right people to assume leadership positions at all levels of the company.

Toward a Leadership Pipeline Definition of Succession Planning

Traditionally, succession planning is equated with replacement planning. In the 1960s at General Electric, for instance, group managers identified four backup candidates for their positions: two from outside their group and two from within it. Though GE has progressed far beyond this simplistic approach, many companies have not. Replacement planning is still the norm in organizations, even though the norm doesn't address the leadership issues these companies face.

Most jobs must change to keep pace with ongoing changes in markets, products, business structures, and leadership requirements. Anyone attempting to designate a replacement now for a job that might open three years from today will be basing their decision on specifications that will be woefully out of date when the transition takes place. In addition, mergers, acquisitions, downsizing, delayering, globalization, and the Internet are profoundly impacting organizations, causing "important" jobs to become unimportant or even unnecessary. Peter Drucker said that people entering corporations now must understand that they may outlive these corporations. In this environment, replacement planning makes little sense.

The concept of a talent inventory drives some succession planning, but it's a flawed concept from a pipeline perspective. The underlying assumption is that if you gather a good group of talent, you'll have strong backups to replace departing leaders. The problem, of course, is that talent inventory advocates equate potential with performance. We've found that high-potential people don't necessarily translate into high-performance people.

Therefore, we'd like to suggest the following alternative definition for succession planning:

Succession planning is perpetuating the enterprise by filling the pipeline with high-performing people to ensure that every leadership level has an abundance of these performers to draw from, both now and in the future.

This definition is designed to provide you with a way to use the Pipeline model to increase your succession planning effectiveness. To that end, here are four rules to follow in keeping with this definition:

The Focus Should Be Performance High performance in the present is the admission price for future growth and development. Some candidates may fit the profile of a leader, but if they haven't demonstrated an ability to perform at a high level, put a question mark in their files. Too many organizations push high-potential people into the leadership pipeline, and this can cause damage because many of these individuals will be unable to perform at appropriate leadership levels. Full performance *now* across *all* leadership levels is the succession planning objective.

The Pipeline Demands a Continuous Flow As a result, you can't just do succession planning for one leadership level. All levels must be included. In fact, we've found that it's difficult to find and develop a CEO internally unless there's a good supply of leaders developed at all levels and an organized method for getting from the bottom to the top. Although not everyone aspires to be CEO, some people do, and a solid group of candidates should be developing and moving up the pipeline so that when it's time to find a CEO there will be a number of internal candidates who have not skipped levels. You can thus avoid the disastrous consequences that follow when people take the CEO job less than well prepared.

The Pipeline Turns Must Be Fully Understood People need to be working at the right level, and this cannot be determined unless the skills, time applications, and work values for each level are clearly communicated and assessed. To make the right judgments about who should be developed for key leadership positions, this understanding is crucial. If you examine or measure skills only, the values will fail under pressure later.

Short-Term and Long-Term Must Be Considered Simultaneously It's not enough to do succession planning to meet immediate needs. Nor is it sufficient to build a reservoir of leaders for the future. Both are critical if you want to stay in business today and ensure success in the future.

To test your definition of succession planning, see whether it answers the following three questions:

- Does it help you understand how any employee can move from an entry-level position to CEO?
- Does it enable you to focus on short-term and long-term performance, including skills, time applications, and values?

- Does it force you to work at succession continuously (rather than once a year)?

Transforming Potential from a Negative to a Positive

Businesses are full of intelligent, good-looking people from top schools who are failing because they don't know how to get anything done. Succession programs often place these people in leadership positions based on their potential—they look the part, they have the right pedigree, they impressed someone with their ideas and ability to articulate them. *Potential,* however, doesn't have to be a bad word in our Leadership Pipeline lexicon. In fact, if you start to think of potential as *the work one can do in the future,* you can use the concept constructively.

Potential actually is a useful succession term if you filter it through the Leadership Pipeline model. For instance, consider the following list.

Three Categories of Potential	
Turn potential	Able to do the work at the next level in three to five years or sooner.
Growth potential	Able to do the work of bigger jobs at the same level in the near term.
Mastery potential	Able to do the same kind of work currently being done, only better.

From selection and succession perspectives, these categories offer distinct benefits. First, they provide a common target for decision makers, who are often armed with diverse data from a variety of contexts. Instead of talking about how Jane has potential to be a good leader, the discussion can be more tightly focused: Does Jane have potential for a turn, growth, or mastery? There's a huge difference, and it helps decision makers determine appropriate development paths for appropriate leadership positions.

Second, these categories provide a way for managers to talk to direct reports about their future. Succession planning is a two-way street, and it's important to have meaningful discussions with people so they receive a clear picture of how they're viewed by the organization. Once they know whether they're seen as having turn, growth, or mastery potential—and once they know the requirements for each leadership level—they can make realistic choices about what to do next and how aggressively to pursue their own development. As a result, these potential employees are fully engaged in the process because they're clear about management's perception of their future and what they need to do to get there or higher.

Third, incorporating this language into succession planning helps banish the term *fast track* from everyone's vocabulary. Managers and HR typically communicate to young people fresh off the campus that they're on the fast track, hoping to induce them to join or stay with the company. Unfortunately, many "fast trackers" become intent on preserving their elite status and avoid taking difficult assignments for fear of failing and falling off the fast track. Hence, succession planning may tab a "fast tracker" for a key leadership position, but that "fast tracker" has avoided the growth and change necessary to make the turn at each leadership level. We believe someone may be on the fast track to a leadership turn but not to the top. The pipeline isn't a straight tube but one with six ninety-degree bends or turns. At each one of these, people need to slow down, reflect, learn, and develop. When people realize the type of track they're really on—when they know whether they have turn, growth, or mastery potential—they are much more willing to tackle assignments appropriate to their future.

Of course, some people lack any type of potential; they don't have the capacity to do their job better at their level. These people need to be taken out of the succession system and placed at a lower leadership level where they once were a full performer. Or they need to be let go.

Setting Clear Standards to Assess Potential

How do you know whether someone has turn potential versus growth potential? Growth potential versus mastery potential? In succession planning, it's not always easy to eyeball a candidate and pronounce that he's ready to move up to the next leadership level in the next few years. What makes this judgment easier are standards for each category of potential. With these standards in place, management can talk in a common language about people and whether they possess or lack the requirements for each category.

Before looking at these standards, we want to stress that the performance standards we talked about in the previous chapter must also be considered when judging someone's potential. When an individual can sustain a high level of performance (three years at least), then she certainly should be considered as a turn potential candidate. If someone has erratic levels of performance, then she is probably a growth potential candidate. There are also individuals who produce results but are working at the wrong level, and they may develop turn potential if they're coached into working at the right level.

Beyond performance, potential hinges on an individual's capacity to develop the new skills and willingness to take on the challenges that come with bigger positions. The skills and challenges are much greater when someone is moving from one leadership level to another than when they're simply taking on a bigger job at the same leadership level. In thinking about standards for potential, therefore, we need to focus on how willing and able someone is to step up. If they're at a turn in the pipeline, the question is whether they're willing and able to tackle the new skills, time applications, and values. If they're just taking on more

Exhibit 10.1. Standard for Judging Potential.

Turn Potential (can be promoted through the next passage within three to five years)

- Exhibits operating, technical, and professional skills that are extremely broad and deep.
- Exhibits managerial skills that are expected at the next highest organizational level.
- Demonstrates leadership skills that are expected at the next highest organizational level.
- Regularly works at building new skills and abilities.
- Aspires to higher level challenges and opportunities.
- Demonstrates "fire in the belly."
- Has a business perspective beyond the current organizational level.
- Is oriented toward total business results, not just focused on the success of own area.

Please note: This designation needs at least one-over-one confirmation, as the immediate boss has not hired people for her own level but her boss has.

Growth Potential (can be promoted to a bigger job at the same leadership level within three years)

- Exhibits operating, technical, and professional skills that are high for the current organizational level.
- Exhibits managerial skills that are high for the current organizational level.
- Frequently demonstrates leadership skills that are high for the current position.
- Adds new skills when the job calls for it.
- Aspires to greater challenges but primarily at the same organizational level.
- Is motivated to do more than is expected.
- Has a business perspective beyond the current position.
- Is focused on the success of own area and the team.

Exhibit 10.1. Standard for Judging Potential, Cont'd.

Mastery Potential (can improve in current role with same effort)

- On balance, exhibits operating, technical, professional, managerial, and leadership skills that are acceptable for the current organizational level.
- Demonstrates little effort to build new skills but keeps current skills sharp.
- Aspires to stay with the company, as opposed to assuming bigger challenges or higher personal contributions.
- Is motivated to do what is needed in the current job.
- Understands the job.
- Is focused primarily on technical success.

Please note: The individual may have the desire, but may not yet have demonstrated the ability, to progress to bigger jobs.

Source: Drotter Human Resources. Inc.

responsibility at the same level, it's obviously a more modest challenge, but the changes required shouldn't be overlooked.

Use the standards in Exhibit 10.1 as a guide for evaluating the potential of your people during succession planning.

As you apply these standards and discuss them with people, don't devalue growth or mastery potential. Although turn potential is essential if your company is large or is growing, growth and mastery potential are also important for organizations. In most large or even medium-sized companies, individuals with growth potential are perfect for taking on larger assignments as their companies grow; there's a parallel individual and organizational growth taking place. This potential also serves a key purpose in global companies, where managers need to ascend from small to bigger countries. Similarly, mastery potential paves the path toward exceptional performance. Everyone is on a mastery track at some point in their careers, and though succession planning shouldn't point them in the direction of bigger jobs, it should help them master a given skill or job as a way to assure high performance for the organization.

How to Do Succession Planning That Fills the Pipeline

We've found that the following five-step plan will greatly facilitate your succession planning with leadership pipeline goals in mind:

1. Tailor the Leadership Pipeline model to fit your organization's succession needs.

Substitute your own titles for the ones we use in the model. You should also feel free to turn our six leadership passages into five or seven if that better fits your organizational structure. We've found that smaller companies often combine the group manager and enterprise manager levels and that they sometimes merge the manager of managers and functional manager layers. Similarly, you should add leadership levels if that better reflects how your company is set up. Global structures frequently require additional levels, for instance. Be clear about the differences in skills, time applications, and values. All this is designed to help you plan succession for real positions rather than trying to shoehorn your planning into a generic model.

2. Translate standards for performance and potential into your own language.

Clear, detailed, unambiguous standards will greatly enhance both your succession and development planning. They provide direction for people who want to grow as leaders. They offer managers better ways to communicate with subordinates who are underperforming or who believe they should be on a faster track. If your company can set out highly specific standards that everyone subscribes to, you can achieve a consistency of judgment about succession that will strengthen your leadership pipeline. Most corporate succession databases are worthless because they're not based on common standards. If you establish these standards, you can create a succession database that is actually worth something.

3. Document and communicate these standards throughout the organization.

When everyone is aware of the standards for judging potential and performance, they know what they have to do to move up a level and be qualified for a given leadership position. We've found that training sessions help communicate these standards by giving employees opportunities to learn about them and ask relevant questions. In large companies, especially, misconceptions are common, so it's important to have training sessions on this subject. It may also be necessary to communicate revised standards along the way, as changing business conditions often mandate new behaviors and results. Communicating what the new standards are and why they're necessary will help people adapt to a changing environment.

4. Evaluate succession candidates through a combined potential-performance matrix.

For a number of years, some companies have been using this type of matrix as part of their succession planning (Figure 10.1).

	High Performance	Medium Performance	Low Performance
High Potential	1	3	6
Intermediate Potential	2	5	8
Minimal Potential	4	7	9

Figure 10.1. Potential-Performance Matrix.

Note: Do not include in this process people with less than six months' tenure in their current positions.

Source: Drotter Human Resources, Inc.

This is a useful tool for gaining snapshots of a leadership layer. Companies can determine, for instance, that their functional managers cluster in the Intermediate Potential-Medium Performance box; this tells the company that they don't have many highly promotable people at this level and they had better remedy the situation. Though this snapshot is useful, it's not particularly valuable from a pipeline perspective. The performance and potential language is too general; it doesn't suggest specific development actions. But look at what happens when we reformulate the same matrix with our potential and performance categories (Figure 10.2).

Likely Future Work Contribution	Sustained Performance Level: Exceptional Performance	Full Performance	Not Yet Full Performance
Turn	**Exceptional/Turn** Box One	**Full/Turn** Box Three	**Not Yet Full/Turn*** Box Six
Growth	**Exceptional/Growth** Box Two	**Full/Growth** Box Five	**Not Yet Full/Growth** Box Eight
Mastery	**Exceptional/Mastery** Box Four	**Full/Mastery** Box Seven	**Not Yet Full/Mastery** Box Nine

Figure 10.2. Leadership Development Matrix Definitions.
*Turns who exceeded expectations in last job but have just been promoted.
Source: Drotter Human Resources, Inc.

Suddenly you have much more insight about an individual's current and future leadership capability as well as how to develop them as leaders. Just as important, this enables senior managers to consider all direct reports during their succession planning and not just the supposed high-potentials. The following key translates each box into a specific assessment and action:

Box One—Exceptional/Turn Individuals with this combination of superior performance and potential are ready for an assignment at a higher organizational leadership level. Action should be taken immediately because of the unstable nature of this situation; the individuals know they've mastered the position and are anticipating movement. In most instances, they are prime targets for recruitment by other companies.

This high level of performance often isn't sufficiently rewarded. These managers often feel as though they've pushed back the boundaries of their job, and they know they can and should be earning more. When they don't, they become restless; they are usually as driven in their career as they are in their performance and believe they should be moving up.

When moving such people, give them a position with a great deal of room to grow so they can keep climbing a steep learning curve. From a pipeline perspective, this means funneling them into the next leadership passage or an assignment in a new (to them) function or business. They also deserve an increase in rewards commensurate with the new challenge. Certainly you don't want to overstretch them or swell their heads with titles and riches. The key is to keep them learning and growing while maintaining a fair deal.

Remember, these people are stars, and they're likely to be offered more money and status by another employer than they currently are receiving. If you don't move these people quickly and continuously—or at least discuss what's possible for them at your company—you'll probably lose them.

Box Two—Exceptional/Growth Although this person should remain at the same leadership level for the time being, she should be developed in ways that help her prepare for the next level. This means giving her stretch assignments in addition to her job that help her acquire new skills, time applications, and work values.

Challenges that come right off the boss's desk provide good tests. Because this work is from the next level up, you can see whether she can handle work from the next leadership level. Cross-functional projects are also a good idea, building the breadth of her experience as well as testing her ability to make multifunctional decisions.

This is a valuable contributor who probably will play a significant role in the future at higher levels. If she can't handle the test you give her while maintaining her performance level, you haven't lost anything now and you've avoided a major mistake later. It's possible that she will end up as a functional leader at a higher level rather than a business track leader. Development-based attention, new and challenging work, and meaningful discussion all help to convey to this exceptional performer that she's appreciated.

Box Three—Full/Turn This category consists of managers who will be as valuable to the company in the future as they are now. The focus now should be on helping them improve their performance; they should not be asked to make a leadership turn until they've significantly increased their performance.

If you're dealing with someone in this box, give him stretch goals. Ask more of him than you would of his peers—more sales, more profit, and so on. Encourage innovation to achieve these goals, and if you get stretch results, recognize that this person has great upward mobility. If you don't get these results, he may still have upward mobility, but not be of star caliber. Be aware that this manager may be in a situation that makes success difficult or impossible, hence the full performance rating. But you should also consider that this person may belong in box five.

Box Four—Exceptional/Mastery These seasoned pros should remain at their current levels, but their contributions should be recognized. Though development probably isn't as relevant, they should be involved in the training of others. Put them on study teams for new products, programs, and processes. They have demonstrated that they can do more than is asked, so performance shouldn't suffer. Also, just asking them to participate is an excellent form of recognition.

Recognize, too, that such a person is very valuable. She is performing at the highest standard and isn't restless about moving on.

You can build around her. At the same time, she may withhold performance at some point, and it may be because she feels unappreciated or underappreciated. Resist the tendency to take this person for granted. Pay sufficient attention to her that she maintains her performance level. No one stays in this box without effort, so you need to make sure they feel that this effort is worth it and well recognized.

Box Five—Full/Growth Performance improvement is the key here. These individuals should be considered for a bigger job at their level if they can deliver better results. Again, stretch goals work with people in this box, and if they achieve them, they may be able to make the jump to box two.

If you're working with this type of person, you may have difficulty determining what box is appropriate for her. In our experience, managers load this box with people who really belong in box seven or eight because they don't want to offend them or make tough calls. If you find yourself with more people in box five than any of the others, double-check your assessments to pinpoint their performance and the skills they're building. In addition, look at your own motives in assigning people to boxes. Are you hoping someone will get to this box, or is his performance such that he really belongs there?

Box Six—Not Yet Full/Turn People who were recently promoted often receive this rating, and they usually just require some time and experience—coupled with some coaching—to improve performance. In time, they may be good candidates for the next leadership level. If, however, their performance shortfall is not a result of a recent promotion, they may have a serious flaw that requires more analysis.

Even in a large organization, you shouldn't have many people in this box. Reassign box-one people to this box after they've been promoted around a pipeline passage. For the following year, track their performance and see whether they can continue to sustain their level of performance over time. At that point, you'll know whether they're effectively moving through the leadership passage.

Box Seven—Full/Mastery These individuals could go either way, depending on whether their performance improves or declines over time. They may become valuable in their current role or slip and become marginal performers. Though you want to appreciate their performance, you also should provide sufficient coaching or development opportunities so they may improve performance and potential.

Frank discussions with this person are useful. Communicate why complacency is risky for him and that career progress results from growth and effort. If this individual is relatively young, he is more likely to fall to box nine if the problem is motivation. With this in mind, you might want to keep your eyes open for another function or business where this person can excel (rather than allowing him to slip into box nine in middle age when it's harder to get a job elsewhere).

Box Eight—Not Yet Full/Growth Tight performance management is crucial here. These people can't afford any slippage in how they do their jobs. A box-eight designation usually means that something is wrong because these people have the ability to add skills (growth potential) but aren't applying the skills they possess (not yet full performance). Still, these are talented individuals with the capacity to take on a bigger job in the future if they deliver better results.

You might want to consider helping this person apply her energy more appropriately and manage her time more effectively. It's possible that too much of her energy is being applied to learning new skills; check her calendar to determine how she's spending her time. It's also possible that she feels her boss or job isn't a good fit for her, and she's devoting herself to skill or knowledge growth rather than confronting a problem that's impacting her performance and potential. If this is the case, you might need to call in a boss two levels above her or a skilled human resources professional to intervene.

Box Nine—Not Yet Full/Mastery These individuals are frequently working at the wrong leadership level and should be reassigned to a lower level or asked to leave the company. Pipelines become clogged when these people are allowed to remain in place and block others who have higher performance and potential.

Before writing this person off, however, do some additional analysis (especially if a full employment economy exists). Examine why performance is at this level; confront the individual directly with this question. It's quite possible that management or organization factors are inhibiting performance and can be addressed. Factors such as poor job definition, insufficient resources, or a lack of integration with surrounding work might be responsible for performance shortcomings.

Factor this person's performance trend into your action plan. Make this individual a partner in your trend analysis and part of the action planning process. You certainly should discuss whether skill training or coaching has helped improve this person's performance in the past, and you should explore what else might be needed.

5. Review the plans and progress of the entire pipeline frequently and seriously.

Don't allow succession planning to become something you do once every few years or once a year. Please don't view it as a relatively minor responsibility. Organizations are still fighting a losing war for talent, despite all their talent inventories, human resource reviews, stock option plans, and other tools. The problem: discussions about talent are too soft, the framework is inadequate or inappropriate, and the reviews are too sporadic. People tend to turn reviews into a mechanical process in which honesty is missing. In short, organizations fail to exert pressure to produce in this key area.

Ideally, your organization will have at least one annual succession meeting that will revolve around this performance-potential evaluation, and you'll also schedule quarterly reviews and monthly action reporting. In addition, the CEO and his or her direct reports should be privy to the performance-potential ratings for the entire leadership pipeline. Just as important, each leadership level should be looking at the ratings for at least two of the levels beneath them. For example, group executives should review reports on business managers and functional managers because they need to know which functional managers are qualified to become business managers; they should also hold business general managers responsible for developing functional managers and managers of managers.

Creating this two-level-down accountability and using the definitions and standards will greatly increase the odds of selecting the right people for key leadership positions and developing them properly. What is more important, it will help organizations achieve their ultimate goal of getting the right people in the right jobs with the right preparation while producing targeted results now and in the future.

Frequently Asked Questions

Q. How exactly do I use the Leadership Pipeline model to improve succession?

A. First, make clear to everyone involved what it means to make a turn. Understanding the required learning and changes helps avoid judgment errors and conveys realistic criteria for moving up. Second, the Pipeline model provides definition, language, and a framework that enables better dialogue around succession issues. Third, the model helps individuals understand what the requirements are for higher-level work so they can make better development choices for themselves. Fourth, good succession work requires consistency of judgment across all businesses and functions. The Pipeline model helps everyone associated with succession see the same challenges and needs. Many people have told us that they don't know how they did succession planning without it. The emerging definition of succession is "preparing pools of talent to make the next turn."

Q. What makes the biggest difference in developing good succession plans?

A. A thorough analysis of organization competence is essential, as the Alignment Triangle in Chapter Five suggests. Organization competence is about making sure that all the work required to execute the strategy is assigned to someone. Any contemplated or planned change in strategy must be accounted for in new structures, changes in job design, process changes, culture renewal, and so on. The people part of succession has more meaning when we can ask about the ability of our people to do the required work. The focus on people therefore is to determine not whether we have good people but whether we have the right people—individuals who can and will do the work no matter how much it changes. People shouldn't be judged in the abstract. We need to have anchor points for making judgments. Organization competence provides that anchor.

Honesty of dialogue is another difference maker. Honesty about current performance and honesty about where people can go are critical needs. Wishful thinking about potential adds nothing.

Q. How far down should succession planning go?

A. All the way down to entry level. Succession is about the upward flow of talent, especially leaders. Every layer is dependent on the layer below it for succession candidates. Therefore we must be sure that the recruitment of entry-level technical and professional employees includes many who aspire to leadership positions. Otherwise we won't be able to fill the manager of others positions properly from the inside. Although going outside for talent to fill leadership positions is necessary at times, hiring from within should be done 90 percent of the time to reduce risk. The exception to the 90-percent rule is entry into a new business or market, when we need to hire people who are already experienced and knowledgeable but don't have them.

Observations from the Field

- Use of the nine-box matrix to convey the company's succession strength, or lack of it, has been widely adopted around the world. This tool has captured people's imagination. They are proud to show us their nine-box filled with names. Unfortunately, when we press for the underlying judgment—that is, how the box was chosen for a particular person—we learn that they relied on their intuition to support the choice. They have not relied on evidence of performance or standards for potential. Companies that rely on intuition only mistakenly believe the nine-box provides the analysis. The nine-box is meant to portray judgment made on a group of individuals. It is not a substitute for standards and hard evidence. The nine-box is frosting, not cake.

- Struggling with the idea of potential continues to be an issue. We are asked about it everywhere we go. There aren't any magic answers. We stick with the definition we presented earlier in this chapter: *potential* means *the work one can do in the future*. The Leadership Pipeline model provides some qualifying language that makes potential easier to discuss and do something about: *turn potential*—should be able to do the work around the next turn in three to five years; growth potential—able to do a bigger job at the same layer in three to five years; and mastery—can continue to grow capability in the current or a similar position.

Thinking that you can know potential absolutely, however, is a trap. Our three distinctions help you make an approximate judgment at a given moment in time. Customer needs change, competitors shift, new products come on the market—all of these result in new products and services, which in turn require new skills. So potential today may not necessarily be potential tomorrow. The worst-case scenario is assigning positive or negative halos that never change. Working at succession and identification of potential requires at least semi-annual review and a willingness to change the judgments based on new facts about the person and the work.

- Recognizing the connections up and down the line impacts a company's ability to choose the right CEO. The Leadership Pipeline model was developed originally for use in succession planning. It enables those working on succession to visualize the whole system and the connection points. Understanding the starting point—appointments to manager of others positions—is the first step toward building great leadership succession. Unfortunately, most of the succession planning energy is focused on the other end of the pipeline—that is, CEOs. Nowhere near enough energy is focused on the starting point. If your company cannot produce a CEO, you are having problems at the manager of others level. Although boards of directors should focus on CEO succession, that doesn't mean the company's succession planning effort should focus entirely at the top. There is no substitute for seeing and addressing the whole pipeline. In fact, an analysis of CEO succession strength will tell you how the whole pipeline is working. All of the problems at lower levels are visible at the top, just as a poor assembly line produces cars with many problems.

- Working on succession continually and effectively is a hallmark of successful companies. Some of the world's top companies have engaged us to help them with succession issues. They say they are always looking for ways to keep their industry-leading position. The Leadership Pipeline, they tell us, helps them sustain a competitive edge by enabling better succession planning.

11

Identifying Potential Pipeline Failures

Up until this point, we've focused on how you can use the Leadership Pipeline model to build a strong leadership pipeline. We've emphasized how it can be used to increase performance and success at all levels. But we would be remiss if we overlooked the reality of failure in leadership development. In company after company, people who have been counted on to assume key leadership positions don't live up to expectations. Some fail in first-time manager positions and some as CEOs.

Although there are many reasons for failure, and some (such as abrupt changes in consumer preference) can't be completely avoided, a significant percentage of them can be prevented or dealt with effectively. Here we'd like to examine the most common causes of individual and institutional leadership failure. We'd also like to suggest ways you can use the Leadership Pipeline model to remedy these failures.

We're going to concentrate a significant part of the discussion on failure at senior levels. Although the Pipeline model is useful for preventing failure at all levels, senior executive failure has a ripple effect that can cause pipeline weakness all the way down to the first-time manager level. When a high-profile CEO doesn't deliver on expectations and leaves the organization, the media coverage of this failure is intense and damaging. The public humiliation filters down through the pipeline, and other senior executives may also lose their jobs. At the very least, the loss in shareholder value harms the institution, and lowered morale harms individual leaders. What is more important, when senior executives don't perform, they often fall short in the leadership development area; they don't nurture and coach their direct reports to move up a leadership level. These direct reports, in turn, aren't prepared to groom their own direct reports.

Failure, then, is something that needs to be addressed as part of this process. We're going to begin by looking at the four most common causes of individual failure:

- Selecting the wrong person
- Leaving poor performers in the job too long
- Not listening to or seeking feedback
- Defining jobs poorly

Selecting the Wrong Person

Jerry and Tim's Story

Jerry, the CEO of a major consumer products company, made two selection decisions during the previous five years that each cost his business $1 billion. He had chosen two group executives from the business manager ranks, and though they had seemed like superior candidates with strong leadership potential, they had not worked out. Jerry chose Tim, one of these executives, because he'd demonstrated strong results in both revenue growth and earnings improvement as a business manager. In that capacity, Tim had introduced products and services to fill gaps in the portfolio and had leaped over the competition. Jerry hoped Tim would be able to lead revenue growth and earnings improvement for several businesses as a group executive.

When Tim took over his new job, he immediately was aware of the white space around his new portfolio of businesses, and he instinctively fell back on his previous method for success. He focused most of his attention on unaddressed markets and customer segments and required his direct reports to do likewise. Because of his company's strong cash position, Tim secured financing for just about all of the growth strategies his direct reports presented. It was almost as though Tim were betting on all the numbers on the board, believing that at least one of them would hit and more than compensate for the ones that didn't. Rather than think strategically and selectively about which projects he should back, Tim pushed everything through.

As a result, Tim's group entered businesses that they either didn't understand or lacked the resources and skills to compete in effectively. In addition, Tim's talent was spread dangerously thin because of the myriad of projects, and the execution suffered as a result. The losses piled up, and after eighteen months in his new position, Tim was dismissed.

With the Pipeline model in hand, Jerry recognized where his decision making had gone wrong and how the model could prevent this failure in the future. As he reviewed the skills, time applications, and work values at the group executive and business manager levels, he saw a big difference in strategy requirements. As a business manager, Tim correctly filled unserved markets, but he did so within the framework of an existing strategy. As a group executive, however, Tim followed the same basic course of action, not realizing that the group executive's universe is too large to do so in the same way. Group executives need to use a more

> disciplined approach to strategy, analyzing their options and then choosing a few (rather than many) to pursue. Tim's thinking and especially his values were actually two levels below those of a group executive. He was operating out of a purely functional value system: *Can we do it?* This is different from the value system of a business manager: *Should we do it?* And it's quite different from the value system of a group executive: *Which choice will give us the best result now and in the future?* Jerry's thinking when he promoted Tim had a certain logic: Tim's skills and success as a business manager should be rewarded with a promotion, and those skills and successes would serve him well in his new position. The flaw in the logic, of course, is that there are subtle but meaningful differences in the requirements for success at different leadership levels.

To avoid selection failure, therefore, keep the following in mind:

General Requirements for Two Adjacent Levels May Be Similar, But Specific Skills, Time Applications, and Work Values Reveal Significant Differences Strategic thinking certainly was necessary for Tim in both his positions, but at a group executive level this thinking had to be much more selective. The unaddressed customer segments and product areas are frequently huge and enticing. The limitations of your business must be considered.

Generating Results at One Level Should Not Be the Main Reason to Select Someone for a Higher-Level Position Obviously, those who deliver results should be considered for leadership positions, but it's often a mistake to make results the only criterion for selection. Tim, for example, didn't spend sufficient time analyzing and prioritizing his options; he didn't value looking at all the company's limitations that would make many choices inappropriate now and in the future. In making a selection decision, focus on whether a candidate is likely to produce results in a significantly different context. Ask whether an individual is likely to make a smooth transition to a new set of values. Has he acquired the targeted skills, and will he find it easy to change how he spends his time? Some candidates have relied on the same set of skills, time applications, and work values their entire career, and if you know this to be true, know that you're setting them up for failure by promoting them to a higher leadership level.

Leaving the Wrong Person in the Job Too Long

This problem is ubiquitous in the corporate world. Out of loyalty or a false sense of compassion, managers allow people to get away with murder. Or they fool themselves and hope against hope that someone who once was a star can rediscover the magic and become a star again. As a result, a minor failure turns into a major one and the leadership pipeline suffers serious damage.

Jerry and Vince's Story

Jerry, the CEO from our previous example, made a second selection error when he promoted Vince from business manager to group executive. If you based a promotion on only one performance factor (which Jerry essentially did), then Vince more than deserved to be named a group executive. He had done a tremendous job building a business in which the company was the first to offer its product in several countries. A well-designed product combined with ubiquitous marketing fueled the business's growth, and the larger they became, the easier it was for them to use their size advantage to bury the competition that tried to follow. Vince controlled the market.

As group executive, Vince was in charge of a range of slow-growth, stable businesses. Although revenues were large, market share was small and competitors were strong. Vince, however, was a bull in a china shop. From the start, he insisted on stretch goals, expansion plans, and product changes designed to lure customers away from the competition. Though some of his ideas resulted in incremental gains, they fell short of his ambitious goals. Consequently, he removed two of his business managers, and a third quit in disgust when Vince essentially took over one of the business manager's responsibilities. Losses began to mount, but Vince saw the solution to the group's problems as a matter of speed. Consequently, Vince changed the group organization structure so that it became one business with Vince as its business manager, a model he enjoyed. When he restructured during the middle of his third year on the job, things went from bad to worse. His lack of experience in several product areas and markets resulted in expansion decisions that failed miserably. By the end of the third year, market share, margins, and customer satisfaction were in free fall.

Jerry was certainly worried by what was happening, but he did nothing about it. He felt he owed Vince because of his previous record-setting performance, and he believed that Vince would turn things around with a bold move. Unfortunately, results continued to deteriorate in the fourth year of Vince's reign, two more good business managers quit, and Vince seemed close to a nervous breakdown. Jerry ultimately removed Vince and reassigned him to a project.

Though it might seem as though Jerry was naive or even stupid, he was nothing of the kind. In fact, he was brilliant. What he lacked, however, was a framework

> for preventing and dealing with human failure. If Jerry could have assessed Vince's performance with a list of skills, time applications, and values for group executive and business manager positions, he would have quickly understood that Vince was operating at the wrong leadership level. Vince had plateaued at business manager level but had been promoted to group executive level. Because Jerry wasn't aware of the specific differences in level requirements, he let his loyalty to Vince and his hope that Vince would pull a rabbit out of the hat blind him to the seriousness of the problems. What became clear in hindsight was not so clear in the heat of the moment. Leadership is a very difficult concept to assess objectively, especially when hope and friendship color the lens with which you view someone.
>
> The cumulative effect of Jerry's tolerance of poor performance was a record low share price for the company, a capital crisis requiring billions in cost reduction, and thousands of people being laid off. And the board asked Jerry to take an early retirement.

The failure of leaving people in jobs too long can be prevented by the following actions:

Assessing Whether a Manager Is Relying on Skills, Time Applications, and Work Values from a Previous Level This is a cardinal leadership sin, but it's difficult to identify unless you're aware of the requirements for each level. When managers begin to replicate behaviors almost identical to those that brought them an earlier success, a warning bell should go off.

Looking at How a Manager's Direct Reports Are Developing and Performing Sometimes it takes a while for the damage done by a poor leader to emerge. Sometimes poor results are excused because of external circumstances. When direct reports aren't growing and performing, however, that's a sign that a leader isn't fulfilling the level's requirements. When Vince's business managers began dropping like flies, Jerry should have taken action.

Failure to Seek or Listen to Feedback

This is an especially acute problem for senior executives. It's not that they're averse to certain types of feedback; they're always asking for feedback on new programs and products. What they don't actively seek—or what they turn a deaf ear to—is unsolicited feedback about themselves. Specifically, they're not interested in hearing how they're leading or how and why they should do things differently. In some instances, they're not interested in this feedback because it doesn't fit their definition of leadership. To them, being a leader means staying the course in the face of adversity, which is appropriate up to a point. If they were to listen to every negative comment or critical suggestion, they'd never follow through on an initiative or get anything accomplished. As we'll see, leaders who avoid failure are open to feedback and skilled at analyzing whether it has merit.

Tom's Story

Tom was a recently appointed business manager at a large aerospace company. After a very successful tenure as a marketing and sales executive in a division selling aerospace equipment to the government, he was promoted to the new job. He appointed his trusted subordinate Gloria to take over his old position. Though high quality, reliability, and on-time delivery have always been crucial requirements for the business, cost control was becoming increasingly critical. The CEO wanted Tom to help achieve cost reductions in order to open up commercial markets for the business's products.

> Unfortunately, the various functions in the business all had different ideas about how to reduce costs, and these ideas were often in conflict. For instance, manufacturing wanted to cut inventory of parts and move to a demand-pull scheduling, whereas engineering opted for cheaper materials for which manufacturing methods had not yet been proven, and marketing wanted to sell spare parts for existing equipment.
>
> Gloria, who was aware that the various functions didn't have a clue about how to work together as a cost-reduction team, told Tom she wanted to meet with him about this issue. Tom, however, studiously avoided this meeting for weeks. When Gloria finally pinned him down and presented the situation, Tom said, "Don't worry, you'll work it out. We've always been able to do so in the past, and this isn't the first time we've faced such challenges." Gloria tried to explain how this situation was different, but Tom maintained that if they just kept working at it everything would work out.
>
> Tom was fired after being in his position for fifteen months because not only were cost conflicts escalating but product quality was slipping and a critical product delivery date for a space mission was missed. If Tom had simply listened to feedback from a trusted subordinate, he probably would not have failed. As it was, he not only failed but also stalled the careers of other promising leadership candidates in his business.

Here's how to prevent this type of feedback failure:

Keeping One's Mind as Well as One's Ears Open It wasn't a big secret that Tom's functional heads had trouble working on cost control issues together. The real problem was that Tom tuned them out. If he had not only listened to Gloria but also solicited feedback from other functional heads, he could have obtained a more complete picture of what was needed and worked with his people to solve the cost problem.

Being Aware of What One Should Listen For If Tom had known that a crucial requirement at his level was functional integration, he would have been attentive for feedback suggesting he wasn't meeting this requirement. Tom's boss was negligent by not communicating this requirement to Tom, and Tom was negligent by not asking his boss to define a business manager's responsibilities. If he had had the Leadership Pipeline model in hand, he might not have been any more receptive to feedback, but at least he would have been aware of what he should be listening for.

Defining Jobs Poorly

At the business-manager leadership level and above, it's assumed that people taking on these executive roles know what to do. This assumption results in failure. As the previous examples made clear, leaders don't always know all the requirements of their positions. Or rather, they may think they know them, but they're actually relying on old definitions of earlier positions. Group executives are most likely to fall victim to undefined roles. CEOs and business managers usually have some inherent structure to fall back on. Group executives usually do not; the level is often defined around the individuals who populate it.

All managers, on being appointed to a new leadership level, should take it upon themselves to define their job. This means defining not only the skills, time applications, and values for the level but also the performance standards for that level. In this way, they will increase the odds that they'll develop their direct reports properly, not usurp their direct reports' responsibilities, and address the key requirements of their job. In most cases, failure doesn't occur because people are lazy or incompetent; it occurs because they really don't understand their roles when they move to new leadership levels.

To avoid failure because of poor job definition, managers should remember the following:

Never Take Their Job Definitions for Granted Relying on assumptions and general job descriptions or following in the footsteps of the person who had the job before them will frequently lead to failure. People need to take the initiative to define jobs for themselves and to define them with specificity. This means not only defining what their contribution should be but also establishing how they will be measured and identifying the differences between their role and those of people above and below them.

Obtain Validation for Their Definition In other words, managers need to present their bosses with their understanding of what their job entails and ask, Is this right? This isn't a question they should ask just once. They should discuss their role with their boss on a regular basis. As they take on a new leadership position and grow into the job, they need to solicit feedback about whether their performance fits the leadership level and their boss's expectations.

Institutional Failure

Companies make mistakes and experience downturns for many reasons, but leadership failure is often at the root of these problems. When customer service is unresponsive or there isn't a stream of profitable new products, the culprit is usually a lack of leadership. It's not just one leader who fails but a number of them. In these companies, leadership is often a vague and undifferentiated concept.

For instance, we were providing executive coaching for a major computer company, and we were talking with a group of senior managers about innovation. The topic came up because the company seemed to lack many new, innovative products and services. Their response: "We have plenty of new products being developed in our research labs. The problem is that they're stuck. We can't get them through the other steps required to move from the laboratory to the marketplace." When we inquired who was responsible for this situation, these executives claimed that it was impossible to pinpoint exactly who was responsible because so many people were involved. Then the discussion naturally turned to leadership and why no one had taken responsibility for this problem. The group explained that the main tenet of leadership and how leaders were measured revolved around sales: all the company's leaders were expected to sell, and as a result they spent a great deal of time with customers.

This company, like many others, lacked three key ingredients that can prevent institutional failure:

A framework for leadership.

Without a framework, leadership becomes an overly simplistic, generalized philosophy. In the computer company, "everyone must sell" was the beginning and end of their leadership understanding. Individual leaders didn't recognize how their particular roles and responsibilities fit into a larger whole. Without a framework, several levels of leaders are all doing the same basic things while important tasks are being neglected.

The Leadership Pipeline model provides companies with a leadership framework. At the very least, it defines requirements by levels and makes clear distinctions between what is required from one level to the next. Typically, large companies go through crises or embark on special projects that demand the involvement of different levels of leaders. As you might expect, if all these levels are focusing on the same thing, other aspects of the business will be neglected and failure will ensue. Crises, for instance, are successfully resolved when leaders at all levels integrate their efforts to deal with the problem. A balance is struck among the enterprise manager, the business manager, and the manager of managers as to how they can best lead their people in the face of the crisis. This is differentiated leadership, as opposed to the situation with the computer company, where all the leadership levels simply tried to sell harder in times of crisis. A framework doesn't guarantee that a company will succeed, but it increases the odds.

Language for discussing problems.

Without appropriate language, organizations lack precision for diagnostics and solutions. Again, let's return to our example of the company where everyone is out selling. This reaction seems to be responsive to the leadership directive, but in fact is nothing of the kind. Or rather, it's an unthinking, undifferentiated response. In all likelihood, having some leaders pushing products through the bureaucracy at an accelerated pace might fulfill the "everyone sells" mandate better than calling on a customer. If these new products are more competitive and provide more value, they will quickly create demand. But such subtlety of language doesn't exist at this computer company. With the Pipeline language, however, people can discuss this problem in terms of skills, time applications, and values for each level. For instance, business managers, according to the model, should value future-oriented work and spend time planning for the future. The ability to craft five-year strategies is a critical skill requirement. Therefore, one of their tasks in terms of this sales directive is looking ahead and coming up with ideas that will build sales not just now but in the future.

With the language of the Pipeline, people can talk about their leadership requirements by using the same categories (skills, time applications, and work values) but define them according to their particular leadership positions.

Standards for judging performance.

As we discussed in Chapter Nine, performance standards help leaders set goals and create true measures on which their performance is judged. The computer company lacked these standards, in part because they made no distinction among leadership levels. Hence a first-time manager was measured in the same way as a business manager. Failure is inevitable if all leaders are being measured in the same way. With just one uniform measurement standard, leaders don't maximize the particular gestalt of their leadership level. In the computer company, everyone is measured by how well they "get out and sell." This standard does not provide much incentive to approach the issue from a variety of angles or with a variety of interlocking resources and ideas.

Frequently Asked Questions

Q. How can HR use the Leadership Pipeline model to help me avoid any failures by the leaders who work for me?

A. HR should be your "early warning system," vigilant for Pipeline danger signs. Because they're involved directly in a variety of processes involving leaders—training, coaching, hiring, promotions—they are often well informed about the attitudes and behaviors of various leaders. They can use the Pipeline model to identify those who aren't making turns properly, for instance. They can be among the first in the company to recognize that a newly promoted leader is struggling with the new requirements of his managerial level, as delineated by the Pipeline model. With full knowledge of the leader, HR can gather feedback on how the leader's output is being received. HR can then have a conversation with this leader or consult with this leader's boss about possible interventions.

Q. I work in HR. What should I do if a leader is about to make a bad promotion decision but won't listen to me?

A. You are obligated to escalate the discussion to the next level of management. If they too don't listen, keep escalating until you find someone who will. The consequences of a bad hire can spiral beyond the individual to the team or even the entire organization. Stopping this spiral is critical. Focus on the specifics, like the job elements or required results that won't be met and why. Examples of the candidate working at the wrong level or failure to change work values in the previous job or other concrete evidence is required.

Q. How do I avoid job design problems that might lead to failure?

A. We have had great success in job design meetings that involve a leader and his team each defining their job as they see it and putting the definition on a flip chart. With the flip charts on the wall every team member can look at every job definition. Interdependencies, required service agreements, overlaps, holes, accountabilities from the wrong level, and so on are readily apparent. Leaders in industries as diverse as financial services, manufacturing, mining, and health care have done this exercise effectively. Everyone has problems in job design, and having a relatively simple, easy-to-use method to fix them is welcome.

Observations from the Field

- Accepting that some leaders will fail is good, but accepting that nothing can be done about it is bad. Work requirements change, people's motivation diminishes, competitors evolve. As a result, some people no longer can do the right work. Mismatches are inevitable, and they should be expected. Although failure or mismatches are unpleasant for everyone, ignoring them has tragic consequences and, unfortunately, is commonplace. We have seen failed or mismatched leaders become isolated from the rest of the organization. This kind of treatment is cruel and hard to watch. It is also bad business. A person who is failing and left in place creates a situation in which communication, productivity, development, morale, and business results all suffer. Failure has to be treated as what it is: a business problem. Examine the facts, make appropriate adjustments, remove obstacles, and, if necessary, move the incumbent. It doesn't matter how good the diagnostics are if the boss won't address the problem.

- Recognize that lack of candor is the most important danger sign of imminent failure. Telling the boss what he wants to hear, being reluctant to put problems on the table, withholding important negative information and the like are indicators that the organization is failing and individual failure isn't far behind. Though we didn't discuss it in this chapter, creating an inappropriate work environment is a fifth common reason for failure. Here we want to emphasize that a lack of candor in important conversations and key meetings creates an environment that invites failure. When the real conversation takes place in the hallway after the meeting rather than in the meeting itself, leaders will fail sooner or later, opportunities will be missed, or both.

- Understand that the higher a position sits on the pipeline, the less likely it is that this leader will receive clear direction and meaningful role definition. Janitors get very specific information about the job to be done and lots of feedback when things aren't done right. Business managers and group managers, on the other hand, are "supposed to know." So are CEOs. These critical leadership positions are complex, and execution can be difficult. As companies become increasingly volatile, complex places, more definition is urgently needed at these layers. We've found that organizations need to examine role clarity, priorities, and performance expectations beyond the financials. Senior executives conducting this examination also require strong support in their efforts. Boards should be asking about it, and CEOs should be particularly vigilant. A leader's actions or inactions are often driven by untested assumptions. These assumptions don't really get tested until after a mistake or a failure. "I thought she knew" is a common post-failure comment. Don't wait until there is a failure to check on the underlying assumptions about role, priorities, and so on.

- Notice that failure or the path to failure is more visible at lower levels. Consider these common warning signs: managers of others who sit in their office all day with the door closed; managers of managers with long lines at their door; functional managers who spend all their time solving technical problems. These leaders are on the path to failure. More senior leaders should walk the premises and observe the activity so they can have firsthand information about the health of their pipeline. Recognize that the source of the problem may be not the particular employee but his boss, who has made a poor selection decision, hasn't designed the job clearly, or has been a poor coach.

12

The Functional Career Passage

The leadership pipeline branches out in a second direction at the passage from functional manager to business manager. Instead of moving from functional manager to business manager to group manager to enterprise manager, some managers move upward on a functional path. For the majority of people who work in large companies, this is the relevant upward path, as very few are selected to be business managers. For some of you, this path may seem irrelevant. The six major passages we've discussed tend to be the ones that command the greatest attention. However, this functional offshoot is one most people will follow. We include this chapter because we have encountered problems with functional heads feeling that their career is cut short in our model.

The functional branch of the pipeline becomes clogged as easily as the business leadership portion, and it's important to use this model to understand requirements and prevent the clogs. In fact, most organizations have a significant number of critical functional positions above Passage Four, and it's crucial that a process be in place to help them go through their leadership passages successfully.

The functional leadership path roughly parallels that of business manager, group manager, and enterprise manager, but there are important differences and distinctions along the way for group functional managers and enterprise functional managers. Let's examine what these differences and distinctions are and how organizations can use the changing skills, time applications, and work values at each level to create strong functional leadership.

Group Functional Manager

This position is not the same as that of a functional manager; it is closer in skills, time applications, and values to the business manager level and also contains elements of the group executive leadership level. Rarely do companies provide a neophyte group functional manager with the coaching and development necessary for him to master the new requirements of this leadership role.

In looking at the following three requirements, note the similarities between group functional managers and business managers.

Integration Business managers integrate functional strategies into a comprehensive business plan, whereas group functional managers integrate functional strategies from each of the group's businesses into a cohesive group functional strategy, making sure that their group receives appropriate support to meet its business goals. Both types of managers aim for cohesiveness among various functional strategies.

"Will We Make Money?" Mentality Like a business manager, a group functional manager must make the shift from "Can we do this?" to "Will we make money if we do this?" He needs to develop and value a results mind-set and strong business thinking. This requires sufficient functional depth to analyze various functional strategies, helping the group manager to determine whether a strategy will produce desired business results. A group functional manager must provide the group executive with business-based critiques of functional strategies and of the strategies' results in existing or new businesses.

Matrix Management Functional managers often report to both group functional managers and business managers, especially when the former run support services such as human resources, finance, information technology, and legal. Group functional managers conduct formal reviews of plans and programs as well as reviews of hiring decisions, rewards, development plans, and so on. The fact that business managers usually have these same responsibilities creates a matrix situation. Group functional managers must develop excellent relationship skills and communication skills. If they don't, they're likely to clash with business managers. What is perhaps more important, they must learn to value functional integration on business teams just as their business manager does and must spend the time necessary to help the business manager achieve functional integration with the business without compromising functional excellence.

Broad and Complex Requirements

Unlike business managers, who run largely self-contained entities, group functional managers must grapple with an enormously complex set of relationships that cross a variety of boundaries. In fact, they have performance accountability and demands on their time from at least five people or areas:

- The group executive (their line boss)
- The corporate functional leader (their functional boss)
- The business managers in their group (to critique functional strategies and provide advice)
- The group functional staff (their own functional direct reports)
- The functional leaders in the business (oversight, development)

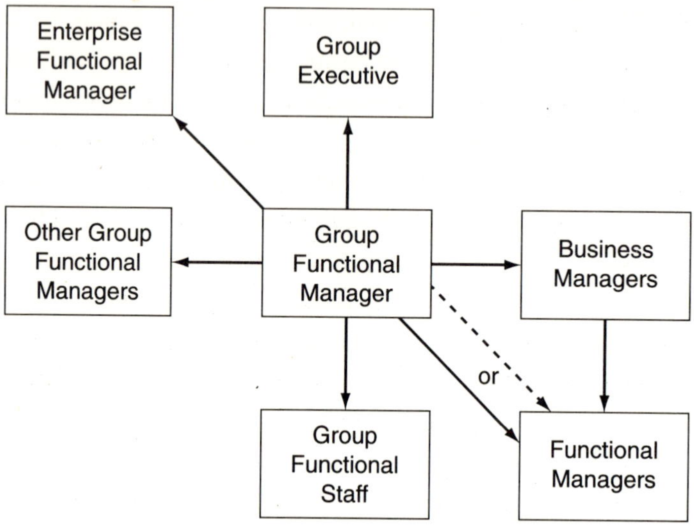

Figure 12.1. Complexity of Relationships for Group Functional Managers.
Source: Drotter Human Resources, Inc.

On top of all this, group functional managers may also be working with other group functional managers to deliver products or services internally. In essence, they support other group functional managers when they deliver human resources, financial advice, and other services to them. As a result, a sixth area of responsibility exists, as Figure 12.1 indicates.

As you can see, group functional leaders face a diversity of relationship challenges. Not only must they understand each separate business strategy but they must also assure each business manager that the assigned functional manager's strategy supports the goals of the group and the business. Because the group functional manager reports to both the group executive and the enterprise functional manager, there's significant potential for tension and conflicts. Balancing these two relationships requires dexterity. At the same time, group functional managers must manage and nurture not only their direct reports but also functional managers.

Juggling these various people and interests requires dexterity in relationship building, decision making, and especially compromise. Group functional managers must learn to value finding common ground. If they don't, one business or another with whom they interact will be shut out and feel resentful. Without a good deal of maturity and a broad business perspective, group functional managers make serious mistakes.

For instance, they allow functional managers to become "caught" between themselves and business managers for a significant period. Functional managers are put in the position of having to choose between their two bosses. If the functional manager chooses the business manager, the functional connection is broken. If he chooses the group functional manager, the business manager often ignores the function, which harms not only the function but the functional manager's development as well.

A key skill in this particular leadership position, therefore, is anticipating problems and being proactive about dealing with them before they blow up. Remember, functional group leaders have to balance six points of contact, and these myriad relationships create all sorts of potential for disputes. Unlike business managers, who can sometimes sidestep problems because of the relative simplicity of their relationships, avoidance isn't an option for group functional managers. They must learn to manage the complexity of their relationships by being acutely aware of their various audiences' special needs and by nipping potential conflicts in the bud.

Jane's Story

Jane is a group human resources manager for the consumer banking arm of a large global bank. With over twenty-one years as a bank employee, and well-respected by her colleagues, Jane is astute about balancing her many points of contacts: the head of the consumer bank (her line boss), the corporate HR head (her functional boss), her direct reports within the consumer bank, senior business leaders within the consumer bank, HR professionals within the consumer bank, and corporate staff reporting to the corporate HR head (compensation, development, staffing).

The bank selected a new corporate HR head from outside the bank and gave him a mandate to make significant changes in the HR function. When he started to impose HR standards on the consumer bank, he and the head of the consumer bank came into conflict, as the consumer bank had operated with relative autonomy in the past.

Jane was placed in a difficult position. Others might well have chosen sides and played politics. Still other people might have tried to avoid the conflict altogether. Jane, however, was operating at the right leadership level and recognized that she needed to keep her points of contact in balance. To that end, she implemented what she considered the "more feasible" HR standards and pushed the head of the consumer bank to implement some additional ones. This position satisfied the new corporate HR head. At the same time, however, she protected the consumer bank from what she considered unreasonable corporate HR requests. This position pleased the consumer bank head.

Certainly there were other situations involving these two contacts that demanded Jane balance a complex series of factors, but she was able to do so because of her ability to find common ground.

Jane was also very thoughtful about her job, which brings us to our next point. At this functional leadership level, people need to value the cerebral aspects of their jobs. Many times, they serve group executives in an advisory capacity rather than through products or other outputs. They guide group executives on a wide range of topics, such as choosing people, removing people, reorganizing, allocating capital, and entering into new markets. Reflection, analysis, and strategy all make this a thinking person's job.

For instance, group managers often are called upon to create group functional strategy. Typically, the group executive has a concept for a new business or wants to address an unserved market. Group functional managers work on developing the actual plan for building the new business or serving the unserved market. It's also possible that the group executive wants to raise the functional contribution of the entire group, and he asks the group functional manager to create a strategy to raise the overall competence of the function quickly.

In either of these strategic assignments, group functional managers need to have strong cognitive skills and truly value the thought processes required to be successful at these assignments. Assessing the functional requirements, developing them, and working through a matrix structure to implement them are just some of the mental gymnastics that must be performed. Increasing the degree of difficulty, these strategic assignments also demand knowledge of state-of-the-art practices in new or different functions and an ability to work in a variety of time frames (tight deadlines and long-term projects) to accommodate a variety of needs for application or training programs.

Signs That a Group Functional Manager Is Not Performing

There are several ways to identify a group functional manager who is not performing. Watch for the following three signs that we have observed:

A First Sign: Acting Like a Politician

The group functional manager responds to the complexity of relationships by promising everyone something but delivering nothing (or delivering very little). Typically, this individual talks in ways that suggest he is responsive to each of his six constituencies but is unable to please any of them. Here's a common scenario: Functional managers believe they are being mistreated by their business manager and ask for the group functional manager's support. Business managers, who want more functional help than they're receiving, ask the group functional manager for better people. The enterprise functional manager insists on budget cuts and innovation simultaneously. While peers are lobbying for assistance, the group functional staff is requesting clearer direction, raises, and better assignments.

What's a group functional manager to do when all these requests come pouring in simultaneously? Many respond by becoming politicians, assuming that's their key to survival. They just don't say no to anyone. If you observe this trying-to-please-everyone behavior—or if it's clear that a group functional manager has been reduced to figurehead status—then you need to intervene through coaching and other development tools and communicate the following:

Unravel the Complexity of Relationships The group executive should discuss these relationships with group functional managers and emphasize that the relationships need to be managed rather than juggled. It may help to use scheduled meetings such as the group executive's regular staff meetings to discuss roles and talk about the various requirements. It isn't realistic to expect the group functional manager to manage all the relationships and requests on his own. A collective agreement based on group strategy, business strategy, and functional resource levels is needed to manage expectations. For example, define what constitutes a reasonable request of a group functional manager. Help define what problems can be brought to him and which ones should be taken elsewhere.

Teach Priority Setting Based on Business Impact Explore the often conflicting priorities involving the six points of contact with group functional managers. Group functional managers need to learn to be tough-minded about holding to their top priorities. They should obtain buy-in from the group executive and the enterprise functional manager about priorities early on—ideally during the first week or two on the job. They also need buy-in from the business managers in the group. From time to time, they should check to make sure that the priorities are still valid. Emphasize that they're going to have to persevere to maintain their priorities, and that part of perseverance is making tough decisions rather than trying to please everyone.

A Second Sign: Excessive Dabbling in the Functional Manager's Work

Watch for group functional managers who retreat to functional manager assignments. Sometimes they're simply overwhelmed by the complexity of this new leadership position and respond by spending much of their time doing the things they did when they were functional heads. By looking at their daily calendar, you can tell whether they're fulfilling their leadership role. If they seem to be spending an inordinate amount of time either with the functional manager who has taken over their old position or alone in their office, then it's likely that something is wrong.

Set the Agenda on Group-Level Work To ward off the retreat to functional manager level, discuss the difference in skills, time applications, and values. Because most people respond better to goals and plans that are concrete than to "values" discussions, establish goals and work plans at the right level to help the group functional manager stay in the role. You may even need to talk about how goals will be met in order to get at appropriate time application. Although this may seem extreme if your company relishes empowerment, it's the best way to get focused on the right agenda. Empowerment means freedom to do the right things rather than what one feels like doing. No one will value the new work if he doesn't do it.

A Third Sign: Being Captured by the Group Executive

Devoting enormous amounts of time to the group executive can also be a telltale sign that the group functional manager is not working at the appropriate level. Certainly it may look like an impressive use of one's time: the group functional manager appears to be the indispensable right-hand man of the group executive. Though there may be critical business needs that demand that a group functional manager spend a great deal of time working with the group executive, these will be the exception rather than the rule. The group executive isn't the only customer. Other customers will understand that you aren't there to serve or help them, so you will be ignored.

Set the Calendar Decisively and Courageously Helping a new group functional manager succeed requires helping him spend time in the right way. Inordinate amounts of time may be spent on rehashing the same old problem with the group executive. Typically, this is done because the group executive can't make a decision. Group functional managers need to say words to this effect: "We have discussed this thoroughly twice and are at the point of a decision by you. Further discussion isn't going to result in a decision, so there's no real point in talking about this any longer." At this leadership level, courage rather than hand-holding is necessary, especially given the premium on time. Private conversations of an advisory nature with the group executive are important, but there are probably other matters of equal or greater importance that must be addressed.

Enterprise Functional Managers

These managers include the chief financial officer, the chief information officer, the general counsel, the corporate human resources officer, and the heads of departments such as research and development, marketing, manufacturing, and operations (though some of these strategic functions may be centralized). Like group executives, enterprise functional managers report to the CEO (or COO or president), and their main purposes are to connect their function to the enterprise, to provide staff support to the CEO, and to scan the horizon for new developments in their discipline. They are responsible for everything from standards of performance to adopting enterprise methods and values.

Like group executives, enterprise functional managers must value setting direction, spend a significant amount of time doing it, and develop the skills that enable them to set direction effectively. As you might expect, this is a significant transition for group functional managers who are enmeshed in the internal spider web of constituencies. Instead of just serving their function or business, they now must learn to serve the entire enterprise. The key to this enterprise functional leadership level is understanding the external world and the forces impacting the enterprise so that plans and responses can be structured. Some of the external requirements are as follows:

- Recognizing how the competition is using the function to gain competitive advantage
- Being aware of the state of the art for the function in a broad range of applications
- Gathering advance information about events or actions that might threaten the enterprise or provide them with opportunities in your functional area or in general areas

In addition, enterprise functional managers must derive the same satisfaction as group executives from developing a key leadership stratum. Just as group executives develop business managers, enterprise functional chiefs develop functional managers. They must make sure the right development systems and programs are in place and that appropriate people are being hired into the function. Much more so than group functional leaders, people at this higher functional level must deliver the entire development package. This means that everything from college recruiting to job rotations to standards for performance and promotion are their responsibility. Valuing the entire functional development process is something people may not have done at lower functional levels, and it's something they need to believe in if they want to be successful at this high leadership level.

Distinctive Skill Requirements and Work Values

Enterprise functional managers, though similar to group executives in certain ways, have their own requirements that give them a special place within the leadership pipeline. Though we've discussed some of these requirements, two are absolutely unique to this functional leadership role.

First, these managers must represent the enterprise rather than a group or function. In fact, it's fair to call the chief information officer the CEO of technology or the finance head the CEO of finance. They must think and evaluate like a CEO relative to their function. The problem, of course, is that in earlier leadership functional roles this was not the case. In the past, they may well have championed programs, processes, events, and rewards that were good for the function but not necessarily good for the enterprise. But for someone serving as the top functional person in an organization, this parochial championing is inappropriate and can lead to major failures. People who try to get their "fair share" for their function will create pipeline blockages, instilling a partisan mentality that is at odds with enterprise leadership. Hence individuals who are promoted to this high functional level must shift away from a functional value system and toward one that is enterprise-focused.

Second, they must rethink the function's role, determining what and how it should contribute. The role may need to be reshaped, given the new economy, increased turnover, and volatile markets. For instance, the human resources functional chief may need to take action to prevent inappropriate hiring decisions because of labor shortages in the United States. The finance head has to sense when targets won't be met because costs, sales, or new products aren't flowing properly. The information technology functional leader needs to fight hard to avoid one business's dictating systems that may be poorly matched to other businesses. An enterprise functional manager needs to have both the vision to see that the function's role must be changed and the courage to change it.

Signs That an Enterprise Functional Manager Is Working at the Wrong Level

Again, we've noted specific skills, time applications, and work values that are appropriate for leaders at this level. The most obvious sign that there's a problem is if someone embodies the wrong values or is missing critical skills. The next three most obvious danger signals are the following:

Being Captured by the CEO Enterprise functional managers can become close to CEOs—especially powerful, highly influential CEOs—and they can end up devoting most of their time and energy to helping the CEO fight fires. As a result, they lose their objectivity and don't address the spectrum of issues facing the function. They no longer lead or represent the function. Others can tell that this enterprise functional manager will not be objective.

Becoming an Ambassador The ego-gratifying activities involved in being a functional ambassador include dinners, speaking engagements, industry conferences, world tours, and the like. Though it's important for functional chiefs to represent their companies in the outside world, they can easily lose sight of or devote insufficient time to their internal responsibilities. It is easy to lose touch with the true challenges their function faces.

Preserving the Status Quo These signs are a result of someone who has been seduced by the "glamour" of the job and is turned off by the more daunting aspects of the leadership position, such as reenvisioning the function's role or upgrading the talent. When enterprise functional managers aren't taken seriously by others in the organization or when they're used by others to send messages to the CEO, they are creating leadership pipeline problems. They need to be coached and developed in such a way that they lay out their own corporate leadership agenda, are rigorously objective, and are fully informed about the company's businesses.

We have observed enterprise functional managers who become so involved in politics, transactions, board of director committees, and the like that they don't have time to read, research, or think about where the function should be headed. They also don't devote much time to considering the function's current state or what must happen so that the function makes an appropriate contribution throughout the company. When they become caught up in politics, enterprise functional managers lose touch with the functional state of the art and spend their time preserving the status quo. They become reluctant to change what is working because of the risks associated with change.

Developing Enterprise Functional Managers

At this level, self-help is the norm. The CEO usually provides direction, but it rarely suffices. The following development suggestions are geared toward self-help because it's the most realistic course of development action:

Obtain an Early, Expert Assessment of the Function Valuing expert opinion other than your own is a basic requirement. Very early on, this expert should look at contributions being made, the skills of key functional people at every level, state-of-the-art functional status, and the needs of the business. An expert—especially one who works with companies in your area specifically or top companies in general—can provide insights. With this expert's information in hand, you can make better choices about where to spend time, energy, and money.

Validate Your Game Plan and Goals with the CEO and with a Cross-Section of Key Leaders at Every Level The CEO isn't your only customer. Because everyone in the company relies on the services your function provides, obtain input and confirmation from all levels. Being aware of perceived versus actual value of your function is crucial. You can't take ownership of the function unless you stay in touch with users at all levels.

Make Time on Your Calendar for Touching the Enterprise at Every Level Personally You require firsthand information from your internal customers, and they need to hear your message directly. Schedule visits at least once per month on an ongoing basis (start out with weekly visits). Don't get stuck on the enterprise executive floor; you must make a conscious effort to resist its pull and move around.

Separate the Important from the Urgent Quick response to urgent problems is mandatory for functional leaders. Of course, everything comes across your desk with an "Urgent" label attached. Determine whether each urgent item is for you. Although dealing with urgent issues may make you feel needed and valuable, that is not what will make you a true enterprise functional manager. Focus on important matters—issues that have a direct impact on key strategies. *Urgent* simply means someone wants it now. Investigate who wants it and why; measure the time impact. Don't spend more than half your time responding to urgent matters. Like the CEO, you're responsible for long-term results, so strike the right balance between important and urgent. If you're drowning in urgent projects, ask yourself whose agenda you're responding to, what the impact on strategy is, and how you might restore an appropriate balance. Successful managers at this high functional level aren't seduced by short-term, highly satisfying victories. They learn to value real progress toward sustainable long-term goals.

Frequently Asked Questions

Q. What is the most common mistake you see made by people at the higher level of the functional track?

A. It's the same mistake we've emphasized throughout the book: doing functional work for its own sake. Although high-level functional work is critically important, it must enable current and future business and enterprise success. Here are a few examples of functional tasks the enterprise functional manager should resist: pursuing state-of-the-art information technology that doesn't really help the business improve, taking executive education courses that are off-the-shelf from a training provider and don't enable the students to improve performance in their job, and making information requests that are repetitive or redundant but satisfy a functional need. High-level functional people must realize that they are responsible for short- and long-term profit to the same degree that line executives are. Functional investment, functional programs, functional data requests, functional reports should help the business compete in the market now or in the future. They should also help to perpetuate the enterprise. Satisfying functional standards isn't enough by itself.

Q. In framing my work as part of the corporate staff or undertaking a specific task, how should I make sure I am on the right track?

A. "How would the world's leading expert do this work?" That is the first question you should be asking yourself. You have to produce high-quality work, not just complete the task. Too often, low standards or average work are the norms. Although you don't necessarily have to adhere to an expert standard—cost or speed may put this standard out of reach—you should know where you are compromising and why so you can share it with the recipient of the work. The second question you should ask yourself is, "How will I add appropriate value?" Your true "customer" must be defined and consulted on the three or four things you should deliver. The customer should have a say in the projects you undertake. Truly understanding that you have to add value will force you to look at your work from the end user's point of view. The third question should be, "What are the options?" Communicate that if we spent a little more or took a little more time or were more clear about what we wanted, we could have achieved 2X instead of X. Seeing your work as a profession rather than a job makes a big difference.

Q. What complaints do you hear from CEOs or group managers about the functional work they receive from group or corporate functions?

A. The most common complaint is that the work wasn't finished. Factual errors that could have been checked were not. Alternatives were not considered; the only option thought of was the one submitted. Business leaders need to trust their support teams. They really don't want to be the fact checker or the proofreader. Time pressure, lack of resources, and hiring people too junior for the roles are common elements that seem to account for the unfinished work. Handing the CEO or the group manager the latest functional tools without adapting them to the business is also a frequent occurrence.

Observations from the Field

- Clogging of the Leadership Pipeline on the functional career path at the corporate level is a universal problem. Placing junior people into senior staff positions seems a likely cause. We're not biased against younger employees, and we recognize that management wants to reward their best and brightest junior people and increase the odds of retaining them by including them in the corporate group. Yet since this book was published, we've seen junior people placed in these positions inappropriately. Although there is room in most corporate staffs for junior people to spend a year or two to see how the function works, learn the standards, and broaden their perspective, the corporate staff is no place for kids to hold permanent positions. They develop a false sense of their importance and expect big jobs as their next assignment. In fact, most junior people in the corporate staff don't have meaningful accountability. They support, administer, follow up, count, collate, sit in meetings, and so on. It takes twenty years of experience to make a real contribution to the corporate staff. Most of the work should be done at an expert level. So, younger people should start at a "manage self" position in a business where they have real accountability and can learn and contribute while developing a peer group. Understanding how the business works demands an environment in which everyone is focused externally on serving customers, understanding competitors, and learning market forces. The corporate staff doesn't offer this environment. Corporate staff may appear to be a glamorous career stepping-stone but can actually be a career trap for a junior person.

- Choosing to join the staff of a group manager doesn't necessarily eliminate anyone from becoming a business manager. In fact, being the group CFO or group marketing leader can be excellent preparation for becoming a business manager. You get the opportunity to look at several businesses simultaneously, which enables comparisons of all kinds and opens a window on best practices. You also receive the group manager's business thinking on the things that make businesses successful. And you have a chance to work with several business managers and can learn from their work as well. All of this adds up to a solid platform for preparing to be a business manager.

- Adopting the work values of a group manager helps facilitate success as a group functional manager. Portfolio strategy, helping business managers succeed and grow, connecting the businesses to the corporation, and taking accountability for the "uncovered" all apply to group functional manager. Many group functional managers become puppets for the corporate staff heads and focus only on their functional work. Although the functional work has to be done well, it isn't the whole job. Specific tasks that help the business are also part of the job. There is a significant learning opportunity here. Real business knowledge and acumen can be gained if the effort is made to connect properly with the group manager and business managers. Gaining the business knowledge will make you a better candidate for corporate functional head.
- Locating individuals on the Pipeline model is most difficult for lower levels in the corporate staff; that is, those reporting to the CFO or CHRO. As we mentioned previously, the model was designed for operating work from entry to CEO. Corporate staff is an offshoot that requires tailoring of the Pipeline model. It is easy enough to figure out whether the functional manager line in the Pipeline model is extended up to the level of enterprise manager.

13

Coaching

One of the biggest challenges of coaching is communicating information in a motivating manner, and the Pipeline model greatly facilitates this goal. It's sometimes very difficult to get through to people—even highly intelligent, successful managers—and get them to change their values, add new skills, and adjust the way they spend their time. The pipeline is motivational from both a carrot and a stick perspective. In terms of the latter, it shocks them into realizing they're not operating at the right leadership level (given their position). In terms of the former, it's very specific in delineating the behaviors and attitudes they need to demonstrate to achieve specific career goals.

The pipeline also helps managers locate themselves on a leadership continuum. During most coaching experiences, the following question comes up (though not in these exact words):

Where am I on this journey?

People want to locate themselves; they want to know where they've been, where they are now, where they're going, and what they have to do to get there. The six passages in the pipeline help them mark their place on the journey. What is more important, they do so not by job title (which can be misleading—in Silicon Valley, it seems as though everyone is a vice president) but by leadership level, a milestone that most people intuitively recognize as valid. In many ways, these six leadership passages correspond to psychological developmental stages—the developmental stages of children, for instance. They represent the progressive growth stages of a leader, and when they're presented in that manner, people become much more coachable.

Finally, the pipeline is a great coaching tool because of its clarity and simplicity. People "get it" right away. They realize that if they want to be successful at the manager of managers level, they need to let go of certain values and skills that made them successful at the first-time manager level. Certainly letting go is difficult, but helping people become aware of and reflect on why they must let them go is relatively easy using the Leadership Pipeline model.

Coaching Framework

We've found that one of the best ways to use the pipeline in coaching is via a three-question framework. What follows are the three key questions to ask during coaching sessions and the purpose behind the questions (the type of information you need to elicit relative to the pipeline):

Question	Purpose
1. Tell me about your career—your jobs, the work you did, achievements, key challenges, and learning.	1. Locate the positions this person has held on the pipeline. Has this person skipped a level? Has she mastered each level's skills, time applications, and values?

Question	Purpose
2. Talk about your current position. What are your issues, challenges, and achievements? What does your calendar look like, what skills do you rely on most to get the job done, and what beliefs govern your work?	2. Determine whether this person understands and is mastering the appropriate skills, time applications, and values for his level or whether the person is just beginning to get them. Assess whether there are obvious development needs, based on responses and objective information such as a supervisor's perspective, 360 degree feedback, and so on.
3. What are your career aspirations?	3. Identify future development needs, given this person's current state and the leadership level to which the person aspires. Suggest types of experiences that will help achieve this level. Based on the answers to questions one and two, convey your sense of how realistic making the next leadership passage might be.

Use the graphic of the Pipeline model with the people being coached. It's usually wise to wait until question two or three to introduce it, as you don't want people to filter their initial responses to fit the pipeline. Once you feel you have a good sense of the person's skills, time applications, and values, it's appropriate to introduce the pipeline graphic and this person's place on it.

Sam and Linda's Story

Let's translate this framework into the real world through the experience of Sam and his in-house coach, Linda (an HR executive), who was attempting to coach him through some problems he'd been having at a leading pharmaceutical company. Linda, with the help of an outside coach, had already identified Sam as possessing turn potential. He'd joined the company four years ago after getting his MBA from a top school, and he'd been placed on a fast development track. When Linda began coaching him, Sam was leading a product development team with five direct reports and thirty other people in the organization. Unfortunately, there was a great deal of tension among his team members, and morale was low.

When Linda met with Sam for the first time, she discovered that he'd never been coached before. To help put him at ease, she emphasized that coaching was meant to be developmental and that the goal was to identify an issue that was impacting his performance and gain a commitment from him to a development plan that would help him address this issue. At first, Linda's questions focused on his background and previous work experience. She discerned that his first job with the company was in corporate staff and that he had later moved to a strategic marketing position in a line organization. For the past two years, he'd had his current job. As they talked, Linda discovered that Sam had skipped the first leadership passage: he'd never had the chance to develop as a first-line manager. Though Sam did well as an individual contributor in significant positions, he'd never really managed at the first-line level.

Based on Sam's answers to questions as well as 360 degree feedback reports, Linda learned that Sam had difficulty managing the performance of subordinates and other organizational members. Although he was skilled at communicating direction and mapping strategies, he was not particularly adept at providing feedback, setting specific objectives, and dealing with poor performance from his people. It turned out that the high performers on the team were frustrated with Sam's inability to deal with underperforming team members who were holding the organization back.

After some discussion about these issues, Linda showed Sam the pipeline graphic and explained what the different leadership passages entailed. When she explained why it seemed as though he had missed the first passage—and how many young, fast-track people miss it—he became less defensive and more receptive to making changes. As soon as Sam saw the skills, time applications, and values spelled out for the first passage and viewed them in the framework of the other passages, he was eager to listen and learn. When he expressed his career goal as "becoming a business manager at the very least," Linda was able to show him how his leadership development might progress to that capstone position.

Clear, Complete, Compelling Feedback

More than ever before, managers are expected to coach their subordinates. The theory—which we subscribe to—is that the best way to learn and grow as a leader is through on-the-job "stretch" experiences. To get the most out of these experiences, people must receive and reflect upon feedback. Managers, however, often aren't trained in giving developmental feedback and may not take to this role naturally. Typically, they rely on books and training that suggest certain coaching techniques (such as making a development contract with the person being coached) but struggle when it comes to providing insight and specific action steps to further leadership development.

The Pipeline model is an excellent vehicle for feedback. To maximize its value when coaching subordinates, keep the following rules in mind:

Clarify Expectations by Using the Passages One way the Leadership Pipeline becomes clogged is when managers are unclear about what is expected of them. Either they're given a vague sense of what they need to do to develop or they're given false or misleading advice. As a result, they become frustrated and fail to develop, or they leave the organization.

With the Pipeline model in hand, you can be very precise about development actions. After pointing out the skills, time applications, and values for a targeted leadership level, identify where subordinates possess the right traits and where they fall short. Be sure to connect their behaviors and attitudes (either from what they've said during coaching sessions or from other sources such as 360 degree feedback) to skills, time applications, and values. For instance: "We expect you to value developing others and seeing them succeed on their own at this level, but as you yourself said, the most satisfying moment of your career here was rescuing that project single-handedly when your team let you down."

Keep It Simple Coaching often is articulated in HR language. It's not only HR people who are guilty of this sin but also managers who think there's some magic in using complex or overly formal terminology or creating elaborate leadership development plans. As you've probably noticed, the Pipeline model relies on straightforward language that everyone can understand. Everyone relates to the concepts of skills, time applications, and work values. Rely on those terms when talking about what's required to make a successful passage through that level.

Be Comprehensive About the Context Don't limit your focus to one leadership passage. We've found that people respond much more positively and enthusiastically to coaching when they have access to the big picture. By discussing not only the leadership passage relevant immediately to the individual but also the passages above and below it, you give this person a frame of reference for his development. We've also found that sharing information about turn potential and using the performance circles model discussed in Chapter Nine help provide this comprehensive context.

Focus on a Few Developmental Items It is easy to overload the person being coached. A comprehensive model can trigger a long list of needs. Focus on two and sometimes three items at most. When they are mastered, add two more. Don't forget that this person has a full-time job.

Bob and Martin's Story

Let's look at how this coaching and feedback helped a functional manager at a global corporation. Bob was the financial head of a large operating unit of a major consumer products corporation. Martin, the head of the unit, felt that Bob was a terrific financial guy, provided excellent support for the business, and was respected by his peers. Yet Martin also recognized that Bob wasn't providing him with much help as he attempted to articulate a new strategy and vision for the business. This was a critical responsibility for Martin, as competitive pressures were such that a new strategy was not only necessary but needed fast. Though Bob certainly was supportive of this new strategy, he wasn't playing an active role. Martin put on his coaching hat and began to work with Bob, not only because he needed help with the strategy now but also because he regarded Bob as one of the brightest and potentially most important young leaders in the company. Over the past two years, however, Martin had become convinced that Bob was not connecting with the dynamic issues that the business was facing.

Martin had talked to Bob about these issues before, going so far as to say that he felt Bob thought of himself as a "finance guy" rather than a full partner in the business. Though Bob said he'd try to change, he really hadn't made much progress. Then Martin began using the Leadership Pipeline model as a tool to help develop Bob. When Martin introduced the pipeline graphic to Bob, the first thing Bob noticed was that he had mastered certain requirements at this leadership level. State-of-the art financial thinking was his strong suit, and he was also adept at the longer-term thinking requirement. But when he came to the requirement for complete understanding of the business, long-term strategic direction, and goals, he shook his head and admitted that this was where he was falling short.

It wasn't the words on the page that caused Bob to admit this as much as the comprehensiveness of the model. As Bob said, "I never really thought of myself on any sort of leadership continuum. I just thought of my career from a position standpoint." Bob told Martin that he was convinced that he was the "best damn functional head" in the company, and he may well have been the best technician. But Bob realized that he was not the best from a leadership standpoint; not only did he lack certain skills and time applications, but his values were more appropriate to a first-line manager.

That was a shock to Bob, and it helped open his eyes to what he needed to do to be a full performer at his current leadership level. He also came to understand that these requirements were a prerequisite to moving on to the next leadership passage. With the Pipeline model, Martin pointed out that a common failing of functional managers is "not valuing what they don't know." Bob had never really articulated his work values before, and he told Martin that what he valued most was using his financial skills to solve a knotty problem the business was facing. Rather than valuing what he didn't know, Bob devalued things such as spending time on business strategy. Up until this point, he had studiously avoided learning much about this area. With his new awareness of its importance, Bob made a commitment to Martin to try to get up to speed and contribute. As a result, Bob and Martin created an informal (and accelerated) development plan that identified three terrific business strategists in the organization and solicited their help in turning Bob into a strategist. (Martin arranged interview sessions with them as well as Bob's participation on a strategy development team.) Within six months, Bob was much more willing and able to contribute in Martin's business planning meetings.

Letting Go

A great frustration of many coaches is that people refuse to let go of certain negative behaviors and attitudes. No matter what a coach says or does—and no matter how serious someone seems about wanting to change—individuals often hold fast to certain ways of managing. Jammed pipelines often are filled with managers who can't let go of behaviors that made them successful at lower leadership levels, and coaching should be an excellent way to help them drop these behaviors.

But no matter what coaching technique you use, it really won't have much lasting impact unless you reach people on a deeper level than the typical negative warning or positive reinforcement. Telling someone they'll be fired if they don't cease and desist or promising them a chance at a promotion if they change their ways is rarely enough. Or it may be only temporarily effective. People respond to these warnings or promises by changing short-term behaviors, and they may well move up a level and seem as though they're growing and developing. In fact, they are simply creating even more serious clogs in the leadership pipeline, because now they're still working at the wrong leadership level but it's a higher level. Invariably, they'll revert back to old, comfortable skills, time applications, and values. Coaches need to convey a deeper understanding of why the managers need to let go of these old, comfortable ways of doing things and to reflect on why letting go is crucial for their careers and their organizations. The Pipeline model facilitates both goals:

Encourage a Deeper Understanding There are many "surface" reasons why managers are asked to change. They're told that they're not getting enough out of their people or that they lack a skill that's important for them to do their job effectively. Although these are valid reasons, they don't always have much impact. The Pipeline model offers coaches a way to reach deeper. There's a logic to the pipeline that helps people recognize that a request to change is not merely a subjective or trivial request. When a coach tells someone he must stop competing with his direct reports, he can put the request in the form of a leadership development imperative. *If you're going to make it through the second leadership passage, you need to let go of value A and adopt value B; you have to let go of skill C and acquire skill D; you have to let go of spending your time that way and learn to spend your time this way.* A coach can talk about what's appropriate for a given manager in his past, current, and future leadership roles. The notion of maturing as a leader and leaving "younger" leadership approaches behind as you grow makes giving up cherished behaviors easier.

Facilitate Reflection It's shocking to realize that you're not performing up to your leadership level. It's one thing to be told that you're doing something wrong and something else entirely to be told that you're performing one or more levels below your assigned job level. The pipeline concept is thought provoking. Coaches can jolt managers out of their complacency by pointing out where they are falling short from the standpoint of skills, time applications, and work values. Remember, many of the managers we're talking about are the best and the brightest. Typically, they've enjoyed a great deal of success up to this point in their careers. It's likely that they assume they'll continue to enjoy the same success in the future if they continue to do the things they've done before and work hard. What they need to reflect on is that leadership is a series of passages, and for one reason or another they have failed to make it through at least one passage. Coaches need to communicate that for the managers' own careers and for the company's future, they need to sit down and think about what type of leader they are and what type they want to be. The pipeline provides a fast and effective graphic tool to achieve this end.

Redefining Coaching from a Leadership Development Perspective

Coaching often devolves into a problem-fixing activity. Managers turn to a coaching approach when they have a talented but troubled direct report and they want an alternative to the usual (and usually ineffective) way of dealing with her. Therefore, they schedule time with this direct report and attempt to talk to her on a more "personal" level. Rather than talking to the direct report as a boss, the manager attempts to talk to her from psychological, emotional, and career standpoints. Though this is fine, it doesn't get past the fact that the focus is still on fixing the problem.

Tina's Story

Pipeline coaching certainly can fix individual problems, but its real focus is on developing well-rounded leaders. Put another way, problems are examined within the broader context of the Leadership Pipeline model. For instance, less than a year ago Tina was promoted to a business manager position in her mid-sized organization. In her previous job as a functional manager (of sales), Tina had been extraordinarily focused, and she'd done a terrific job of revamping the function and making it more responsive to a new and more diverse customer base. But she'd had problems in thinking differently about the business; that is, from Can we do it? to Should we do it?—a crucial requirement at the business manager level. On more than one project, Tina had moved from strategy to action prematurely, committing resources to getting the job done as quickly and effectively as possible. She had failed to pause and think about whether the project was really worth doing in the larger framework of the business's goals and whether the results would be sustainable. Her boss also had noticed that Tina rarely contributed ideas in meetings that addressed issues such as profitability or long-term growth; she was still stuck in a tactical, sales-focused mind-set.

Tina's boss coached her using the Pipeline model. Rather than trying to gain a commitment from her to

> "work on" her problems or challenging her to talk about why she had made these mistakes, he explained the values of a functional manager versus those of a business manager; he also talked about how values changed at other leadership levels. Almost immediately, Tina recognized that though she had many of the skills required at the business manager level, she lacked appropriate values. Once she came to terms with how her problems emanated from her functional values, she was willing to reassess those values in light of her new position. After some thought, Tina began making a conscious effort to adopt the values consistent with her leadership level and began to change what she worked on.

Coaching with the Pipeline model rather than the problem in the spotlight is not always an easy task. Managers often are tempted to "fix it" and deal with the problem rather than with the individual's leadership capability. To avoid a pure fix-it mentality, concentrate on attempting to achieve the following through coaching:

Help People Achieve Their Full Potential Whether it's turn, growth, or mastery potential, design coaching interactions around this potential. Discuss what managers need to do in order to fulfill that potential on their current leadership level. Don't forget that potential (both defining it and recognizing it) is often a moving target.

Provide an Honest Assessment This means communicating to managers where they are on the pipeline in terms of their skills, time applications, and values, even if where they are personally is nowhere near where they are assigned. By making people aware of how they stack up as leaders, coaches can foster a leadership mentality and an interest in developing level-appropriate attitudes and behaviors.

Communicate the Benefit for Both the Individual and the Organization When coaches focus on the problem, they are also focusing exclusively on the organization. In other words, they're essentially saying to the person they're coaching: If you stop causing this problem, the organization will be better off. Coaching also should encompass how the individual will be better off, and the Pipeline model provides insight about how a behavioral change might benefit a career.

The Leadership Pipeline model, however, is a tool that will facilitate coaching people at all levels of a company. Its clarity and perspective will help coaches communicate their points with the maximum amount of impact. As we have pointed out, coaching is a critical leadership task at every leadership level.

Frequently Asked Questions

Q. What criteria should we use when selecting a coach?

A. Experience at the level of the person to be coached is key. The next most important criteria is experience with the problem at hand. Coaches who have personally solved the problem(s) facing an individual possess the practical knowledge that can benefit that individual. Other important criteria are the knowledge and experience to understand the layer, communicate knowledge clearly, build a coaching relationship, and instill confidence in the coachee. A good coach should be able to tell the difference between accepting the advice intellectually and actually making change. Price and geographic proximity are not relevant criteria. This is about improving a person's ability to achieve results. If the results matter to the business's success, price should be a secondary issue. We have found that few coaches are evaluated in terms of their knowledge of how to solve the problem at hand, and this factor is far more important than cost, given what's at stake.

Q. When should we focus on the current job, and when should we focus on the next job when coaching anyone?

A. Focus on success in current positions until you are sure people can sustain their performance at their layer. Coaching on the future should be reserved for exceptional performers. Coaching for potential (coaching for the future) is not a legitimate consideration until performance in the current role exceeds expectations. Be sure that the coaching doesn't encourage people to look past their current assignment before they have delivered what is required. The most ambitious people are the most likely to be coached. Don't overinflate their egos and push them to think about the next position until they have satisfied current position requirements.

Q. What is the difference between coaching and mentoring?

A. Coaching generally has to do with success in the current position, with some emphasis—say, 10 to 15 percent—on the next position. Mentoring is the reverse. Most of the emphasis is on the future, probably 80 to 85 percent; only 15 to 20 percent is focused on current performance. These terms tend to be used interchangeably, but there really should be this much of a difference in emphasis.

Observations from the Field

- Coaching is often mediocre to poor in quality. Specifically, here are some of the problems we've found: practitioners without credentials, coaching engagements without goals or measurements, standards that are too low, managers abdicating their responsibilities to untrained coaches, and employees expecting the process to provide magic answers. In our first edition, we were not sufficiently specific about what it takes for a coaching engagement to produce results that help the business. Making the coachee feel better is not a valid outcome.

- Don't underestimate how important coaching is to being a good leader. In our work with companies since this book was published, we've gained a greater appreciation for coaching as part of a leader's responsibilities. Leaders also come to appreciate the value of coaching when they understand that coaching subordinates to perform more effectively fosters improved business results. Delegating coaching duties to a well-meaning but uninformed external provider requires involvement by that boss if it is to be of value. Hiring a professional coach doesn't relieve the boss of responsibility. The boss must (1) make the expected outcomes clear, (2) spend time with the coach to be sure the coach is up to the task, (3) track progress, (4) measure results, and (5) decide when the coaching assignment is complete—or fire the coach if improvement isn't happening.

- Selecting a coach requires a good frame of reference. Unfortunately, we've observed many leaders who lack this frame of reference. Instead, they hire coaches based on (1) fame as a world-renowned coach, (2) local availability, (3) price, and (4) the recommendation of a middle person or "coaching company" executive. Leaders seldom seek out a coach with a track record of fixing the specific problem that a coach is being engaged to address. We believe that generalist coaches are of little value. A specialist in the needed area—such as a strategic planning specialist for strategic planning coaching, a selection expert for selection coaching, and so on—is the way to go. If you can't define the specific coaching need(s), you should not hire a coach. Do the coaching yourself until you are convinced that a specific skill or ability that you don't possess or can't teach is the real answer. Generalist coaches—who were, for example, in executive search last year, organization development the year before, and outplacement the year before that—probably won't help. Coaches who have experience in executing the work you want done provide the most value, even if their skill as a coach isn't perfect. That's why you are probably the best coach for your people.

- Learning is highly valued; being taught isn't. Most people like to learn but don't like to be taught. Leaders who do coaching as a normal part of the dialogue with subordinates seem to do the best job. Sharing ideas and previous successes while discussing a problem with subordinates can be really powerful. A special session called "coaching" isn't really needed. Leaders who coach effectively often do so in the flow of managing. Employees seem to enjoy this approach more than any other. Admittedly, some employees relish having a "coach." It conveys a sense of importance and high priority for their success. What matters is improvement, and the boss usually holds the keys to improvement, which he can use without incurring extra cost to the business for an outside coach.

14

Benefits Up and Down the Line

To create a leadership pipeline requires more than words and diagrams. Significant behavioral changes are required from a wide range of people. This is especially true for people at the top of the organization. The CEO, group executives, and business managers need to examine their own skills, time applications, and work values. If they discover that they're working at the wrong level, they need to take that first step themselves and raise their skills, time applications, and values to the appropriate level.

Formidable obstacles loom that may make it problematic to make these changes. Many senior executives are reluctant to change "what got them there." Coaching at senior levels isn't valued in many organizations. So the incentives and support to make behavioral changes may be absent. Just as significant, human resources sometimes doesn't understand executive level work and isn't sufficiently involved in business strategy and requirements to provide much assistance.

Nonetheless, these obstacles are eminently surmountable. The Leadership Pipeline model offers theory *and* practical tools for changing your own leadership behaviors and those of others. We believe the theory of the case—that there are six distinct leadership passages that demand mastery of certain skills, time applications, and work values—will compel organizations and individuals to look at leadership differently. There's a war for talent going on now, and it's going to become only more intense in the future. The Leadership Pipeline model provides a way to win that war.

No matter what your position in an organization might be, you can use it to think, talk about, and decide on actions to build your group's talents. In doing so, you may need to convince yourself and others that it's worth adopting this Pipeline model. Some people will prefer buying stars; others will be reluctant to move from a traditional leadership development model.

For these reasons, it's helpful to conclude with a real example from Marriott International of how it is applied and a discussion of the many-faceted benefits of the Pipeline model to the individual and the organization, now and in the future. To a certain extent, we've communicated the most obvious benefit of having the right people at the right leadership levels: performance throughout the organization is enhanced and a competitive advantage is realized and is sustainable if the pipeline is filled and flowing. There are a variety of other positive results for specific groups and individuals that we haven't explored and that can help you facilitate the construction and use of this Pipeline model.

Making Leadership Development a Core Competency: Best Practices at Marriott International

One company that is establishing itself as a "leadership pipeline" powerhouse in the new economy is hotel giant Marriott International. The Marriott success story has been well chronicled in other places. From its start as an A&W Root Beer franchise in 1927, Marriott has developed into an $18 billion global corporation today that manages and franchises over two thousand hotels under ten brand names as well as senior living communities, vacation time share resorts, and executive apartments. Recalling the words of his father and company founder that "success is never final," in 1997 Marriott's chairman and CEO Bill Marriott asked president and COO Bill Shaw and HR head Brendan Keegan to build a corporate capability in leadership development. Marriott knew that he would need a strong talent pool of diverse leaders to continue to fuel the company's aggressive growth plans and prepare it to compete in an increasingly complex and technologically networked global business world.

Keegan recognized that even though the company was well known within the lodging industry for the strength of its management team, a new mind-set and skill base were required to accelerate and strengthen the leadership pipeline. In early 1998, he hired David Rodriguez, a senior human resources officer at Citicorp with a doctorate in industrial and organizational psychology. At Citicorp, Rodriguez played an integral role in a global transformation initiative that resulted in the company's highly benchmarked leadership development system. Moreover, he focused on applying the Leadership Pipeline concepts and engaging managers at all the levels of the organization in the leadership development process. As Citicorp's system evolved, Rodriguez began to envision how the leadership development process could be engineered so that employees, their managers, and human resource professionals could play complementary roles. The framework and language provided by the Leadership Pipeline model made it possible. Hired to lead Marriott's leadership development initiative, Rodriguez has collaborated with his colleagues at Marriott to apply prior lessons learned and to identify emerging best practices. They have created a system that works within the context of Marriott's corporate culture and global operating challenges.

Marriott's efforts are impressive indeed and are likely to pay off in more than a deeper reservoir of exceptional management talent. Marriott wants to be recognized by Wall Street as a great global brand with stock valuations more akin to other great brands than to the lodging industry. Their case is quite persuasive when one considers the strength of their brands and track record of earnings growth. Recent research suggests that "quality of management" is becoming an increasingly important factor in investor decisions. This may be because investors believe that a company that has a strong and predictable leadership pipeline is more likely to be able to generate sustained earnings growth. For this reason, a company's "leadership brand" can be a very valuable asset in today's investment community. By this measure, Marriott's position as an innovator in leadership development, in addition to its strong global brand position and balance sheet, bodes well for the company's future.

Marriott's leadership development system is based on simple shared beliefs, practices, and language that are powerful because of their interdependency and common foundation on the Leadership Pipeline model.

A fundamental principle of Marriott's system is that the quality of a company's senior management team is the strongest influence on the talent pipeline. A second, strongly related idea is that senior managers must be held accountable for skilled stewardship of the talent pool under their management. Bill Shaw, president and COO, was personally involved, played a direct leadership role, and clearly demonstrated that he held himself accountable for developing the talent pool. The same was true of each of his direct reports. Candidates for Marriott's 250 senior-most positions participate in a structured leadership assessment interview. Job specifications are used to guide the assessment and selection processes as well as development planning for newly appointed leaders.

Marriott's efforts in leadership development are spearheaded by its executive council on human capital. The council is chaired by the president and COO, and its members are the most senior executives in the company, responsible for business strategy, management of other forms of capital (for example, financial), and important decisions such as business acquisitions. Consistent with the imperatives outlined by McKinsey & Company's 1998 War for Talent study, Marriott has elevated leadership development to the very top of this corporate agenda. The council is actively involved in identifying, assessing, and developing leaders for the future and in shaping strategy and policy to strengthen Marriott's leadership pipeline.

The cornerstone of Marriott's leadership development system is the Leadership Talent Development Inventory (LTDI). The LTDI is a process by which Marriott can assess the strength of its talent pool at each leadership passage and identify managers "ready now" for accelerated development. The process ensures that all managers are engaged in developing leadership capabilities in alignment with the Leadership Pipeline framework. Marriott used the LTDI initially with its top 250 managers and is currently engaged in implementing it at every level of the organization.

Senior HR professionals at Marriott are expected to possess strong skills in assessing and developing management talent, creating job specifications, and diagnosing organizational issues that facilitate or impede human performance. High-performing senior line managers at Marriott are also increasingly being trained in these same skills. This is in recognition of the fact that in the new economy, human resource effectiveness—and leadership talent development in particular—will be a competitive dividing line. Training for both HR and line managers starts with the Leadership Pipeline model.

Marriott's leadership development system provides managers with tools to make informed decisions about the allocation of scarce development resources. As is the case in most companies, this requires a significant mind-set shift about leadership development. Rather than primarily relying on external education or the latest fads, Marriott's leadership development system emphasizes using the job situation to cause development to happen. In addition, managers are trained to think about development within an ROI framework that takes into account the likelihood of achieving the desired performance target. This ensures that precious development resources are allocated in an optimal manner. Based on the level of the incumbent's position, as defined in the Leadership Pipeline model and the specific contributions needed from the incumbent, the individual and his or her manager identify opportunities to demonstrate and strengthen the new skills, time applications, and values on the job. The manager is expected to take a strong coaching role and provide feedback on progress. There is a heavy emphasis on moving top performers who are "ready now" into new and challenging assignments. External and internal development programs are used to supplement the on-the-job development process.

In addition to using the Leadership Pipeline model as a framework for its leadership development system, Marriott has created a concise set of executive competencies to describe specific outcomes that are required from its 250 most senior managers. In essence the competency model is formulated around the following equation that has been advanced by leading thinkers in the area of leadership development:

Leadership effectiveness = Attributes × Results

For example, to take advantage of its scale of operations, Marriott requires its leaders to "improve bottom-line performance by working collaboratively with others to leverage shared resources." Marriott has realigned its internal executive education programs and its use of external course offerings against the Leadership Pipeline model and the Marriott executive competencies in combination.

Perhaps most impressive is Marriott's effort to create a leadership development system that is scalable. By using a variety of Web-based tools, Marriott enables individuals to provide input on their past career experiences, current job challenges, development needs, and career aspirations while their manager and peers provide input about the demonstration of leadership competencies and related management skills. A Web-based psychometric tool is also used to gain insight about key success enablers such as creativeness and assertiveness. In talent review sessions, senior managers integrate the various sources of information, discuss the development progress of all managers, and identify high-performers who are now ready for larger assignments and the individuals about whom they need to know more. Human resource professionals trained in assessment conduct in-depth interviews with the latter group. Throughout the process the governing question is "What development action will yield the greatest return on investment?" (especially on extremely precious development resources such as management time and challenging assignments). The Leadership Pipeline model is an enabling force in that it provides a common view of what is required.

In-depth interviews build on the information assembled through electronic means and review sessions. In addition to validating recent accomplishments and determining whether the demonstrated skills are appropriate to the leadership passage, the interview focuses on assessing factors that are important to senior leader effectiveness: learning agility, because today's fast-changing business environment requires leaders to experiment, learn quickly, and adapt to the next situation; dealing with adversity, because high-performers tend to work through obstacles instead of using them to explain away failure; and emotional intelligence, because the technological world we live in has made effectiveness in working with others even more important.

Under its overall leadership development initiative, Marriott has endeavored to align other related processes and systems. For example, because the quality of the leadership pipeline is dependent on the caliber of talent at the lower levels, Marriott has instituted a "portfolio management" approach to university relations and recruitment. Under this approach, Marriott evaluates several relevant areas, such as retention of students hired, to determine resource allocation and optimize its yield of top campus talent. As another example, in 1999 Marriott held its first worldwide women's leadership conference and in 2000 cosponsored a similar event focusing on diversity leadership. Finally, like many other leading companies, Marriott is working to create Web-enabled staffing and learning management systems that will allow it to do many functions more efficiently and effectively while allowing resources to be reallocated to higher-value activities.

The rate of progress has been exhilarating, thus reinforcing the company's commitment. In a few short years major improvements have been made through the combination of executive-level effort, high-quality staff support, and the enabling power of the Leadership Pipeline model.

Making Development Actionable and Understandable

Everyone talks about how people must be accountable for their own development, but not everyone shows people *how* to be accountable. Similarly, every organization has individuals who are considered high-potentials who are put on accelerated development tracks, but the very idea of a high-potential person is relatively meaningless, especially from a development standpoint. One high-potential individual may have very different development needs from another high-potential person, but they're lumped together because of their status and developed as though they were clones.

Let's look at the two ways the leadership pipeline addresses these issues:

Establishing a Common Language "Potential," "development," and "full performance" are soft and fuzzy concepts that are virtually useless in real-world situations. The Leadership Pipeline model makes these concepts much more definitive. For instance, the very specific divisions of potential into turn, growth, and mastery provide a very precise language to describe the type of work someone is capable of doing in the future. On a number of occasions, we've observed two people (usually a senior executive and his direct report) poring over succession planning documents and arguing over the potential of a subordinate. They are arguing not because they lack knowledge of the person in question or respect for each other's opinion, but because they each have a very different definition of what potential is and what the underlying requirements are. If they had access to more specific language regarding potential, this argument wouldn't take place (and poor successions decisions would probably not be made). In the same way, talking about six leadership levels and specific skills, time applications, and work values for each offers people a productive way to communicate whether someone is fulfilling their role effectively.

Building a Framework for Self-Management Honest self-assessment and personal awareness of gaps in performance are powerful forces for self-development. Unfortunately, most organizations lack a framework that makes self-assessment easy to do and that gives people the confidence that they're doing it in ways that jibe with organizational expectations. The Leadership Pipeline model, when communicated to everyone in the organization as the gold standard, provides universal measures and requirements. An individual manager can very quickly determine what skills, time applications, and values she needs to acquire to move to the next leadership level; she can also immediately determine whether she possesses the skills, time applications, and values for her current level. Often and throughout the world, we've seen managers who have made extraordinary efforts to take on new and challenging assignments in order to develop their leadership capacity. Just as often, however, we've seen managers unwilling to take on these assignments if they feel that the organization won't appreciate their effort or if they're uncertain about whether they're tackling the right type of assignments. They don't have an effective framework for making the decision.

Providing Boards with Insight and Information

Up until this point, we've said very little about how the Leadership Pipeline model assists boards of directors. We would be remiss if we didn't address how the Pipeline model serves the board in a number of ways, none more crucial than decisions on CEO succession. In recent years, boards have a mediocre record in choosing CEOs, as evidenced by the frightening number of chief executives who fail. We've found that boards can make better choices if they use the Pipeline model to address the following failure-producing factors.

Lack of Job Specification for the CEO Position When mulling over CEO succession issues, boards almost reflexively focus on the people rather than the requirements of the position. Because board members are often current or retired CEOs themselves, they often feel they know exactly what those requirements are. Though there are similarities in requirements for these positions, there are also major differences based on corporate cultures, competitive situations, and specific challenges facing a given company. The sixth leadership passage in the pipeline can provide a great starting point for defining specifications. Candidates can be assessed by using the skills, time applications, and values necessary for this passage. Then the board can factor in the specific needs of a particular organization and adjust the requirements accordingly. The Pipeline model, however, provides an objective starting point, untainted by board members' past experiences as CEOs in their own companies.

Exclusive Focus on the CEO Position CEO succession should not be just a matter of selecting a new CEO, especially in today's highly complex, diverse environment. Effective leadership at the top requires a team, and boards should focus on the CEO and her direct reports as a team. Nonetheless, boards often focus only on the CEO position, for a variety of reasons. To evaluate and question the senior executive team seems to be a mammoth task that the board is ill-equipped to handle. The Pipeline model makes this difficult task doable. The board can assess group executives, the chief financial officer, the head HR person, and others by using leadership-passage requirements (including the functional branch of the model). At the very least, the board can gain a snapshot of who is and who is not fulfilling their leadership roles. It should be asking who, if anyone, can make the passage to CFO, group executive, and so forth.

Neglect of the Health of the Larger System Even when boards do concern themselves with other senior leaders as part of their succession responsibilities, they often ignore broader succession issues. Boards are caretakers of the pipeline, and they need to be vigilant that it is flowing smoothly from top to bottom. Rather than addressing a few senior management appointments, the board needs to ask questions about whether people are being prepared to make all six types of leadership passages. These questions include the following:

- What steps is the company taking to identify the right people to go through passages?

- How is the company helping individuals move through these passages?
- When and how does the company assess the skills, time applications, and work values appropriate to each passage?

We've found that boards that use Pipeline tools as part of a human resource committee do a much better job ensuring that there is a solid pool of leadership candidates up and down the line.

Now let's examine the benefits of the pipeline for individuals at our six leadership levels.

Enterprise Leaders

Obviously a CEO will reap the benefits of an organization that enjoys superior leadership performance at all levels. Any company that can avoid getting into a bidding war for talent and "grow their own" will see direct bottom-line impact, and CEOs responsible for this new leadership approach will receive kudos from various stakeholders. Leadership strength is well understood to be a prime driver of share price.

Less obviously, the Pipeline model serves enterprise leaders as a risk management tool. Managing risk when new products or services are introduced is well understood by many CEOs. There aren't many CEOs who would introduce products without being sure that preparatory steps like market research, quality checks, and pilot testing are done properly. These actions help manage the risks. Oddly, organizations frequently don't apply the same rigorous risk management methodology when making important selection decisions. Part of the problem is that organizations don't know their people well enough to understand what risks they're taking when they promote someone. They don't realize that new skills, time applications, and values are required and that it's a big risk to promote someone to a position if he lacks these required qualities or is unwilling to develop them.

Let's say an organization is moving a functional manager into a business manager position. This is a difficult leadership passage, and one of the difficulties is learning how to integrate functional plans and actions into a coherent business team effort. To do this effectively, business managers must value all functions. To manage the risk inherent in this leadership passage, CEOs should be able to ask group executives key questions such as these:

- What do functional managers say about the treatment they received from this new business manager?
- How well are products that he's responsible for flowing through the organization from concept to customer?
- Do his business plans reflect an appropriate level of understanding of each function's ability to contribute?
- What evidence do we have that he is making this passage appropriately?

Based on the answers to these questions, the CEO can then insist that a plan be created to remedy any obvious problems that someone is having (or might have) with this leadership passage and thereby manage the risk. The Leadership Pipeline provides CEOs with a tool to demand accountability of group executives for leadership development of business managers. If group managers can't answer these questions pertaining to skills, time applications, and values, they're putting the company at risk by not developing business managers—a crucial requirement at their leadership level. Hence the risk may be at the group executive level rather than the business manager level. One way or another, the Pipeline model identifies what the real risks are.

Functional excellence is another benefit. An organization's fortunes rise and fall based on how well functional people do their work. In many instances, however, these fortunes mostly fall because there's not enough functional accountability at all leadership levels. The Pipeline can help ensure this accountability by communicating what each level of leader should do and how they should do it. The following requirements for functional success and accountability at various levels may serve as a guide.

Item	Accountability
Right individual contributors in place to do the work; job well defined	First-line manager; enterprise functional managers
Individual contributors trained properly	First-line managers
Coaching and feedback improving performance; rewards appropriate and timely	First-line managers taught by manager of managers
Work properly connected and integrated within the rest of the function and the business	Manager of managers
Appropriate state-of-the-art technology used as part of functional strategy	Functional manager strategy
Clear business strategy properly communicated for right motivation; appropriate resources available	Business manager
Likely future requirements of the function made clear	Group functional managers
Appropriate standards used, including role in immune system that protects the company	Enterprise functional manager

Group Executives

These organizational leaders are best qualified to take responsibility for succession up to the business manager level. In reality, group executives sometimes shy away from this responsibility because they don't know what to do. When leadership succession is a haphazard or ad hoc activity in organizations, group executives are perfectly happy to allow HR to usurp this task. The Pipeline model, however, can facilitate succession planning by providing clear requirements for each leadership level. What was an onerous task becomes eminently doable.

We've also found that group executives benefit from the Pipeline model because it clarifies their role. More than any other type of leader, group executives are confused about what they should be doing. They're especially unclear when it comes to their responsibilities versus those of the enterprise leader and business managers; it's common to find gaps and overlaps among their own responsibilities and those of their boss and their direct reports. With the Pipeline model in hand, group executives can define exactly what their contribution to the organization should be.

Business Managers

This leadership level is responsible for generating short-term profit as well as strategies that produce long-term success. As a result, revenue and costs are of great concern to business managers. The Pipeline model can prevent or reduce one of the greatest costs to any organization: people working at the wrong level. Getting people to work at the right level not only reduces transaction costs but also reduces the number of people needed to do the work. Eliminating many of the overlapping responsibilities and gaps between levels creates a much more efficient business in which more can be accomplished with fewer people.

Just as important, this leadership passage can be extremely difficult, and the action that best facilitates this passage is coaching from a group executive. In most instances, however, business managers don't receive this coaching. Instead, new business managers are sent to a development course for business general managers that lasts several weeks. When they return to their jobs, these managers have to coach themselves and often struggle, no matter how good the training was. The Leadership Pipeline model mandates that group executives coach business managers; it makes it clear that this is something group executives need to value and devote a significant amount of time to doing.

Functional Managers

The passage from functional manager to business manager is challenging, and many functional managers don't meet this challenge because they don't understand the skills, time applications, and values involved. The Pipeline model provides them with knowledge of what will be required of them and what their developmental targets should be. It particularly signals the need for management maturity. It also helps them make important career decisions, especially about whether they want to pursue a functional or business leadership track. When they're aware of the specific tasks they need to do on each track, they can make a more informed choice.

Managers of Managers

This tends to be the most anonymous of leadership positions, and the more anonymous a position is, the more self-management tools are required. A disturbing number of managers of managers suffer from an identity crisis: they're not quite sure what their responsibilities are and how to meet them. The Pipeline model makes it clear that managers of managers should value teaching and coaching first-line managers—that as developers of talent, they hold the strength of the pipeline in their hands. They're the ones who must help individual contributors adjust to their first managerial job, and they must make sure that these neophyte managers value being managers.

Without the Pipeline model in place, many managers of managers don't know what to do or how to do it. Training programs are often in place for first-line managers, functional managers, and business managers, but not for them. Managers of managers derive a sense of purpose from just seeing how they fit into their organization's leadership pipeline, and it also gives them a sense of career direction.

First-Line Managers

First-line managers must seek clarity on their decision to become a manager, and the Pipeline model forces them toward this clarity by asking them to adopt certain values, develop certain skills, and adjust their calendar accordingly. When they face these changes, they naturally ask themselves, Do I really want to be a manager? If they don't have to face these changes, they may become managers only for the money or the prestige, and thus may do a poor job at this leadership level.

The Pipeline framework is also important from a career standpoint. First-line managers are full of questions about how they might develop their careers and whether they're doing a good job. They can measure their performance with the Pipeline model and also figure out what training and development they need to pursue in order to master the skills at the next leadership level.

A Flexible Pipeline for Changing Organizations

The six leadership passages we've discussed and the attendant skills, time applications, and values aren't set in stone. Even now, we find that some requirements need to be tweaked to conform to specific environmental realities. In some companies, five leadership levels are a more accurate reflection of the organization; in others, seven are a better fit. We want to emphasize that not only is it OK to tailor the Pipeline model, but you should by all means do so if that will better suit your organization's structure and culture.

In fact, we've found that the Leadership Pipeline model—with minor adjustments here and there—is especially well-suited to three types of organizations that don't fit the traditional business model. Let's briefly explore how the model addresses the leadership issues of e-commerce, health care, and mega-corporations.

E-Commerce These companies are going to be taking major risks as they fill their leadership positions with talent from the old economy. As these organizations become sufficiently large, they'll need leaders with traditional business talents—strategic ability, operations strengths, and so on. The Leadership Pipeline gives these companies a tool to manage the risks. They can identify the specific requirements for any leadership position rather than just finding someone with the right "title" experience. Making the transition from an old economy company to a new one will be tough enough for any leader. The transition can be facilitated, however, if the right selection criteria are used.

Health Care Failure of CEOs in this industry is almost a daily occurrence. We don't need to spend time here recounting all the problems involving HMOs and other health care providers. The health care industry, especially doctors' groups, hospitals, and HMOs, is desperately in need of better leadership models. The industry requires leaders who can provide clear direction for care, enhanced efficiency in delivering service, effective case management, and stronger relationships with partners. Because many people in leadership positions at health care facilities have been trained as doctors, they often lack any leadership model or training whatsoever. The Pipeline model can help these doctors appreciate the needed changes in skills, time applications, and values as they move to new leadership levels. The model also helps them understand what they have missed developmentally and provides them with a road map for defining and planning their own development.

Mega-Corporations Especially in the areas of telecommunications, automotive, and financial services, the size and scale of corporations resulting from mergers, acquisitions, and partnerships presents unprecedented leadership problems. Never have there been companies so large, so global, and so fiercely competitive. There's a great deal of confusion about how to run these companies effectively.

One problem is the duplication of leadership positions that results when companies merge. Typically, one duplicate goes and the other stays, but this decision is largely based on politics rather than leadership ability. Sometimes the decision is made almost randomly: "We've taken ten leaders from Company A but only four from Company B, so now we must take the next three or four leaders from Company B." Similarly, if the two companies have different leadership systems, there often are conflicting standards.

The Pipeline model provides standardization for leadership requirements and also helps organizations make decisions on who is really right for the one job opening.

Ultimately, perhaps the Leadership Pipeline's greatest value is that it provides a framework on which new organizations can be built and old ones can reconfigure themselves. In the future, it may be that the six passages we've delineated will change. As e-commerce affects almost every company and other major trends force companies to rethink what they are and what they must do, leadership passages will evolve. Nonetheless, the Pipeline model will remain viable because its essential message is timeless: leadership entails a series of passages that come with very specific values, skills, and time requirements, and leaders must not skip passages as they take on more responsibility and influence in an organization or they will end up working at the wrong level and will clog the pipeline.

With these principles in mind, any organization can develop their own talent to maximum leadership capacity now and in the future.

Frequently Asked Questions

Q. How do we obtain the major benefits from the Leadership Pipeline model?

A. You have to define your own Leadership Pipeline model using your terminology, your passages, and your desired business results. As previously mentioned, companies that have done so make observable progress in both performance and development. This book should guide you in this effort; our next book will provide even more guidance because it has an even stronger "how to" component. In our work with companies, we have found that those that tailor the pipeline to their particular organizations realize a much greater benefit than companies that fail to do so. Like basketball or any other competitive endeavor, businesses must practice to truly see benefits.

Q. Do you recommend using the Leadership Pipeline model in small companies?

A. Very small companies, such as an owner or leader supervising a small number of individual contributors, won't get much benefit unless they are growing or plan to grow rapidly. Owners in particular must learn to make turns as their business grows and they add layers. Our clients have revenues from $20 million to over $100 billion, and they have all benefited from the Pipeline's language, definitions, and diagnostics. Small-growth companies seem to benefit the most because they don't have specialized staff functions. The model enables managers in these small companies to help themselves get the best from their employees.

Q. Is there one particular passage or layer you worry about the most?

A. Although most of the energy and effort in leadership development is focused on CEOs, business managers, and managers of others, the biggest problem lies in the functional manager layer. It is harder to detect the shortfalls. In particular, functional managers look successful by solving technical problems and championing their functions in the battle for needed resources. What they should be doing is extricating themselves from functional work and pursuing competitive advantage. They should be allowing their people to solve the tough technical problems. Functional managers often hurt their business by focusing on functional success, not business success.

Observations from the Field

- We've found that the Marriott example in this chapter is still relevant and useful despite the passage of time. Some of the people mentioned have retired or changed roles, but they continue to use excellent leadership development methods and practices. Despite a downturn in travel caused by the September 11, 2001, terrorist attacks and the collapse of the financial system in 2008, Marriott continues to grow and prosper.

- Leaders who have used the Pipeline framework keep referring to its importance at two levels in particular. Differentiation between the layers gets substantial recognition as a vehicle for improving role clarity and job focus—this is true at all levels, but particularly for managers of managers and group managers. In company after company, these two passages have been the most poorly defined. Both are frequently viewed as span-breakers rather than roles that can add substantial value. Managers of others and business managers are probably the two roles hardest to fill. The manager of managers (for managers of others) and the group manager (for business managers) play a vital role in the success of these tough-to-fill positions. Conversely, they can and do play a big part in the failure of new manage others and business manager incumbents.

- HR functional members at every level have told us of the utility of the Leadership Pipeline model in their work. They commonly use phrases like "my leadership development bible," "my north star," and "my road map." Many HR practitioners understand that they don't have a central architecture such as the general ledger, the budget process, and the cost accounting system that enable financial practitioners to do their work. Behavioral science has some utility, but it doesn't explain the work of a leader or help HR understand the business. It doesn't constitute useful architecture by itself. The Leadership Pipeline model is the core of the architecture for the human side of the business. The big benefit to the whole company is that it helps to integrate HR's programs and services. It also helps all the other functions and businesses understand what is on the human side of the business and how they should contribute.
- The Leadership Pipeline model and the associated terminology have entered the lexicon of business, underscoring the value of language for thinking about or discussing anything. In fact, the model's terminology has become almost universally used in succession planning, leadership development, and coaching by HR and all the other functions. Clearly there was a

gap in the language—and therefore a gap in the thinking and discussions on the human side of the business. Problems were sensed or felt but not defined or addressed. We take real pride in having helped to create this language, even if it's only with hindsight that we've come to appreciate its true value.

Acknowledgments

I have learned tremendously from a large number of participants in executive education programs, in-house programs (at GE, Unilever, DuPont, Ford, and other places), and university-conducted programs (at Harvard, Columbia, Wharton, Northwestern, Duke, and Penn State). I am deeply grateful to them.

Over the years, professor Noel Tichy of the University of Michigan and Patty (Stacy) have influenced dramatically my thinking in this area.

The greatest insights have come from working with CEOs whose valuable judgments about people—what they do best and what they lack—were uncluttered by biases and fancy language. These are the people who know how to grow leaders. Their trust was absolutely essential to my learning and I'm deeply grateful to all of them.

—*R.C.*

Walt Mahler introduced me to the concepts underlying *The Leadership Pipeline*. He made it come to life and cared enough to get me to understand it.

The proof of *The Leadership Pipeline*'s value comes through successful application. I would like to thank many who have successfully applied the concept. Thanks to Tom Flanagan at Southern

California Edison; Sam Wassaerman at Gap; Jane Howard and David Burrell at BAT; Lance Hockridge, Jo Best, and Tracey Waters at QR Limited; Steve Bonner and Matt McGuire at Cancer Treat Centers of America; Doros Constantinou and Bernard Kunerth at Coca Cola Hellenic; Kjetil Kristiansen at Aker Solutions; and Carrie Olesen at Microsoft.

Colleagues and members of my network who have successfully advanced the concepts include Barry Venter, Peter Ivanoff, Adriana Gontariu, Terry Gilliam, and Greg Waldron.

Barbara Kostka did a great job of converting my scratchings into a legible manuscript.

—S.D.

Many people have had an impact on my thinking about how organizations develop the leadership potential so critical to their success. One individual, however, has profoundly affected both the development of my thinking and my career. That person is Ram Charan. It has been my privilege to coauthor this book with Ram, a truly gifted talent who has given so much to so many over his career.

I also extend special thanks to David Dotlich, who was so helpful to me as I established my consulting practice. David introduced me to his two partners in CDR International, Steve Rhinesmith and Peter Cairo, who have also influenced my thinking about coaching and development. Finally, I gratefully acknowledge the special enjoyment in working with Neil Johnston over the years.

Many clients have given me the opportunity to work in a field that brings so much personal pleasure. I thank all of you.

Finally, thanks to my wife Sarah, a very special person, and to our children Allison and Amy, Amy's husband Ted, and our grandson Jeb, all of whom give meaning to my life.

—J.N.

The Authors

Ram Charan is a world-renowned adviser to corporate boards and business leaders, a best-selling author, and an award-winning teacher. He is known for his keen insights into business problems and his real-world practicality in solving them.

For nearly four decades, Ram has counseled some of the world's most successful business leaders on far-ranging issues, from corporate governance and building a leadership pipeline to pursuing organic growth. Most recently he has been deeply involved in helping boards and managements with the financial crisis and global economic slowdown.

Boards of directors were Ram's specialty and the subject of his doctoral thesis at Harvard Business School. He has deepened his knowledge of corporate governance ever since. For the past fifteen years he has been helping boards and CEOs deal with the practical challenges posed by rising societal expectations. He works with managements and boards to improve the functioning of the board and its contribution to the company. He assists boards in conducting self-evaluations, peer reviews, and evaluations of the CEO. He helps key leaders make executive sessions productive and effective. Through retreats and facilitation, he helps managements and their boards get on the same page regarding company strategy, including its operational side. He also helps boards keep their composition in tune with the changing landscape through director succession planning and recruiting. He himself is a director serving on three boards: Austin Industries, Tyco Electronics, and Emaar MGF in India. *Directorship* named him one of the top 100 directors of the year.

Ram, a prolific writer, is the author or coauthor of seventeen books, including *Boards That Deliver, Owning Up, Leadership in the Era of Economic Uncertainty, Know-How,* and *What the CEO Wants You to Know. Execution* was on the *New York Times*' best-seller list for nearly three years and has two million copies in print. Ram has contributed to lead articles in *Fortune, Harvard Business Review,* and many other publications.

Ram's interactive style and real-world approach have made him a favorite among executive educators. He has taught for thirty consecutive years at GE's John F. Welch Leadership Center in Crotonville, New York, and Wharton's Insurance Institute. He has won best-teacher awards at Crotonville and Northwestern's Kellogg School of Management.

Ram has MBA and DBA degrees from Harvard Business School, where he graduated with high distinction and was a Baker Scholar. He was elected a Distinguished Fellow of the National Academy of Human Resources. He is based in Dallas, Texas.

Stephen Drotter is chief executive of Drotter Human Resources, an executive succession planning, leadership performance, and organization design company serving a large global customer base. He has completed over forty enterprise level CEO succession plans for corporations such as Marriott, Citigroup, Goodyear, Ingersoll-Rand, Newmont Mining, DeBeers, and Cancer Treatment Centers of America. In-depth assessments of over 1200 senior executives have created much of the information for this book. He has worked at over one hundred major corporations for more than one week.

Steve has over forty-five years' experience in organization and management. As an organization and management practitioner at

GE, he was one of the early designers and implementers of GE's succession planning system. As Head of Human Resources, first at INA (now called Cigna) and then at Chase Manhattan, he focused on executive succession, leadership performance and development, and organization design. He was a member of the Policy Committee at both companies.

Steve holds a degree in economics from Amherst College and is a graduate of GE, Human Resources Program.

Jim Noel is a retired independent consultant and leadership coach. He is the former manager of Executive Education and Leadership Effectiveness at GE's famed Leadership Institute in Crotonville, New York, and later Citibank's vice president of Executive Development. Early in his career, Jim was assistant dean of the College of General Studies at The George Washington University in Washington, D.C. His consulting firm, Noel and Associates, assisted companies in the selection, assessment, and development of key leadership teams. He is coauthor of three books on leadership including *Leadership Passages* and *Action Learning*, and is coeditor of *The 2008 Pfeiffer Annual: Leadership Development*.

Index